CLEANSING
THE
TEMPLE

RESTORING THE GLORY OF THE LORD

*And the Lord, whom you seek, will suddenly come to
His temple…For He is like a refiner's fire and like
launderers' soap (Mal. 3:1-2).*

BERT M. FARIAS

CONTENTS

"These things says He who has the sharp two-edged sword..."
(Rev. 2:12b)

ENDORSEMENTS

In early 2016, we were introduced to Bert Farias' books and couldn't read them fast enough because they really spoke to our hearts. Being pastors, we handed them out to our church leaders, primarily (at that time). An immediate hunger for a move of God was sparked in them, and our monthly church prayer turned into weekly prayer. Our people have read nearly all of Bert's books since then.

We were blessed to be able to bring Bert and Carolyn here to minister soon thereafter, and they left a deposit that has only grown and still continues today. Our pray-ers pray in a new place in the Spirit; people are in the Word like never before, with many operating in new giftings and boldness. At the meetings, one 72-year-old woman received new knees and now shovels snow and hauls wood!

And the healings continue...a man healed while in Mexico of a large blood clot in his leg (then he got on the plane and flew home!). One woman healed of advanced asthma/COPD. A man healed of chronic pain and totally off Vicodin and morphine.

Something changed in the spirit realm when Bert and Carolyn came. Our pray-ers can't wait to get to prayer now. They are all operating at a different level of faith and truly have an "exaggerated expectation" as Bert spoke over us. The presence of the Holy Spirit is so strong during worship, our pastor teaches with a new anointing, and we are so anticipating Bert and Carolyn's return.

—Pastors Randy & Sue LeBlanc, North Pointe Church, Bend, Oregon

---

Our church was blessed to have Bert and Carolyn minister recently. In addition to ministering in our regular church service, they also ministered to area pastors and leaders as well as to a group of intercessors. As a church, we have been praying and believing God for a move

of His Spirit. However, as is the case in many places today, we were very weary — especially the intercessors. We had been praying for the Lord to strengthen us, and Bert and Carolyn were an answer to that prayer. The Holy Spirit is very real and active in their lives, and they imparted a hunger for that to our church. Many speakers come and just talk; Bert and Carolyn IMPART — they leave something tangible.

Our church is different — the Holy Spirit is moving in a new way. Our prayer group has been spiritually stretched, and the intercessors are moving in a new anointing that we have not seen before. God uses His people, and He used Bert and Carolyn's ministry to help us and strengthen us. In a day when Pentecostal/Charismatic churches are pushing the Holy Spirit out — the very One that brings life — Bert and Carolyn bring an acute awareness of His Presence.

—Pastors Rick and Paulette Robison, The Meeting Place, Blacksburg, South Carolina

---

The Lord used Bert and Carolyn to ignite a fire in us that is having lasting effects to this day. Our praise has gone higher, our worship deeper, and our love and devotion to God and one another seems to be growing fonder daily. Over the years, we have been blessed with many fine men and women of God, but none with such a holy impartation as Bert and Carolyn brought.

—Pastors Pete and Theresa Barby, Lighthouse Church, Rochester, Minnesota

---

Bert and Carolyn Farias have been a huge blessing to our church here in Houston. The anointing that they flow in and their powerful ministry of the Word has brought a transformation to our church that is still evident today. They minister out of love but without compromising the life-changing true gospel. They reveal Jesus with joy and a godly fear.

After being with them for a short time, they immediately were like family, and my wife and I are truly thankful for this relationship. We cannot wait to see them again this year, and our congregation misses them as well.

I would highly recommend not only their ministry, but this wonderful, loving couple. It's not just the gifts they carry, but it is who they are that has impacted us so deeply.

—Sidney and Cathy O'Pry, Senior Pastors, Overflow Fellowship, Houston, Texas

---

My wife and I have been pastoring Resurrection Life Church in Vidor, Texas, since 2007. Our hearts have been stirred for revival and awakening since our days at the Brownsville Revival and the Brownsville Revival School of Ministry, where we first were introduced to Bert and Carolyn Farias. Their passion and love for Jesus that they modeled was absolutely admirable and contagious.

The past 11 years have been spent laboring and crying out for a move of God in a very dry religious land. We had almost given up. In prayer, the Holy Spirit led us to contact Bert and Carolyn about a speaking engagement. They arrived in Texas with just as much zeal, passion, and intensity as we remembered from 20+ years before in revival. What a testimony in itself! The fire had not gone out.

They ministered with such sensitivity, boldness, and accuracy, and left a lasting impartation in our church body. As a matter of fact, that was the weekend of turning in our church. Our church, once struggling, is now thriving! Souls are being saved and discipled, the addicted are being set free, the gifts of the spirit are in full operation, and there is LIFE all around us. We are so incredibly thankful to the Father for sending the Farias' to the body of Christ. What richness they possess.

—Lead Pastors Todd and Mendi Short, Resurrection Life Church of Vidor, Texas

Our church has been greatly blessed by the ministry of Rev. Bert and Carolyn Farias on three different occasions. They flow accurately and proficiently in the gifts of the Holy Spirit. They teach and sing prophetically, bringing a practical, challenging, strategic, accurate message. Their words carry such weight and their songs propel us into a very special place in God's presence.

We have received many testimonies from people in our congregation who were greatly impacted by their ministry. Bert and Carolyn are a tremendous blessing to the body of Christ. Their ministry is powerful, passionate, and prophetic!

—Pastors W. Carlton and Elvi Rogers, Dynamic Life Ministries, Front Royal, Virginia

PREFACE

8-5-21

I was watching a YouTube video recently in which the late Kenneth E. Hagin, whom I reference a few times in this book, shared about how God told him to preach and carry the message of faith to the Church nearly a century ago. Through many hardships, he obeyed that call and eventually prospered in it. Because of His obedience to God's mandate on his life and ministry, millions of people worldwide have been blessed by his life, example, and teachings. He preached and taught on many other topics, but faith in God's Word was his primary message for much of his life.

What most of the general public doesn't know about Kenneth Hagin Sr., also affectionately known as "Dad" Hagin by those taught and fathered by him, is that he never desired a large ministry or the attention of the limelight — indeed a rarity today. In fact, this outstanding quality so moved me as a young student in his school that I have kept one of my favorite quotes of his tucked away in my Bible for years to remind me of it.

"I could care less if God used me. I wish He'd take me off the platform. I'd be perfectly happy in a prayer room, never being seen or heard. If you want to be seen or heard, you shouldn't be on any platform. The people don't need to see or hear you but Jesus, anyway."

This quote will become increasingly significant throughout the pages of this book, so you may want to remind yourself of it now and then. The polar opposite of this statement is the modern-day scourge in the Church today, where self-aggrandizement is king. Hagin's quote is the anchor of truth, representing the posture of true humility and prayer that will keep you from what you will come to know in a later chapter as the mystery of iniquity.

immoral or gross behavior / wickedness

One time, someone asked "Dad" Hagin how it was that his ministry just seemed to spring up out of nowhere and then propelled to national and international prominence. In other words, what was the secret to his success? Very humbly, he replied: *"All I've ever done is obey the written Word of God and follow the leading of the Holy Spirit in my life."*

What Hagin said reflects a simple yet profound wisdom that, due to the prayer-less spirit of the age, many have veered greatly from. If we follow Brother Hagin's stellar example and Biblical principle, we will also fulfill God's plan and purpose for our lives, which should be a priority for every believer and minister. But this is nearly impossible to do without pure motives. This is one of the emphases of the book you now hold in your hands and one of the chief themes in some of my other writings. The fact that you're browsing through it or have begun reading it is proof to me that the Spirit of God is drawing you to what we believe is a critical word from the Lord to the Church in this hour.

HOW THIS BOOK WAS BIRTHED

In prayer one day, while my wife Carolyn and I were praying in the Spirit, three scriptures flashed before her that instantly bore witness with both of us. The first one was Acts 5, with Ananias and Sapphira; the second was Acts 8, with Simon the sorcerer; the third was Acts 19, with the burning of the magic books at Ephesus. Immediately we discerned the message from the Lord, and we sensed a burden and a commissioning to write a book on the impurities and iniquities that are prevalent in the church world today and how judgment and cleansing must come before the glory can be restored. He highlighted to us His desire to burn up the greed and covetousness for money, position, and power that rules so many.

This revelation led me to read the various gospel accounts of Jesus cleansing the temple. As I meditated on this cleansing, I became acutely aware that this is a work God endeavors to do in every generation, but it will be most intense in the days prior to His return. One of God's primary works has always been to move the Church from being a house of merchandise and even a den of thieves to a true house of prayer. This is another one of the emphases of this book.

"And He found in the temple those who sold oxen and sheep and doves, and the money changers doing business. When He had made a whip of cords, He drove them all out of the temple, with the sheep and the oxen, and poured out the changers' money and overturned the tables. And He said to those who sold doves, "Take these things away! Do not make My Father's house a house of merchandise!" (Jn. 2:14-16).

"Then He went into the temple and began to drive out those who bought and sold in it, saying to them, "It is written, 'My house is a house of prayer,' but you have made it a 'den of thieves'" (Lk. 19:45-46).

Whenever the Lord speaks to His churches as He did, for example, to the churches of Revelation, we read this phrase: *"He who has an ear, let him hear what the Spirit says to the churches (Rev. 2- 3)."* This phrase is always preceded or followed by some kind of promise to the overcomer. Although this book contains strong truths and many warnings, it also promises a reward to all who overcome. It is our assignment from the Lord to trumpet these things now, for too many have followed the love of money and the pride and esteem of an honored reputation among men and inordinate desire for public ministry — instead of serving the Lord with the purest of motives and following the Spirit of God through prayer and communion with Him.

This book touches on a few other topics, but these two issues are the heart of the book.

A LENGTHY BOOK TO BE READ IN PORTIONS

Finally, some of you may not be ready for the spiritual food contained within the pages of this book — at least not yet, or certainly, not all at once. Similarly, when you buy your weekly groceries, you don't consume them all at once as soon as you arrive home. You will eat them in portions one day at a time and stock the rest in your pantry.

What you will read in this book may need to be chewed on for a while or put aside until a day when you can actually eat it and digest it. It may be a little too much for you to chew on and swallow right away. But sooner or later, as you witness the dawning of a new day, and you are ready for solid food, you will go back into that pantry and say, "Now I remember what that brother said. I'm ready for it now."

I believe that, if you are a serious disciple of the Lord, you will enjoy this book, as it is filled with inspiring prophetic utterances and many stimulating quotes. But unless your spiritual hunger is great, I recommend you read just one chapter per day. The book is divided into four main sections. In a little more than two weeks, you will have read it through and, hopefully, be enriched and empowered.

May God bless the reading of the words on these pages to your ears. May a deep cleansing as well as a new consecration and fresh dedication to God arise in your heart from this message. And may you long for the purity, prayer, and power to fill the true temple of the Lord in this day, which is the heart of man.

SECTION I
THE COMING RESTORATION

INTRODUCTION

While waiting on the Lord in prayer before an evening meeting in a particular city, the communications of the Spirit of God began to flow (Carolyn and I recorded it and then transcribed it). For the last several years, this has been our pattern and mode of operation. We have hundreds of pages of prayer notes — or "prayer jottings," as we call them — that have been birthed from these special times of waiting on the Lord. It is in fact a conversation or dialogue with the Lord in tongues, revelation, and interpretation. Here is one such transcription of prayer jottings that will launch you into this book.

And even here you know something is not right, and you've been picking it up in your spirit, but you're not seeing anything, for it's been masked...

It's very skilled at being deceptive...it's veiled in religion...a mask of religion... and it's only a certain kind of utterance and power that is going to break through this very strong veil of deception.

Tongues...

I see that, Lord. So we can't go in light and fluffy, for it's all disguised in that religious display.

More tongues...

So this, then, is why the demonstration of My power, not with enticing words of man's speech, is necessary here (1 Cor. 2:4-5), for this mask that has been here knows what to say, knows what to look like on a Sunday, knows how to pretend, and is very good at it, but genuine faith must be established in the power of God.

We just surrender now to the Holy Ghost and power, to the One who shows us Your heart and Your will, shows us the sick and dis-

eased, and shows us and penetrates through with the preaching that cuts to the heart and separates the soul.

"For the word of God is living and powerful, and sharper than any two-edged sword, piercing even to the division of soul and spirit, and of joints and marrow, and is a discerner of the thoughts and intents of the heart. And there is no creature hidden from His sight, but all things are naked and open to the eyes of Him to whom we must give account" (Hebrews 4:12-13).

Lots of tongues, heaving...

This utterance must come forth to break through the veil of religion, to break through that deceptiveness that is here, and what Ananias and Sapphira were trying to do; because they saw people doing it (Barnabas was honored in Acts 4:36-37), they did it, too.

But the anointing and the power and the glory were too great at that time to allow deception. That lie could not walk past the anointing and the one who was walking in the spirit of truth (Peter), for it not to be recognized as a covering and a veil to bring in an impure spirit, a falsehood, and a lie.

And what was going on at that time? There was such a great awareness of the truth of Jesus Christ; there was such an anointing and a power in the body.

There were miracles going on outside the church walls with the shadow of Peter...there was demonstration and power that was being seen, yes, that was going on. The demonstration of the Spirit of the Lord was upon My people, My ministers, so much so that they didn't need to be in a building; they just had to walk the streets, and there I was moving. Yes, that same power that raised Christ from the dead was upon them, and the shadow — yes, even the shadow — which was

My Spirit, was healing and delivering and moving through My apostles at that time.

Tongues…

Yes, and even the preaching that came forth was causing hearts to decide either to disbelieve and oppose, and get angry at the words coming forth, or repent, be glad, and rejoice.

Can you not see what it looks like? Can you not understand what it looks like when I am moving? There is power, and there is an utterance and a word that causes there to always be a dividing, and you said it — through your own words and through your own mouth — that I make them either glad, sad, or mad.

This is evidence of My Spirit moving and My Spirit in dominance and of its authority on My ministers.

Tongues…

You see, it's almost like He's highlighted this morning the beginning of Acts, where it started, how there was an anointing, how the Holy Spirit first came through a people who prayed and were consecrated and waited on Him; He came like a whirlwind, and the people automatically went out of the upper room and into the streets — that is automatic, and that is something you should see and recognize, even in the body today.

When the Holy Spirit is poured out, people cannot stay in the pew; they have to go out into the streets, for there's an activation that compels them.

And so you have seen, and so don't you remember when you went to_____. Aahh, I remember when we were moving in the Spirit at _____ and how gifts were activated and how some started waking up when the Spirit was released. Yet that leader stopped it — perhaps because it threatened his sense of being in control and not understanding or agreeing with it — and all of a sudden, it was all stopped. What was the release, and what happened out of that?

It burst, and, instead of life, it brought forth adultery in the body, and it brought forth coldness and people walking away; it brought forth people being taken away, this marriage being destroyed, this one going off into false doctrine, that one moving away from God and becoming cold, and it brought forth a dry, cold monument of religion.

Whenever someone or something comes to stop a move of God, that is the result...the work of Satan, the work of death...but, oh — remember how it all started? How they let the Holy Spirit move and Peter got up and preached, and the word cut to their hearts and there were so many who came to the Lord and believed. Then there was a movement in homes.

But understand that what tried to come in with Ananias and Sapphira was disguised in religion, disguised with a mask of pretension. But because of the sensitivity of the ministers (Peter), they were watching, and they saw it as soon as it moved by. <u>There was a discernment that came because the Holy Spirit was in charge</u>, and He recognized in the disguise that which was false.

Today, we would allow Ananias and Sapphira to walk in the door with their paychecks, with their checkbooks, with their debit cards and credit cards, and their bank accounts, and say: "Oh, God told us to give this to you, pastor." They would be received — and yet it was a messenger of Satan; it was a pride that got in, and then there comes the control through the money...a control of what goes on through the Spirit because of the money.

Tongues...

And so I see the disguise that's gone in and infiltrated the church in this area.

They know what to say, they know what to do, they know how to come in and make havoc of pure things that may have started with the right heart, but oh…

They know how to raise their hands, they know how to dress, they know how to move, they know what to say…

It's a disguise, I say.

But Bert and I pray, for we have a little bit of understanding now. You told us to come in demonstration. For how will they even pay attention? How will their faith even be in the words that are spoken, except they first see the power of God — the pure power of God.

Thank You for this revelation and understanding of what we're dealing with in this religious spirit.

Now let's give place to praying in the Spirit together…

Bert:

Honest with God, honest with God…the honesty and unveiling starts with God. It starts with an individual's relationship with the Lord. It starts with transparency. It starts with an unveiled face. It starts by beholding the glory of the Lord as in a mirror. It starts vertically with every believer's relationship with the Lord. For you cannot hide from God. You can put a mask on, but He sees through the mask.

For nothing is veiled, but all is open and naked before Him to whom we have to give account. Every creature is naked before God. For the sharp sword of His Word cuts through the soul and spirit and the joints and marrow and discerns the thoughts and intents of the heart.

You cannot hide from Him!

So there is the need to walk before Him in purity and integrity and honesty — without defilement, without guile, without hypocrisy, and without malice — as babes in Christ, desiring the sincere milk of the Word so that you may grow thereby.

As babes, as babes...for He hides His wisdom from the wise and prudent, but He reveals them unto babes, so as babes, desire the pure milk of the Word. And receive the wisdom, yea, even the hidden secrets of God.

Tongues...lots of tongues...

I'm reminded that the true apostolic and the true prophetic is of this manner — that it turns the hearts of the people toward God. It turns the motives of the hearts of the people toward God, and that which is veiled and masked is ripped apart. They see even as they should see and are known even as they're known — not even just "through a glass darkly," but in the Spirit they see, even as God sees what He desires for them to see at that moment and at that time.

We forget that that operation is supernatural and is such an integral and critical part of the apostolic and the prophetic. When _____ ministered at _____, his opening statements ripped a veil and ripped a mask off the fake, phony, carnal "prosperity" gospel, and it turned the motives of people's hearts immediately toward God. It put them face to face with God and with pure truth, and then they are able to decide.

For too many have spoken smooth words from smooth lips when there's been war in their hearts.

The truly apostolic and prophetic — even as seen in the early apostles and Peter in the early Church — ripped that mask, that veil, that political-correctness talk right off of people.

So I see that the Church has had on a mask, and many things have been veiled, even as You have shown us today. There is a great need for true apostles and prophets to come with strong words and a certain kind of utterance that would penetrate and unmask and unveil those things which are hidden and that are hindering the Church and God's people and pure truth from seeping through. Those things are hindering the true move of the Spirit of God, for the Spirit cannot be yoked with darkness. What manner of agreement has God with Baal, and how can we dine at the table of God and the table of devils? What accord has light with darkness?

So you see even the need of the hour, even as you're beginning to write, that "My house shall no more be called a den of thieves but a house of prayer."

There must be a cleansing, and there must be a purification before the true power can really come. If the power comes without the purification, the deception would grow. People would say, "Oh, God must be pleased with us, for He's demonstrating His power and pouring out His Spirit." People would continue to walk on in their blindness and in their deception.

For I will not pour out My power on a church that is blemished and full of pride and sin and deception. No, no, no! That would only further add to the deception that already is. So there must be a purifying, a sanctifying, a cleansing of all the impurities that have been veiled and masked.

CHAPTER ONE

TURNING THE HEARTS OF THE PEOPLE BACK TO GOD

I believe that much of what the Lord is doing today is completely counter to Christian pop culture and the flow that we are seeing in the mainstream and most highly visible Western Church. It is typical in such times that there will be a counterfeit that runs parallel to the real. There will be an echo that arises right alongside the authentic voice.

Some of these echoes are very deceptive and hidden from the casual hearer, while others are rather obvious and easy to discern. For instance, there's a false teaching out there, a part of the "hyper-grace" message that says the Christian doesn't need to repent — that God has already forgiven all your past, present, and future sins. Yet there's never been a greater need for repentance in the church world than there is today.

In a recent poll by ChristianMingle.com, single Christians between the ages of 18 and 59 were asked, if, given the opportunity, would they have sex before marriage. A whopping 63 percent stated that they would. How can that be? It's simple. Either they are hopeless backsliders, or they've never repented of their sins and experienced true conversion. This is the kind of damage that extreme messages like this can do. A majority of these deceived Christians belong to a church culture that is perhaps trendy and popular but has no interest in fulfilling the demands of Christ. Many of them serve an "American Jesus," who lets them live as they please and who will, of course, never judge them. Amidst all of the frenetic religious activity going on today, we need the ability to recognize the real Jesus (refer to author's book *The Real Jesus*) and the authentic voice and leading of the Spirit of truth.

In John 3, John the Baptist, who was filled with the spirit and power of Elijah and who ministered with divine authority, declared, *"Behold, the Lamb of God!"* Then he declared again, *"He must increase, but I must decrease."* We must continually behold the Lamb of God in prayer and our walk with Him, especially the attributes becoming to a lamb, such as those of being pure, harmless, holy, and undefiled. Unless we are constantly decreasing in pride and self--assertiveness and cultivating meekness, humility, and teachability in our lives — as well as a ravenous hunger and love for the truth — we will eventually lose our way and drift into deception.

John's ministry was not one of self-exaltation or self-promotion, as is so common today. He was separated by God for the sole purpose of exalting the Lamb of God and preparing a people for Him, a bride for the bridegroom, *"not having spot or wrinkle or any such thing, but that she should be holy and without blemish"* (Eph. 5:27).

"He who has the bride is the bridegroom; but the friend of the bridegroom, who stands and hears him, rejoices greatly because of the bridegroom's voice" (John 3:29).

Those who are true friends of the bridegroom in this hour are hearing His voice, not an echo. The voice of His messengers, who are filled with the spirit and power of Elijah, will point people to the Lamb of God, not to their own ministries, personalities, or agendas. John the Baptist was a voice crying in the wilderness. The entirety of his ministry was focused on the Lamb and His bride.

If a ministry is not pointing people to the One who was, and is, and is to come, it will be judged harshly in this hour. Those who are truly exalting and honoring the Lamb of God have no interest in being seen or heard. They are not looking for a platform or a microphone to promote themselves. The things that denote ministerial "success" in

our day, such as large buildings, large followings, and p(
no interest to the true messengers of the Lamb.

Actually, the Lord is leading His true ministers and f.
bridegroom right now to do the opposite of what it takes to build a
large ministry. He is stripping away human wisdom and all we've utilized in our own efforts to build His Church, for He will not share His
glory with another. He is raising up unconventional ministries.

JOHN THE BAPTIST AND THE SPIRIT AND POWER OF ELIJAH

"There was a man sent from God, whose name was John" (John 1:6).
There is a present-day ministry with a mandate just as John the Baptist
had: to turn hearts back to the Lord and to make a people ready for
Him. Not only did John herald the first arrival of the bridegroom, but
his fiery message prepared he hearts of the people to receive Him.

*"Now John was clothed with camel's hair and with a leather belt
around his waist, and he ate locusts and wild honey"* (Mk. 1:6).

The attire and diet of John the Baptist were significant because
their simplicity confounded the wisdom of man and the vanity of the
false religious leaders. They demonstrated the necessity of man's sur-
vival in connection with dependence upon God and not upon anything else. There was no self-sufficiency in the wilderness.

John could have been a priest in the temple like his esteemed father. He was a direct descendant of Aaron, and he could've had honor,
security, elegant robes, and jewels, but, instead, he went into the
wilderness. The wilderness is the place of separation, preparation, and
training for battle — and certainly not for the weak in faith.

This wild man in the desert, who could have been a prodigy for
the Jewish priesthood, chose a different path, in sharp contrast to the
religious leaders of that day — and actually a total mockery of the reli-

gious system. John the Baptist's preaching and methods were controversial and unconventional.

One of the great emphases of the Lord in this hour is on the preparation of His bride. There must be a distinction made between the church world and the bride of Christ. This is more than a salvation issue. It is about the Lord possessing our vessels for His eternal purposes. This is the spirit and power of Elijah that was upon John the Baptist and would also be a characteristic of those who would minister before His second coming (Mal. 4:5-6).

The Ephesians 4:11 gifts are to equip the saints for service and to prepare a bride for the bridegroom, or a wife for the Lamb.

It was the Lord's provision to meet with God in the days of John the Baptist, to prepare for Jesus' first coming. Likewise, it shall be so in this hour to prepare for His second coming. It is in God's eternal purposes to prepare for His return, for the marriage of the Lamb, to be filled with His Spirit, and visited and equipped by the presence and power of God and the gifts of the Holy Spirit. For there are many who need a fresh infilling of the Spirit and many wise virgins that He is awakening and foolish virgins who need to purchase more oil. God is making a way for those virgins who gave their all for extra oil. They paid a price to burn bright in the darkest hour and to hear the word of the Lord as they heard John the Baptist in the wilderness long ago. I am just one of many voices by the river of living water, aiding and helping those who need fresh baptisms.

God's invitation is to everyone, but that invitation demands a *dedication* and a *consecration. Counting the cost* and *paying the price* are terms we no longer hear today in the marketplace of Western Christianity, but this language is found everywhere in the Scriptures.

It is time to wake up the sleeping church. As I heard one minister say, she can be awakened kindly with a kiss or be shaken with the Lord's severity (Rom. 11:22). It's our choice. If we put it off to the future, it will demand His shakings, which often come in the form of tests and trials — or a crisis that will expose our pride and crooked ways. Pure wholeheartedness is what the Lord desires.

We see this ministry in manifestation in the spirit and power of Elijah as he stood on Mount Carmel and contested with the false prophets of Baal. The fire fell and consumed the sacrifice along with the wood, stones, dust, and even the water. This mighty manifestation caused the people to fall on their faces and declare the Lord as God.

"Now when all the people saw it, they fell on their faces; and they said, 'The Lord, He is God! The Lord, He is God!'" (1 Kings 18:39)

We also see this ministry exercised in the days of Moses as he stretched forth his rod, and the Red Sea swallowed up and drowned the Egyptian armies. The results of this anointing and authority are noted in Exodus 14:31: *"Thus Israel saw the great work which the Lord had done in Egypt; so the people feared the Lord, and believed the Lord and His servant Moses."*

This anointing administered in the spirit and power of Elijah will be seen again and produce holiness and the fear of the Lord in people. Its purpose is always redemptive — to bring forth true repentance and cause the hearts of the people to completely turn to the Lord. We've been in the infancy stages of seeing this on a wider scale. This will include a worldwide company of men and women who have been summoned by the Lord to be His messengers.

In the times of Moses and Elijah, and throughout other stages of Israel's history, great severity was necessary to turn the hearts of the people back to the Lord. Often people quote the scripture in Romans

2:4, properly stating that it is the goodness or kindness of the Lord that leads to repentance, but they fail to read the verses of wrath and judgment surrounding that scripture. When the Lord's goodness does not lead to repentance, then He is forced to move us into the realm of divine severity (Rom. 11:22).

Too many people have taken the Lord's goodness to further their pleasurable, worldly, and even sinful lifestyles and agendas. Too many are building their own ministries today who have little to no godly character because they have never been thoroughly tested or proven and stripped of pride and selfish ambition. Therefore, for the sake of their salvation and the perseverance of their souls, for the sake of their eternal reward, the Lord has to administer His severity.

And so we will see the manifestation of both the goodness *and* severity of God side by side in the days ahead. Bittersweet times are upon us. We will choose our own medicine. These things will come with great cost and great loss to many as well as great glory and victory to others.

I find the scriptural reference to Jesus as the "Lamb of God" very rare until we get to the book of Revelation. There we find approximately 29 references, more than the rest of the entire New Testament combined, to a lion-like lamb (slain but standing, and what a paradox it is to know of the *"wrath of the Lamb"* — Rev. 6:16) which delivers victory in judgment in a manner reminiscent of the resurrected Christ. It was the revelation of the Lamb that ushered in His first coming, and it is that same revelation that will usher in the end of the age, when His wrath is poured out. It is only in the Lamb's meekness and character that we will triumph. With fear and trembling, let us make ourselves ready.

James 5:16

THE CALLING OF A CHURCH AND A NATION BACK TO GOD

If ever there was a time when true apostles and prophets must arise in America and the world, it is now — not only to give prophetic words of what the future holds, but with holy conviction, to call a Church and a nation back to the true worship of God, to drive out the money changers, and to call us back to true Spirit-inspired, fervent, effectual prayer and fasting, and holy character. They must also confront the elite vipers of iniquity and warn the false apostles and prophets of their whitewashed walls and false claims to peace, and to cry out to the people to repent and return to God. Both John the Baptist and Jesus did this as well as the writers of the New Testament.

Now is the time to flee the existing superficial version of Christianity and our false, unholy allegiances and return to a lifestyle that reflects the humility and meekness of our Master. It is an hour when true ministers must move away from the rat race of professional ministry, money-making schemes, and the pursuit of fame, popularity, and media exposure, and be made whole in God's presence and through God's love.

Only true friends of the bridegroom whose character has been shaped in the crucible of their own sufferings and earned God's trust are qualified to lead a Church and a nation back to God. They alone shall know the secret and heart of the Lord.

"The secret of the Lord is with those who fear Him, and He will show them His covenant" (Ps. 25:14).

Notice how this verse reads in the Living Bible:

"Friendship with God is reserved for those who reverence him. With them alone he shares the secrets of his promises."

29

Too many modern apostolic and prophetic voices are tainted because they are too eager for power, popularity, influence, riches, and fame. They seek more the validation and affirmation of men at the neglect of truly living and speaking in the sight of God. The road can be lonely and difficult at times, but we endanger ourselves when we seek the validation of man over the validation of our heavenly Father. We must begin to align ourselves with the heart of Christ and see clearly what is within man, and rather than seek approval in the flesh, prefer at all costs the approval of God. This will keep us preferring purity over popularity, intimacy over influence, and holiness over hype.

A heartfelt reliance and preference for the approval of God over the approval of man is what distinguishes all true apostles and prophets from counterfeits and wannabes. The same could be said for all ministers and all saints. For there will come a time when they must not only speak out against the carnal and sinful status quo, but shake off those religious, political, and cultural traditions that run contrary to what God demands and expects of His people. This cannot happen unless they love and fear God more than man. This also cannot happen unless they have an exceedingly great zeal for the honor of God's house, who we are.

CHAPTER TWO

LET THE ZEAL FOR GOD'S HOUSE EAT YOU UP

"Then His disciples remembered that it was written, "Zeal for Your house has eaten Me up" (Jn. 2:17).

Zeal. It's not an adjective we use very much in common, everyday language. It means "a great exertion, great energy, or enthusiasm in pursuit of a cause or an objective." Some synonyms for "zeal" are passion, vigor, intensity, and devotion. This is what many of the prophets of old demonstrated toward God's house and His holiness. As an adjective "zealous" is primarily used in the positive sense except when it is used without knowledge as Paul did for Judaism before his radical encounter with the Lord (Gal. 1:14). Zeal is a godly attribute when it is used to glorify God and for righteous causes and godly works.

Phinehas turned back the wrath of the Lord from destroying Israel in their sin because he was zealous with God's zeal (Nu. 25:11).

Elijah was full of zeal because the children of Israel had forsaken God's covenant, torn down His altars, and killed His prophets with the sword (1 Kings 19:10).

The psalmist was consumed with God's zeal because his enemies had forgotten God's words (Ps. 119:139).

We are admonished to be zealous for the fear of the Lord all day long (Pr. 23:17) and to be zealous for good works (Titus 2:14).

Jesus was the greatest example of zeal. In fact, He wore zeal as a cloak or a mantle (Is. 59:17). Many don't see Jesus that way.

When He cleansed the temple, His disciples remembered that it had been written of Him in the Scriptures that zeal for the Father's house would eat Him up. The Amplified Bible says that He will be consumed with jealousy for the honor of His Father's house.

"And His disciples remembered that it is written [in the Holy Scriptures], Zeal (the fervor of love) for Your house will eat Me up. [I will be consumed with jealousy for the honor of Your house.]" (Jn. 2:17).

I have written this book in the zeal of the Lord.

THE CONDITION OF TODAY'S CHRISTIAN MARKETPLACE

What are we seeing in much of the mainstream of today's Christian marketplace, especially in the West?

We see seekers of popularity and fame, and those craving a name. We see pursuers of gold and glitter. We see proud, strutting preachers flashing their titles every time they meet you.

We see lying prophets who are leading the simple-minded off to the slaughter. We see false teachers and dreamers who paint a pie-in-the sky picture of a God they've never known.

We see selfish, greedy Word mongers, mammon babblers, sheep fleecers, and un-sanctified vessels unwilling to be tested by the holy scriptures and held accountable by holy men.

We see spiritual adulterers full of iniquity who have prostituted the ministry and merchandised God's house.

The amazing truth is that we could stop all this almost overnight by not supporting these hucksters and charlatans and their carnally minded ministries — whose god is their belly, whose glory is their shame, who mind earthly things, and sadly, whose end is destruction. I tell you with pain in my heart and weeping that they are enemies of the cross of Christ (Phil. 3:18-19), and they are influencing multitudes who are following them to perdition.

It is time to be separated from this rat race of energized flesh, for-profit ministries, and false ministry success.

DEFINING TRUE MINISTRY SUCCESS

In a recent article about "wildly successful" mega-churches, the author referred to some select ministers who have reached the "pinnacle of success in ministry." In a social-media post, a friend moved by holy zeal took this article to task and said something like this:

"Excuse me, but what exactly is this "pinnacle of success in ministry"? How is this success achieved? How is it measured or defined? Is it determined by attendance and numbers of followers one may amass? Is it by the size of building or mailing list one has? Is it based on how influential one is? Is it determined by the size of one's bank account or budget? Number of best-selling books? Social-media popularity and awareness?

What is it that determines who has reached "the top"? Is it CNN? Fox News? TIME magazine? Is it Charisma or Ministry Today magazine? Is it what Oprah Winfrey says? Is there some elite zone where mega-ministry intersects with celebrity status to produce the pinnacle of success? Or could this be a mere carnal definition of man?

"Preachers had better settle this issue of what real success is in their hearts. Because I can tell you that this top-to-bottom pyramid structure is a man-made concept and only a mirage. And if it is a mirage, the illusion will be so attractive that many ministers will do anything to reach it. They will sacrifice their marriages for it. They will sacrifice their children and family. They will sacrifice their time, happiness, and health. They will fill their moments chasing ever-elusive

formulas, blueprints, methods, and plans. We have seen it before, and we will undoubtedly see it again." — Shane Philpott

Here is a scripture that should be the cornerstone for every church and ministry.

"Unless the Lord builds the house, they labor in vain that build it ..." (Ps. 127:1).

Now read carefully these paraphrased words of one young prophet friend of mine with wisdom beyond his years:

"The problem is that ministry today is as addictive as heroin or crack cocaine. Many pursue what they think to be ministry success with total abandonment. We must realize, however, that pursuing ministry opportunities and following Jesus Christ are not the same thing.

"An addiction to applause, platforms, microphones, television cameras, influential ministry connections, and networking is as addicting as drugs or pornography. The pursuit of 'ministry' is becoming the premier cover-up for a dysfunctional marriage, family, and personal life. Too many hide their sins and their private demons behind the pursuit of 'ministry.' Their ministerial success is primarily based on the platform and open doors they've been given and not on the character and integrity of their hearts or the godly order and love in their marriages, families, and homes.

"God is much more interested in changing us on the inside (character) than using us on the outside (ministry).

"Our agreement with this statement can only be found in whether we value the prayer room more than a platform, and private ministry more than public ministry. If we are daydreaming of speaking before large crowds instead of standing or kneeling before the throne of God

and admiring and adoring the beauty of Jesus, our priorities are skewed, and we are more than likely consumed with an addiction to ministry. Many of our Bible colleges and ministerial training schools need to place more emphasis on character, prayer, fasting, having a devotional life, and developing a healthy family life instead of knowing how to network, market, build a ministry platform, and create a culturally relevant ministry or church.

"It's time for a generation of present ministers and future ministers to have character that actually matches the anointing upon their lives. This fruit can only be forged in the fires of prayer and devotion. I don't believe God is interested in who we know, what we know, and what doors we walk through. He wants to know if we are praying, fasting, blessing our enemies, giving and ministering to the poor, and loving our spouses and children — the stuff that doesn't sell books or make very good social-media videos.

"For all the major addictions being addressed in the Church today, why is being addicted to ministry never discussed or even exposed?" — Jeremiah Johnson

That is a word from God that should stir us deeply.

THE SUCCESS OF BIBLE CHARACTERS

Consider many of the Bible's characters in light of what is considered ministry success today.

John the Baptist was alone, imprisoned, and eventually beheaded for taking a stand against sin and speaking the word of the Lord as all true prophets should do. Who in the West do you find who resembles him? Who in the West stands before a king or president and calls him an adulterer?

Paul was abandoned by his so-called "Christian friends" — and even abandoned by the churches he planted — falsely accused, in conflict with other church leaders. His ministry was often slandered and sabotaged by others; he was imprisoned, alone, and, finally, executed.

Do we even know anyone who is suffering this kind of opposition and persecution in the Western hemisphere? Oh, yes. We see plenty of examples of it in nations where the gospel has been outlawed, and converting people to Christ will get you imprisoned and killed. But are we seeing anything close to this in the West and in so-called "free," industrialized Western nations? Often it is quite the contrary, as we are usually persecuted for unrighteousness' sake and our filthy-rich or immoral lifestyles.

Jesus was abandoned by friends, falsely accused, virtually alone, and finally crucified. Where can we find this abandonment, false accusation, and persecution of those who obey God here in the West?

History records that all the apostles were persecuted, too, and that all but one were killed for their faith in Jesus.

John was the only one who supposedly died a natural death, but he also suffered, even into his elderly years — alone, imprisoned, and cast off on a barren island.

How this clear biblical narrative gets transformed into Western Charismatic and Evangelical models of "ministry success" would amaze even Harry Houdini. Jesus said to be leery when everyone thinks you are wonderful, for Israel so loved the false prophets (Lk. 6:26).

The culture of Christian media that oozes over the popularity and success of unholy vessels and charismatic personalities should mean nothing to us if we want to please Jesus. We should hate it. Accurately representing Jesus and the true values of his kingdom is likely to get you slandered and killed by devout religious people. Is it all that important to get your face on the cover of Christian magazines that are owned by secular, un-sanctified, for-profit corporations who are in it for personal gain?

CLOAKS OF CHRISTIANITY

The truth is that such a great percentage of Christian ministry today is characterized by jealousy, envy, play-acting, self-promoting, self-justifying, and self-focused behavior — all of which are hidden under 101 highly choreographed religious cloaks.

Churches are filled with ministries who are wonderfully trained to perform "the liturgical functions" but who are sadly lacking in true spiritual maturity. And our assemblies are consequently full of professing believers who have no eye to discern and differentiate between true spiritual maturity and maintaining a disciplined outward appearance.

In this "*Quid pro Quo*," "I'll scratch your back — you scratch mine," "I'll promote your preeminence — you promote mine," "good-ole-boys club" system, ministries work together very diligently to keep God's people from seeing the little men behind the curtains. We need to draw open the veil revealing that which many ministers and pastors know about one another and work so earnestly to keep the public from seeing. We have a soulish, carnal ministry cleverly cloaked over by a multitude of religious fig-leaves.

The real maturing of the saints (Ephesians 4:11-12) has been abandoned long ago by many and replaced by the drive to expand our ministerial piece of the pie with a guild of salaried professionals.

As the following author so succinctly says it: we must stop protecting our own projects.

"As we turn to the evangelical leadership of this country in the last decades, unhappily, we must come to the conclusion that often it has not been much help. It has shown the mark of a platonic, overly spiritualized Christianity all too often. Spirituality to the evangelical leadership often has not included the Lordship of Christ over the whole spectrum of life. Spirituality has often been shut up to a very narrow area. And also very often, among many evangelicals, including many evangelical leaders, it seems that the final end is to protect their own projects. I am again asking the question, 'Why have we let ourselves go so far down the road?'" — Francis Schaeffer, *A Christian Manifesto*

How can the church be delivered from further generations of soul dominance and energized flesh? Only by walking straight into the bright spotlight of the Holy Spirit, instead of maintaining a strategic business-as-usual distance from it.

THE GLORY HAS DEPARTED

The reason there's no glory in the modern Church has nothing to do with bigger and more attractive buildings, the appeal of outward appearance, the color effects, the decorative staging, the fancy lights, the cool bands, or the skinny jeans, big screens, and fog machines. Nor does it have to do with the kind of music or worship style we have. Nor does it have to do with whether you meet in a home, a building, or another venue, or whatever part of the city or town. Neither has it anything to do with compensation and lack of financial resources or whether you have paid staff or volunteer help.

The glory has departed because we have sinned. Our ministry leaders have sinned.

It was because of the sins in the priesthood that the glory departed from Israel in the days of Eli and his two wicked sons (1 Sam. 4:22). In fact, Hophni and Phinehas, the sons of Eli, didn't even know the Lord, and they were priests (1 Sam. 2:12). I find that there are many in the ministry today that do not know the Lord. I don't necessarily mean that they are not born again. I don't mean that they are not engaged in the work of God, but they are carnal and motivated by pride and popularity. What I mean is that they don't really know the heart and the ways of the Lord.

Hophni and Phinehas had no passion for the presence and glory of God, no love or consideration for people, and no honor and respect for the holy things of God. They were in the ministry for themselves, immoral men who sought only to satisfy their carnal appetites. They also mishandled and demanded offerings from the people (1 Sam. 2:16-17), which is so common today.

God blamed Eli for the wickedness and corruption of the priesthood. Not only that, but the iniquity of his house was so great that God said it could not be atoned by sacrifice or offering forever (1 Sam. 3:13-14). Think about that. God rebuked Eli for honoring his sons more than he honored the Lord — by allowing his sons to be fattened with the offerings of God's people (1 Sam. 2:29). Eli knew the evil dealings of his sons but refused to judge the situation and the fact that they made God's people to transgress (1 Sam. 2:22-25). We are having similar issues today, when no judgment is ever made on sinning ministers and sinning "saints." There are hardly any constraints, restrictions, accountability, and no enforced disciplines for those who practice sin. A minister falls into adultery, and the next week or month, he's back in the pulpit preaching. How sad.

Where is the glory of God today? Why has it departed? One big reason is that we refuse to judge the true condition of the Church and the body of Christ. We actually do the opposite and hold up our thou-shalt-not-judge card when sin and wrongdoing are addressed.

TODAY IT'S STILL ABOUT WHO IS THE GREATEST (Mk. 10:35-45)

It is a true difference-maker to recognize the great need for the restoration of the glory and power of God in the Church today and the issues we are outlining in this book that will either help or hinder God's plan and purpose. On a more practical level, the other difference maker is in the love and honor we have for God and for one another, and for the varying gifts that are to complement each other. Unfortunately, today it's more about, "Who's the greatest?"

The Church is scattered, divided, mired in comparison and competition; in most cases, not all the governing leadership can agree. Pastors bear too much of the burden because they refuse to share their pulpits and pastoral responsibilities with other qualified ministry gifts and local elders. Must the people always hear from the same pastoral gift? Must they preach every sermon? Must they make every decision? Must every buck stop with them? Must they be so controlling, programmed, and restrictive?

Dear pastor, we need your precious gift and function in the body of Christ. We cannot operate without you, but why can't you share your pulpit with other ministry gifts besides those who have the same agenda and message as you? Have you forgotten that it's the entire Ephesians 4:11 ministry gifts that properly equip the body of Christ for works of service? Will you honor the gifts in others?

Train, equip, and delegate. Release responsibility and authority to others. Mobilize the saints for the work of the ministry. Let go and let God.

Can the body be a church if all hell breaks loose in our nation, and we face heartbreaking crises and persecution we've never faced before? Have the Ephesians 4:11 ministers equipped the saints properly and sufficiently? Or are they still arguing over who's the boss, who's the most gifted, who's got the best church or most effective ministry, and who's heard from the Lord? In the day of battle and real persecution, those things will be the furthest from our minds. We need to prepare now for the coming storm.

Can the Church be the Church and move forward in purity, in true prayer, and in greater glory and power? I believe she can, but only if ministry leaders step up to the plate and lay down their concepts, their new ideas, and old conversations that mostly deal with external things, and tend to hinder true unity in the leadership. Once we are united in spirit, then let come what may — crises of all sorts — let everything be shaken; for the Church will then stand in its unity. But if leadership continues to jostle for position and argue, as the disciples did, over who's the greatest — and sell their own ideas through lectures and books for their own personal advancement — it will deter the Church from rolling up its sleeves and getting dirty for Jesus and networking with other ministers.

Lack of true humility is causing ministers to shuck their responsibilities. This is the reason for a lack of readiness for any grave crisis in our culture — which, when it comes, will come in greater measure. In leadership, no matter the cause, it always points back to you.

QUESTIONS TO ASK EVERY LOCAL SAINT AND LAYPERSON

Do you know and understand your responsibility to the local body of Christ? Are you walking in true honor, respect, and keeping opinions to yourself, while functioning in the personal responsibility of what your life and gift requires? This alone will turn much of our division into a harmony that will lead God's Church into unity.

What have you contributed to a team lately concerning the poor, the needy, and the lost?

Have you considered that hanging around believers in social settings, although a necessary part of our lifestyle and encouraged in Scripture, is easier than going out to the streets, projects, drug centers, and prisons, and laying down our lives for the unlovely?

What about widows and orphans? What of single mothers? What about the elderly? Are you making a conscious effort to minister to them, inconveniencing yourself for their benefit? Many sons and daughters don't even take good care of their own sickly or widowed parents, much less others. These things are important to the Lord and speak of pure religion (Jam. 1:27).

The body of Christ has become good at gathering and conducting meetings and conferences but has failed in true discipleship, because it requires more time, patience, and sacrifice.

The issue with most leaders and laypeople is that they don't pray much. So there's no discernment, no direction, and their spirits are hardened to God's agenda and His compassion. We are growing into a Godless culture.

Don't focus on outward things and that which does not matter, but just obey God and take your rightful place in the body of Christ and flow in your gifting. Stop competing, and just work. Stop criticizing and finding fault with your pastor and local leadership and church. Quit following online ministries whose marriages and families are in disorder, or who have no value or respect for local churches and pastors. The only thing most of them care about is building their own following, ministry, and popularity.

Pastor, receive God's plan and purpose in prayer. Do what He says, and speak what He commands you to say. Stop reaching for honor and expecting people to serve you and just serve them. The Church will mature but only if our local leaders grow up first and become true servants.

Are we willing to obey God at any cost? Are we going to unite or still be looking for reasons not to honor one another's gifts in the Lord and serve a lost generation?

The Western Church as we've known it must come to an end. The true Church must emerge, or there will be nothing of any real significance left — only dead orthodoxy, a religious social club, and an entertainment center.

And here's another reality that must change: many churches and leaders are too busy with fluff and programs and non-essentials to make any lasting impact on the community around them. As a result, their members are losing their zeal, fire, and love. Many of them are becoming like the church of Ephesus, who forsook their first love.

SOME COMMENDATION BUT MUCH CORRECTION

I know I am speaking very plainly, but there were several churches in the book of Revelation whom Jesus spoke to very plainly and strongly also (Rev. 2 & 3). Even in His public ministry, He was often direct with his words and speech. There was much reproof and rebuke combined with a little commendation. As strong of a rebuke as some parts of this book are, there is still an incredible amount of good being done every day through the churches around the country. From feeding the poor to housing the homeless to fighting human trafficking to adopting abandoned children to helping addicts get free, to sponsoring refugees — certainly these are commendable causes, and some commendation is in order and deserved. And this is only the tip of the iceberg of good works done by the Church; still, so much correction and reform is needed.

Actually, only two of the seven churches in Revelation received no correction or rebuke from Jesus. We are living in that day. Just like the messages to the seven churches of Revelation, so there must be strong voices in these end times who will speak what God is speaking and bring the heart of God and true direction back into the Church. They must prepare people for the glory of God, for the harvest, and for His imminent return.

In the Old Testament, God even used a donkey to speak when Balaam the prophet wanted to say something else (Nu. 22). In this hour, there are too many voices saying something else. Like Balaam, the wages of iniquity (2 Pt. 2:15), running greedily in his error for profit (Jude 1:11), and the desire for popularity have influenced many ministers and pastors to tone down the importance of holiness, the workings of the Holy Spirit, and what He wants to say and do. Churches must be loosed from their soul ties with money and popularity, for the Lord has borne witness with us that it has been a great temptation for many.

This is a kind of bewitching, where money and the driving desire for popularity have been used as a means of manipulating leadership into wrong decisions and a wrong direction. At the root of the many issues facing the Church in this hour is the love of money and the incessant need for popularity. After all, it is the love of money that is the root of all evil. Too many seem to be following the money.

BE CAREFUL OF BEING MONEY-MINDED

The words of Smith Wigglesworth are more true today than they were when he spoke them:

"There is one thing I am very grateful to the Lord for, and that is that He has given me grace not to have a desire for money. The love of money is a great hindrance to many, and many a man is crippled in his ministry because he lets his heart run after financial matters."

May ministers stay free from this snare so they can preach what God wants them to preach and do what God tells them, regardless of money. True messengers of the Lord are not moved by the promise of money. Becoming money-minded can get you off course in your calling and ministry. It can cause the anointing on your life to wane or be lost completely. It can manipulate you to do things that God has not directed you to do. The pressure of not having enough or constantly reaching and coveting more can quickly kill an otherwise healthy church or ministry.

Our petition has been that the Lord would once again overturn the tables of the money changers and the seats of those who buy and sell — those who utilize the Church as a place of business — religious establishments, and those ruled by filthy lucre. We have also prayed for the protection of ministers, who out of personal conviction, will be forced to leave these religious systems and establishments to obey God. Even in so-called "full gospel" and Charismatic circles this will be so.

For example, we know of some fine couples who've had to step out into their own ministry without any financial support or backing from the large church they've had an active part in for years. There's been a spiritual ceiling placed over so many functioning ministers that it becomes difficult to fit themselves into an existing local body or organization. Often doctrinal differences and suspicion of "sheep stealing" emerges, concerning already fruitful and maturing ministries. Through experience I've found that it usually takes much longer for a functioning ministry to be trusted by a church organization than for the average believer, who doesn't have a functional ministry. It's a system that some can no longer just exist in because it confines them, and so they are forced to leave in order to obey God. But then to compound the problem, finding another fellowship of leaders and believers with similar values becomes difficult for many such ministries.

The key lesson the Lord taught us concerning these things was to always keep our hearts right because you don't want to alienate yourself from those who are still considered to be a part of the body of Christ. There are many within those man-made systems who have genuine gifts and callings but have become stagnant.

GOD IS JOINING TOGETHER KINDRED SPIRITS

On the positive end of things, the people of God are connecting with one another in the spirit of truth and unity, as a divine dissatisfaction with the religious systems of this world and of man fills us. This is the attitude that will bind kindred spirits and those of like-precious faith together and mushroom into a mighty move of God in this hour. The real unity of the Spirit is not ecumenicalism, where people with various religious beliefs are brought together through man's efforts. It's relationship-based Christianity and activity in the Holy Spirit that connects spirits to spirits.

Here is a recent prophecy given by my wife concerning this:

"You see, I've brought you into relationships that are after Me, and you stir one another, for this is what I've ordained for My body to have... spirit-to-spirit communications and activations.

"For it is only then that there is a move of My Spirit and revelation and knowledge of the things I am doing. That is why when you hear of someone who is moving with Me, your spirit is stirred, and it causes you to move with Me, too. For in the past, you've looked at others and have witnessed things that are similar to you, but I've made you who you are and given you what you carry. For those things that are in you stir up others that you come in contact with. So be who you are, be who I've made you to be, for I'm bringing even more of those spirit-to-spirit relationships that stir each other. For if you can see what it looks like in the spirit realm — it is the moving of My Spirit and the activation and the life that comes forth...and it even goes through the phone lines, I see, for there is no distance in My Spirit.

"That's why you can only go to places now where I've made that connection of spirit to spirit through your writings and teachings, for the things that they hear causes an activation of My Spirit in their spirits, and this is what causes the communications and them to reach out and connect.

"For I see now, too, something goes on with you — that you're going to see this moving in you, too. For just as others are moved by you, you're going to be moved by the gifts in others. So, yes — reach out, but don't press, even as you've learned from Me. Yes, reach out, and see if I don't do something within that realm of others stirring things in you. You'll know, and you'll understand, and you'll feel what I'm speaking now, and you'll know that there is a relationship connection.

"Just as I've spoken to you before of how those who have walked away and have been deceived and bewitched, I'm now bringing some of those back in this hour, and there's going to be a reconnection. That is why I've told you not to judge them by where they were, but to listen to My Spirit within your spirit and find that they will say things,

and there will be movement again. So, pay attention to those relation-ships that I bring to you.

"And just as you came back into the fullness years ago, and the things I dealt with you about, I'm doing in others, too.

"Thank You, Father, and we agree as touching this in prayer right now. I see so much activity in the Spirit. That is what happened with _____ and _____. There was instant Holy Ghost activity, and it was so good (tears). And even the pastor in _____, who doesn't know how to flow and operate in the Spirit, he still reached out because he wants it. And so that is what's going on. This is activity in the Holy Spirit, connecting spirits to spirits."

EQUAL YOKES: PRAYER, PURPOSE, AND AGREEMENT

Charles Finney was a great revivalist in the 1800s and a leader in the second awakening. He has been called The Father of Modern Re-vivalism. Most students of revival and church history are very familiar with Finney, but not as many are familiar with the real secret of his power and effectiveness. Finney attributed his success in revival and the high retention rate of his converts to a man named Father Daniel Nash.

Father Nash was a mighty man of prayer who was the engine be-hind Finney's revivals. On his tombstone, part of his epitaph reads: *LABORER WITH FINNEY, MIGHTY IN PRAYER.* Three to four months after Nash's death, Finney left his itinerant ministry. He knew the power to his ministry was almost exclusively in the prayer ministry of Father Nash and one or two others who would partner with Nash in prayer. How many today esteem the ministry of prayer to this degree? And how many really understand what it means to pray with the real anointing of the Spirit and labor in travail for lost souls?

The secret to the power in Finney's ministry was the supply of the Spirit that came from Nash's intercession and travail for souls. But Finney and Nash also walked in great agreement in their purpose for revival and the conversion of souls. So, although prayer was obviously a big key, the agreement in their purpose was vitally important, too.

Here's another inspired utterance my wife and I received in prayer recently:

"I have never denied a man or a woman of power in prayer who aligned themselves with My will and My Word in obedience to the purpose of Mark 16 and Matthew 28 of going into all the world.

"The lack of power comes only when man's plans override Mine. There is power in agreement. Where you have seen lack of power is where there was lack of agreement. The ministry gifts have to be in agreement with the Word and with the purposes of God, and the pray-ers must supply the power.

"In your travels, you've seen there are places where they agree with My Word and the leadership is obeying Me. And even when they've had error in some things you've seen, they've gone with one purpose, and the pray-ers are praying for that purpose. And therefore, there's freedom and there's liberty in that place, in that city. That is what you see — agreement, agreement with Me."

What a tremendous word!

There is power in being like-minded. There is power in being equally yoked. Agreement in the Spirit with those of like-precious faith is vital to our success in advancing the kingdom of God.

Father Nash in his humility released the manifold wisdom of God (Eph. 3:10) when it was attached to a ministry gift who walked in agreement with God's purposes.

I see a pen and a paper — a new document and a new order. I see names written on the paper — those of like spirit who have faith and agreement in the Spirit. No more unequal yokes. It's time now for equal yokes. When you're equally yoked, there's no grind in the flesh. We call forth divine connections and equally yoked hearts for the work God wants to do in these end days.

CHAPTER THREE

THE DECLINE OF THE POWER OF GOD

My wife Carolyn is given to dreams from the Lord. In a recent dream, she saw that I was very upset because there was food being cooked at a friend's house that wasn't prepared right. It was not the kind of wholesome food needed to satisfy and nourish the body. I was actually very vocal about the food's lack of quality. What is intriguing is that she has had several similar dreams in recent years about spiritual food. I believe the reason for this lies in the fact we are living in a time when there is a great departure from the faith and sound doctrine (something laid out below).

In the last part of this dream, there was a pastor present who was very indifferent and uncaring concerning the situation of his church and people. He was so far removed from what the body of Christ was to partake of and do — completely unattached, with no compassion. Carolyn was trying to get the pastor to look and see the dire state of things, but he was too indifferent and said that it was nothing to be concerned about. She tried to warn him before judgment came in the form of fires and floods, but the pastor didn't seem to care. Clearly, he was a wolf or a hireling with no real concern for God's people.

When we inquired about the dream, the Lord said that this lack of nourishing food reflected the state of many churches today and is a fulfillment of the following scripture:

"For the time will come when they will not endure sound doctrine; but after their own lusts shall they heap to themselves teachers, having itching ears; and they shall turn away their ears from the truth, and shall be turned unto fables" (2 Tim. 4:3-4).

Just as the wrong diet and poor eating habits affects the physical body, so, too, the wrong spiritual diet affects the spirit. The Lord told us that good spiritual food and proper spiritual nourishment will now come by His Spirit to correct error and root out problems in the spiritual body and in a spiritual sense. This book is another small contribution to this area of concern in the heart of our Lord.

In the natural realm, eating lots of sugar can cause many problems in the physical body. The same is true spiritually when people feed on messages that tend to produce deficiency, deceit, and delusion. We are more susceptible and vulnerable to deception when these kinds of "sweet tooth" messages comprise much of our spiritual diet.

Here is a word the Lord charged us with that can apply to other ministers as well:

"Be aware of the Lord's utterances that will come in places and in nations where you are preaching. These utterances will contain food and true meat for the people. Some will refuse it, but some will begin to partake again, and there will be a restoration in their spirits, and deliverance, and they will be ready for My return. I will show you more unpleasant things to see, and there will be an opportunity for many to hear the word of the Lord and change."

When religious leaders engage in practices that steal from the sheep, and the deepest spiritual needs of God's people are not being met, it grieves and angers the Head of the Church, the Lord Jesus Christ. This is the reason He cleansed the temple in the manner He did.

"Then Jesus went into the temple of God and drove out all those who bought and sold in the temple, and overturned the tables of the money changers and the seats of those who sold doves. And He said to them, "It is written, 'My house shall be called a house of prayer, but

you have made it a 'den of thieves.' Then the blind and the lame came to Him in the temple, and He healed them" (Matt. 21:12-14).

What we ought to see in the temple: Purity, prayer, and the power of God being manifest to meet the needs of the people.

What is currently being seen as in the days of Jesus: Impurities, prayerlessness, and powerlessness.

(I do recognize that, in the New Covenant we, His people, are the true temple of the Holy Spirit, and the house of God both individually and collectively [1 Cor. 3:16; 1 Pt. 2:5; Heb. 3:6], so when I refer to the "temple" or "house," I'm speaking of the Church collectively.)

Many of the impurities in the Church today lie in the form of a consumerism (money used for man's own interests and purposes) that acts as leaven that defiles the body of Christ. Even when people refuse to heed the word of the Lord and change or make the necessary adjustments, God remains patient and continues to give them opportunities to hear and to change, but eventually He must act. Now is a very serious time for instruction, correction, and reproof given to the Church with the anointing and authority of the Spirit of God and in the love of the Father. People must be prepared and made ready for the storms that are coming, for the harvest of souls yet to be reaped, and for the glory of God — and to meet the Lord, either at His imminent return or at death and the Judgment.

WHAT HAS GONE WRONG

Many pastors and ministers are quenching the Spirit of God and not cooperating with His plans and purposes. Angels are hindered and bristle when ministers fail to carry out their priestly responsibilities and to walk in truth and in their God-given authority. Because many of them are not yielding to the Spirit and preaching the full counsel of

God, which includes correction, not only does deception occur, but people do not get properly nourished or activated in their gifts and callings.

What some local pastors don't realize is that the utilization of the gifts in God's people will cause healing, satisfaction, and fulfillment in their own hearts and lives. Too many are not seeking the kingdom and moving in their gifts and assignments, and doing what they're called to do, and functioning in who they're called to be. Some are in rebellion, but frankly, others are just bored, and spiritual passivity is killing them. Local pastors, in conjunction with the other Ephesians 4:11 ministry gifts, must be ready to assist the gifts and graces in others that will help accelerate divine activity in a body and in a community. This will open doors of utterance in an area. Although under a completely different set of circumstances, this is what the apostle Paul requested prayer for while he was yet in prison.

"Continue in prayer and watch therein with thanksgiving, besides praying also for us that God would open unto us a door of utterance to speak the mystery of Christ, for which I am also in bonds..." (Col. 4:2-3).

Paul was in prison requesting prayer for an open door of utterance to speak the mystery of Christ. Sadly, many local churches have become like prisons today, where control and confinement as well as prayerlessness is holding back doors of utterance from opening for the people to be released to flow in their various gifts. Their spirits are malnourished, and there is no zeal and fire in them, because in many churches, the pastor is the only gift they are given access to. This is the reason many are getting their feeding, training, and equipping online or elsewhere. Most churches are top-heavy with the pastor/teacher and administration gifts, but very light on apostles, prophets, and evangelists. Gradually and slowly, this will produce passivity in people and eventually kill a church.

The book of Acts is our Church model and pattern and purpose for all believers for all time. In the book of Acts, we see what apostolic ministry looks like. We see the evangelistic model in Philip (Acts 8). We see prophets and teachers praying and moving together (Acts 13). We see what the activation of gifts looks like. We see what open doors of utterance look like. We see what moves of God look like. Prayer is a big key.

A century ago, the great apostle to South Africa, John G. Lake, had a mighty angelic visitation. The angel took him through the book of Acts, saying:

" *This is Pentecost as God gave it through the heart of Jesus. Strive for this. Contend for this. Teach the people to pray for this. For this, and this alone, will meet the necessity of the human heart, and this alone will have the power to overcome the forces of darkness."*

When the angel was departing, he said: *"Pray. Pray. Pray. Teach the people to pray. Prayer and prayer alone, much prayer, persistent prayer, is the door of entrance into the heart of God."*

Jesus said that His house is to be called a house of prayer. We know that the temple today is not buildings or houses of brick and mortar, but the people individually and collectively who make up the house of prayer. And it is effectual fervent prayer that opens doors of utterance where the Word is preached in power and demonstration, and the deepest needs of the people are met.

TWO OTHER REASONS FOR THE DECLINE OF THE POWER OF GOD

Smith Wigglesworth spoke prophetically decades ago before he died and said that one of the great moves of God would happen in the

1980s, when solid teaching of the Word would be combined with the gifts and the move of the Holy Spirit. He knew he wouldn't live to see it but that the younger generation of his day would. My wife and I cut our teeth on that move of God and personally benefited greatly from it and enjoyed it while it lasted. That move of the Word and the Spirit laid a solid foundation in both of us that we have carried since that time. The Word and the Spirit should be the plumb line for every generation.

We were also privileged to be a part of a very fruitful Word and Spirit missionary movement in West Africa that took us into three different countries before transitioning in the 1990s back to America. Here in our own homeland, we were privileged once again to be a part of a great outpouring known now historically as the Brownsville Revival (1995-2000). In a five-year period, 4 million visitors came from around the world to that revival with 150,000 experiencing first-time salvation. We were part of the faculty of senior leaders of the ministry school that was spawned from that great outpouring. There we helped to establish students in the Word of God and their respective ministry callings.

Since those special days, however, I have witnessed a steady decline of both the Word of truth and the Spirit of truth in many churches and many places. There's been a dilution of the anointed Word of God and a subsequent diminishing of the workings of the Spirit of God. What should've continued to grow in might, strength, and influence has actually declined, at least here in the West, while in some other nations we are seeing great revival and a harvest of souls.

What has happened to cause this decline and diminishing of both the Word and the Spirit? In prayer the Lord unveiled the two main issues we referred to earlier in the Preface of this book (lack of true spiritual prayer, and impurities such as pride of position, desire for the honor of man, hypocrisy, greed and covetousness concerning money, which all amounts to the worship of mammon). Of course, the Church has other issues and problems, but these were the two the Lord highlighted and wanted us to address at this time. This has led and contributed to the following:

FIRST REASON: WISDOM OF MAN

You've undoubtedly heard it said that a lack of prayer equals a lack of power. Those who are too busy to pray are too busy for power. Lack of true spiritual prayer and true communion with the Holy Spirit causes man to glory in his own wisdom and conceit, which in the end is what diminishes the glory and power of God. The Scriptures give us a description of the true wisdom of God:

"For you see your calling, brethren, that not many wise according to the flesh, not many mighty, not many noble, are called. But God has chosen the foolish things of the world to put to shame the wise, and God has chosen the weak things of the world to put to shame the things which are mighty; and the base things of the world and the things which are despised God has chosen, and the things which are not, to bring to nothing the things that are, **that no flesh should glory in His presence**. *But of Him you are in Christ Jesus, who became for us wisdom from God — and righteousness and sanctification and redemption — that, as it is written, "He who glories, let him glory in the Lord"* (1 Cor. 1:26-31).

Carnal man and those devoid of the mind of Christ have gloried in fleshly wisdom, and in the mighty and noble things of this world. But God has chosen the foolish things, the weak things, and the base and despised things to confound, put to shame, and bring to nothing the things mere men place their trust in. We will see this more specifically in a later chapter, but here is one main way this has happened.

First, this lack of true prayer has resulted in a lack of power with fewer true conversions and a precipitous decline in church attendance. To offset this, church leaders have created new church models subtly based on the wisdom of man and carnal marketing techniques.

For example, there were two leading pastors and churches who were primarily responsible for forming the most popular new church model. I have chosen to conceal their names because they may have changed or repented since then. I will not side with Satan, the accuser of the brethren, and accuse my brothers of something they started many years ago now. Additionally, I don't know their hearts and have never spoken to them personally, and I don't believe blowing out someone else's candle will make mine shine any brighter. These men may be doing much good right now, and my business is not to falsely judge them but to share the history of what transpired through the years that I believe greatly weakened the spiritual condition of multitudes of churches, not only here in America but throughout the world.

At any rate, these two leading men formed their own association of churches, one of them having 9,500 of them espousing to and following his new ideology for church growth, with 100,000 church leaders attending at least one conference. In its beginnings, more than 250,000 pastors and church leaders from approximately 125 countries also attended their church growth seminars, and more than 60,000 pastors initially subscribed to one of their weekly email newsletters. Those numbers may be much higher now, but these figures will give you an idea of the influence these two men and this new church model has had, although I've heard unconfirmed reports that at least one of these men has since renounced this methodology, calling it a big mistake.

Nevertheless, the damage done by this new church model has produced an untold number of churches called "seeker friendly" or "seeker awareness." Their main philosophy is evangelizing through application of the latest marketing techniques. Typically, it begins with a survey of the lost or unchurched. This survey questions the unchurched about the things that interest them and offers ideas that would motivate them to attend a particular church. The results of the questionnaire indicate areas for potential change in a church's operations and services that will help them better attract the unchurched, keep them attending, and win them to Christ. Those who have developed this marketing approach oftentimes guarantee the growth of churches that diligently follow their proven methods. As far as numbers go, this method is working, as many churches are exploding with numerical growth. But is it Biblically based, or is it a gross compromise of the real gospel? (See author's book *The Real Gospel*.)

Though it is noble and praiseworthy to reach more people for Christ, let me show you why these means and methods are clearly corrupt. As a result, the end must also be corrupt. Let's begin with marketing as a tactic for reaching the lost.

Fundamentally, marketing has to do with profiling consumers, identifying what their "felt needs" are (by the way, this has been the number-one reason "Christian" publishers have rejected some of my submitted manuscripts, saying that the message is from the Lord but not a "felt need," which simply means it won't sell), and then fashioning one's product (or its image) to appeal to the targeted consumer's desires. The focus is on getting the consumer to buy into the product. George Barna, whom *Christianity Today* calls "the church's guru of growth," claims that such an approach is essential for the church in our market-driven society. Church growth leaders are convinced that this marketing approach can be implemented without compromising the gospel. I'm afraid this has constituted a great deception, and in my own humble opinion, it is the number-one reason for the decline in the presence and power of God in many of our Western churches (I'm specifically referring to the Pentecostal/Charismatic churches who actually believe in the power of God).

A.B. McMahon explains it so well:

"First of all, the gospel and the person of Jesus Christ are not 'products' to be 'sold.' They cannot be refashioned or image-adjusted to appeal to the felt needs of our consumer-happy culture. Any attempt to do so compromises to some degree the truth of who Christ is and what He has done for us. For example, if the lost are considered consumers and a basic marketing 'commandment' says that the consumer must reign supreme, then whatever may be offensive to the lost must be discarded, revamped, or downplayed. Scripture tells us clearly that the message of the cross is 'foolishness to them that are perishing' and that Christ himself is a 'rock of offense' (1 Cor. 1:18; 1 Pt. 2:8). Some seeker-friendly churches, therefore, seek to avoid this 'negative aspect' of the gospel by making the temporal benefits of becoming a Christian their chief selling point. Although that appeals to this gratification-oriented generation, it is neither the gospel nor the goal of a believer's life in Christ."

I wholeheartedly agree with this viewpoint. Truth be told, this new model is now a monster that is breeding a second-generation semi-believer who lacks passion for God and discernment in the things of the Spirit, and is unskilled in handling the word of righteousness. This is the sad result of man flexing his own muscles and building churches with the strength of the arm of flesh. We have been wise in our own conceits and placed our trust in man's wisdom and ability.

Secondly, if you want to attract the lost on the basis of what might interest them, for the most part, you will be appealing to and accommodating their self-serving desires. Wittingly or in ignorance, that seems to be the standard operating procedure of seeker-friendly churches. They mimic what's popular in our culture such as top-forty and performance-style music, theatrical productions, stimulating multi-media presentations, and thirty-minutes-or-less of positive messages. The latter, more often than not, are topical, therapeutic, and centered on self-fulfillment and how the Lord can meet one's needs and help solve one's problems.

What I have just described at length is the product of man's own wisdom and the foremost reason for the steady decline of both the Word of truth and the Spirit of truth in a large segment of the body of Christ today. I'm sure there are other factors involved, but this is a big one — perhaps bigger than most have considered.

"The American church is guilty of great crimes against the Holy Spirit. We told Him to leave and let us grow Christianity incorporated — the worst thing we could have done. It was a mistake — a terrible, incalculable, ongoing mistake — derailing more truth in less time than any moral plague in history." — Evangelist Mario Murillo

SECOND REASON: A DEPARTURE FROM THE WORD AND SPIRIT

This second reason for the decline of the glory and power of God is connected to the first one and actually is a by-product of it: namely, the lack of solid, Biblically based teaching of the Word of God and genuine demonstrations of the Spirit and power of God (See author's book *Passing on the Move of God to The Next Generation*). This lack has created a void for people to chase spiritual experiences, thrills, and sensationalism outside of the real manifestation of the Spirit of God. Many who are weak in the foundations of the Word are hungry for an experience. That is a risky combination as it often leads them to pursue mystical things and the false prophetic. The devil is all too happy to fill that void and place of barrenness with something else.

Back when great pioneers of the faith like Smith Wigglesworth ministered, one of the devil's big strongholds in the Church was Christian Science. Here is what Wigglesworth said about it:

"The secret of many people going into Christian Science is a barren church that does not have the Holy Ghost. Christian Science exists because the churches have a barren place void of the Holy Ghost. There would be no room for Christian Science if the churches were filled with the Holy Ghost."

Such insight! And make no mistake about it, Wigglesworth's words apply in every generation.

Some examples of filling this barrenness of the true move of the Holy Spirit and His operations would be the obsession with receiving personal prophecy; the abuse of the laying on of hands for everything — for faith, for financial breakthrough, for deliverance, to impart ministry anointings; the overemphasis on warfare, deliverance, inner healing, etc.; and to further complicate matters, there is such a lack of emphasis on holiness, character, and the fruit of the Spirit. These have all greatly contributed to the diminishing of the real power of God. The fact is that many of these blessings come through the Word, personal disciplines to walk in the Spirit and not fulfill the lusts of the flesh, and praying and being led by the Spirit of God. People need to be taught these things.

You can't lay hands on people for everything, and personal prophecy is not the main way you are led by the Lord. Even misguided pastors and ministry leaders fall into the trap of being too loose and letting their services be a free-for-all, or they lean to the other extreme of being too heavy handed and restrictive in their leadership style, which creates its own set of problems. Although I am strongly opposed to strange fire, I've always believed that a little wildfire is better than no fire at all.

Wise shepherds and local elders are like good gatekeepers who watch at the gate of people's lives for thieves who would steal, kill, and destroy them. True shepherds warn their people of wolves in sheep's clothing and false teachings that will upset their otherwise spiritually healthy diet and make them spiritually sick. The primary way they do this is not by constantly criticizing other churches or ministries, but by teaching and demonstrating the truth of the Scriptures. People must be exposed to the solid Word and true manifestation of the Spirit to eventually recognize the counterfeit. An experienced jeweler's ability to recognize a counterfeit diamond comes from his exposure to the real.

This is also the reason God has given us the Ephesians 4:11 ministry gifts — so His spiritual children won't be "*tossed to and fro and carried about with every wind of doctrine, by the trickery of men, in the cunning craftiness of deceitful plotting*" (Eph. 4:14). Wise shepherds and local elders are watchful and faithful to feed the sheep entrusted to their care with good food that supplies adequate spiritual nourishment and strength. They also understand the importance of the other ministry gifts that can help in equipping their local body. Feeding the sheep and pastoring people properly is so important to the Lord and is the reason He emphasized it to Peter in one of His post-resurrection appearances:

"*Peter was grieved because He said to him the third time, 'Do you love Me?' And he said to Him, 'Lord, You know all things; You know that I love You.' Jesus said to him, 'Feed My sheep*'" (John 21:15-17).

If you'll do a word study, you'll find that Jesus first told Peter to feed His lambs and then to tend to and feed His sheep. There is an implication there that lambs cannot feed themselves yet, but sheep can and are to be pastored more than fed.

I'm also finding a growing number of older Christians who are not really grounded in the Word of God. They are like those the Word describes who ought to be teachers by now but have become *"dull of hearing"* and need someone to teach them again the first principles of the oracles of God (Heb. 5:11-12). Oh, many have an intellectual knowledge of the Word, but they are spiritual babies who have need of milk and cannot handle solid food yet.

Don Lynch says it so well in one of his social media posts: *"There is a massive warehouse for millions of saints called 'church-ianity' to care for those who refuse preparation and maturity.*

"The Body drags them around the meadows in mercy, hoping they will grow up some day and be more than consumers.

"We currently have ten times more blubber than muscle. We have cases of eyeballs that cannot see. We have football-field-sized floor-to ceiling pallets for hands that do nothing but suck thumbs.

"We have mouths running continually with baby talk that should release prayer. We have ears filled with earbuds listening to entertainment jingles and syrupy "It's All About Me" songs that should hear the Word of God.

"We have a remnant functioning in ecclesia and a nursery babying tens of millions who are in kindergarten learning to tie their shoes for thirty years.

"The greatest need of the American church kingdom is maturity, and only fathering leaders have the strength of will to challenge that vast riot of consumer-minded babies.

"Fathers are being trampled by two-hundred-pound babies fighting for formula fountain access, while kingdom battles are fought by a Gideon army."

Wow! I couldn't agree more with Don's perspective — so brutally honest and eloquently written. There is a great need for mature elders and true fathers in the body of Christ.

The true anointing of the Spirit must be our Teacher (1 Jn. 2:20,27), for it is a day and an hour where many are being led astray. Seducing spirits and doctrines of demons have been unleashed and are holding sway over so many. Foundational truths must be taught in order for people to achieve stability and balance in their daily lives. Knowing the Word, cultivating godly character, learning the true anointing, and being led by the Spirit of God must become the emphases. Personal holiness in conduct and conversation, overcoming trials and offenses by walking in faith and love, understanding and exercising their authority as a believer, and learning to truly enter into the prayer life by putting on the armor of God should be high priorities for every saint. Additionally, the elementary doctrines of Christ should be ingrained into every new convert (Heb. 6:1-2). These foundations should never get old but need to be rehearsed and renewed regularly.

Through a process of time, hearkening to this practical instruction will turn the tide again and cause a groundswell of maturity, power, and effectiveness in the life of the Church that will once again distinguish it from the false and carnal church. In this way, spiritual ground that's been lost will be recovered.

GONE IS THE AGE OF MAN

In a sense, the age of man is gone. We've entered into the age of God. It is high time to stop grieving the Holy Spirit by doing things our own way and using His principles for our own personal gain, whether it be for fame, honor, influence, or financial gain. God will not share His glory with any man. It's time for the true works of the Father, born of obedience, to be manifest in the earth.

What many ministers need to do is go back to the original place of their calling when they said "Yes" to God and ask themselves the reason and motivation for that "Yes." What will be our end if we are not in ministry out of simple, sincere devotion to Jesus and a pure love for people? It is in renewing our minds and keeping them focused on Him that we will not only receive His peace (Is. 26:3) but strength to resist the world's wisdom, patterns, systems, ideals, and mindsets that have infiltrated the Church.

Here's a vision one of our spiritual daughters had not too long ago that I believe is significant for the hour we now live in:

"I saw a picture of fresh concrete being poured. I knew as I saw this that all the structures of men had already come to nothing. I knew that this was a new day, with new foundations being poured. I knew that we were stepping into the age of God. I knew that He was laying His own foundations for the Church to be built upon.

"Then I saw those who were pouring concrete but did not make Christ the Cornerstone, and consequently their concrete was not being allowed to harden. But for those who made Christ the Cornerstone, their concrete was allowed to harden."

Once again, we are reminded of the scripture: *"Unless the Lord builds the house, they labor in vain who build it..."* (Ps. 127:1).

HOW THE LORD BUILDS

"Through wisdom a house is built, and by understanding it is established..." (Pr. 24:3)

It takes much time and patience to plant and establish a local church or a work. Without effectual prayer and supernatural help from the Spirit of God, it can be burdensome for many church planters, shepherds, and local elders. It will lift the burden immeasurably to understand that we are not called to work *for* the Father but to work *with* Him. It is in hearing and obeying His wisdom and counsel that this happens. The Spirit of God always moves to perform the Father's will, not some concoction of our own will devised by the carnal mind. The *lack* of hearing and obeying the Father's wisdom and counsel produces the works of man. But hearing and obeying the Father's wisdom and counsel produces the works of God.

Jesus is the Pattern Son and our perfect example. He felt no obligation or compulsion to do anything outside of the Father's will and counsel. He knew that He did not come to this Earth to do His own will but the will of the Father (Jn. 5:19). He also knew that He was not here to do His *own* will in the Name of the Father, which is the more subtle and common problem in Christendom today.

The Holy Spirit wants to bring clear communication between us and the Father and Jesus, for He has been sent for such a purpose — *"to speak whatsoever He hears and to show us things to come"* (Jn. 16:13). **The greatest cry of the Holy Spirit on the Earth today is that God's people would learn to wait on the Lord and receive His wisdom and counsel for every situation.** Praying in the Spirit at length, meditating on the Word of God, and ministering to the Lord is the best way to cultivate this ability. This is also the reason I've dedicated an entire chapter later in this book to the subject of *waiting on the Lord*. It is vital that we recover and learn this lost art.

Think about this: All of man's failures are a by-product of a lack of clear communication between the believer and the Godhead. This is the devil's greatest victory — to keep us too agitated, frustrated, anxious, distracted, deterred, entangled, and too busy to wait on the Lord and hear the Holy Spirit's clear communication. He delights in communing with us and sharing the Father's wisdom and counsel. Nothing is impossible to those who've learned to hear and obey the Holy Spirit's communication and His holy written Word.

True ministers of the gospel are those whose thinking has been elevated above the ways of man and who teach and train God's people to receive God's wisdom and counsel. God can move only where His counsel and instructions are heard and obeyed. God wants to move, and He wants to do much more *for* us and *through* us. The problem in this age of man has been that men are doing all the moving. There are few on the Earth who live in the realm of the Spirit and understand these things.

I pray that you would learn the ways of God and truly be among those who are taught by Him and led by Him. God wants the best for His children. The fullness of His blessing, however, is in hearing and obeying what He says to you both from the written Word and by His Spirit. This is how the early Church began when the original apostles chose not to leave their primary responsibility and calling to prayer and the Word (Acts 6:3-4). As I said, we will discuss these things in greater detail in later chapters. This should be the foundation of all ministry established and exemplified first by Jesus and then the apostles.

CHAPTER FOUR

THE RESTORATION OF THE APOSTOLIC

The Church began as a house of prayer (Acts 1 & 2). It is God's purpose for the Church to always remain a house of prayer. Every gospel bears witness to the zeal for God's house being a house of prayer (Matt. 21, Mk. 11, Lk. 19, Jn. 2). The four-gospel witness is very significant, since only 8% of the content in John's gospel appears in the others.

When God's house ceases to be a house of prayer, then, by default, it becomes a house of merchandise or a place of business. Actually, Jesus stated it much stronger when He called it a *den of thieves*. This is one of the strongest and saddest indictments that characterizes the modern-day Church.

Apostles were the first ministry gifts appointed by Jesus. He appointed them after a night of prayer (Lk 6:12-13). Isn't it interesting how the apostolic is released through prayer? We see the pattern again in the early church (Acts 13:1-3). Once apostles do their work, local shepherds are needed (Matt. 9:35-36). The harvest is contained by the shepherds. Laborers are primarily activated and released by apostles.

Jesus was a Shepherd, but He was first the Apostle. An apostle is a sent one. The twelve were apostles because they were sent. Divine work can be done only by those who are divinely commissioned. The Church had its beginnings, and thus its roots, in the apostolic.

We need not fear the word "apostle." It is not a title to be used for personal consumption. It is not a gift to promote greed. It is not a credit card to be flashed for recognition. Rather, it is a glory for the Church. True apostles count themselves last, not first. They don't have to announce that they're an apostle, for the fruit of their character and ministry makes it obvious. This ministry often comes with a humiliation and not an exaltation.

The New Testament and its epistles were laid down by apostles. The Scriptures are holy because they are God breathed and written in the ink of holy apostolic men who hazarded their lives for the Name of Jesus (Acts 15:26). It is interesting to note also that what tradition has labeled as the "pastoral" epistles (1 and 2 Timothy, Titus) are actually apostolic letters written from an aged apostle (Paul) to younger apostles (Timothy and Titus).

The authentic apostolic ministry has been overlaid with crusty layers of man-made doctrines and traditions that are so common today. They are now overshadowed by the insecurities of men who have hidden themselves in the systems and structures which their own hands have made and from which these doctrines and traditions feed and grow.

The scribes and Pharisees devoured widows' houses (Mk. 12:40) and used the resources to strengthen the systems and structures which their own hands made. Let that statement sink in. This is the fly in the ointment or the impurity in the postmodern church. The house of prayer has become a place of business, or, again, as Jesus put it, a den of thieves.

The "give until it hurts" offering definitely holds sway, as does the notion that "God will not bless you unless you give" and, worse still, "You are cursed for not tithing." Men have used such language and these forms of extortion to obtain financial support for essentially corrupt, exploitive, and self-serving religious enterprises. Where in the Old Testament is it written that widows were to give their last mite (Mk. 12:44)? Isn't the reverse true, in that widows and orphans are to be supported and cared for by the body of believers and their leadership? But the scribes and Pharisees twisted it for their own benefit much like what we see today in many ministries and congregations.

In the same manner, Jesus condemned the tradition of Israeli culture when He exposed the practice of dishonoring parents, which was made available to individuals who made a donation to what essentially was the temple mafia system (Mk. 7:10-13). To remove responsibility for honoring parents from their sons and daughters, and transferring the requirement and responsibility of care and love to an organization, Jesus said they made the Law of God of no effect.

Jesus was substantiating this charge by contrasting Moses' commandment with their current tradition of *Corban*. *Corban* is a word denoting withdrawing something from its intended use as though it were an offering made to God. Therefore, if a man wanted to be relieved of his responsibility to care for his aged and sick parents, he could declare his property *Corban*. No one else then could share his possession, although he himself would continue to enjoy the benefits of it throughout his lifetime. Such a practice was deceitful and in direct violation of the commandment of God. Such similar practices are all too common in ministry today.

True apostolic ministry and authority exposes this deception and brings righteousness and order to these types of practices.

In the earliest beginnings of the Church age, money and resources were laid at the apostles' feet (Acts 4:35), men who devoted themselves to prayer and the Word, and who risked their physical lives for the name of Jesus. Today, money and resources are laid at the feet of men who are not as interested in building God's house as they are in building a structure, a system, a ministry, or a place of business. This will never satisfy the cry of God's heart. Sadly, these men often deserve to be called "thieves" for stealing and diluting God's glory. When you conduct ministry to serve your own interests instead of God's interests, the devil has invaded your ministry.

The glory of God will be restored to the Church when we become a house of prayer. Before that happens, there will be a further shaking and cleansing. Man-made doctrines and traditions will be confronted. The dual-character nature and impure motives of many ministers shall be challenged. The pastoral ministry shall cooperate more fully with the other ministry gifts and vice versa, while the authentic apostolic shall enjoy greater prominence.

THE AUTHENTIC APOSTLE

The goal of the apostolic Church is to be conformed into the image of Jesus Christ. That is the greatest burden of genuine apostles (Rom. 8:29) (Gal. 4:19) (Col. 1:27-29).

What or who is an apostle? In simple terms, the word "apostle" translated from Greek means "sent one." This was a term used in the Roman empire for a general who was sent to change the culture of a conquered country to Roman. The term seems to have been used because Jesus sent out His disciples (apostles) into the world to preach the gospel of the kingdom. But He first called His original apostles to Himself for the purpose of being with Him and learning of Him before sending them out, unlike so many ministry leaders today who are more interested in using followers to advance their own agenda.

"And He went up on the mountain and called to Him those He Himself wanted. And they came to Him. Then He appointed twelve, **that they might be with Him and that He might send them out to preach,** *and to have power to heal sicknesses and to cast out demons"* (Mk 3:13-15).

I believe it is safe to say that a true apostle is one who spends time with Jesus and has been sent as an agent of change — anointed by God to spiritually impact a people and a culture. We know from the Word of God and from history the results of the apostles and the impact of apostolic ministry on the earth. Therefore, something that is of an apostolic constitution is something given by God and sent from heaven that produces radical spiritual change.

This apostolic grace that is sent from heaven is for the fabric of the Church that Jesus is building through His ministry gifts and people on the Earth. I fathom that it is safe to reason that a church consumed with being conformed into the image of Christ and functioning or living this way is apostolic, indeed.

The Bible tells us there are both true and false apostles. Let's learn to discern the difference.

For many years, traditional denominations taught that the ministry of the apostle passed away after the New Testament era. It was assumed that the only people who served in apostolic roles were early followers of Jesus who witnessed His resurrection. Cessationists (those who believe that miracles stopped after the canon of Scripture was completed) believe that healing, deliverance, prophecy, and all other supernatural phenomena have also ceased and that apostles are no longer necessary.

But as Christians in recent eras began to experience the supernatural gifts and power of the Holy Spirit, church leaders and even some theologians began to teach that the gift of the apostle is vital if we hope to advance the gospel in our generation. This logic, of course, makes sense and is thoroughly scriptural. If we still need pastors, teachers, and evangelists (all part of Jesus' ministry gifts mentioned in Ephesians 4:11), we also need the apostles and prophets who are listed in the same passage. The Bible never says these functions were discontinued.

One anonymous writer, whose name I failed to find, made this observation, which I also observed and agree with:

"During the 1990s, there was a renewed interest in the ministry of the apostle. Many books were written on the topic, explaining that the Greek word apostolos *refers to God's special ambassadors, or "sent ones," who are commissioned to contend for pure doctrine, preserve unity among the saints, equip leaders, model Christian character, and help the church advance into new territory. But a strange thing happened on the way to recovering genuine apostolic anointing. In true blue American fashion, we began to merchandise it. Here again is yet another impurity that crept into the body of Christ.*

"No sooner had the first book on apostles been written that some men began to claim the title and print it on their business cards. "Apostleship quickly became a fad. Before too long, some men were creating networks of independent churches answerable to a governing apostle who took ownership of their buildings and controlled their congregations. The same type of thing happened with the prophet's ministry, which created its own set of problems and messes today. Do you see how easily man's carnal wisdom corrupts the work of God and His sacred ministries?

"Some charismatic apostles became mini-popes who carved out their turfs and domains. Suddenly the independent Charismatic movement had more invasive authoritarianism than the denominations some of these pastors abandoned 15-20 years earlier." — Anonymous

I've also witnessed this widespread defilement of the apostolic ministry. In some circles, apostles demanded total allegiance from the leaders who were "under" them. Some required a policy of "tithing up," creating a monstrous organizational structure similar to a spiritual "Mary Kay" or "Shaklee." So-called apostles created their pyramids with huge "downlines" and made exorbitant amounts of money. Some leaders even offered pastors the opportunity to become "spiritual sons" by contributing $1,000 a month to their ministry. Personally, I detached myself from one such ministry that I was associated with during this period of time once I clearly perceived the self-serving nature of it. In this commercialized and consumerist version of the faith, an apostolic covering could now be bought, and apostolic grace was reduced to the level of a motivational coach.

Now can you see how, with such unholy practices, what was ordained by God to be a house of prayer can quickly become a "den of thieves"? May God forgive us for making it all about the money, power, and influence and reducing the value of such a precious apostolic gift.

I still believe we need the apostolic anointing now more than ever — and I know many genuine apostles who have planted churches and works in many parts of the world. Others are not sent forth to plant churches per se but are messengers of the Lord who carry moves and messages for His Church. When it comes to error and falsehood, they don't just see the here and now, but similar to genuine prophets, they have an anointing to see years down the road what the harvest of today's sown seeds could potentially grow into.

Paul wrote in 1 Corinthians 12:28: *"And God has appointed in the church, first apostles, second prophets, third teachers, then miracles, then gifts of healings, helps, administrations, various kinds of tongues"* (NASB). When carnally minded people read this verse, they assume God has set up some kind of ecclesiastical hierarchy, with apostles sitting on thrones at the top. But if we view leadership in the way Jesus taught it (Mk. 10:42-45), we know that being first is not about being on top. Apostles and all ministers are at the bottom of the pecking order. They are the servants of all. And because they serve a foundational role, especially the apostle, their work will often remain hidden in obscurity. They are not looking for fame or celebrity, nor are they grasping for a title, for their role is to empower everyone else.

EXAMPLES OF MODERN-DAY GENUINE APOSTLES

When we were missionaries years ago, we were actually a part of a young apostolic team that was divinely commissioned and anointed to establish interdenominational Bible training centers. I've read other accounts of many true missionaries who were also "sent ones" or apostles.

For example, I recently met a man from West Africa who has planted many churches in that region, trained countless young church leaders, many of them former Muslims, in a makeshift Bible school, and led multitudes of people to Christ. This man has witnessed whole villages impacted by the gospel through one miracle of healing. He has never ridden in a limousine, and he lives in a modest village home that he shares with other disciples he is training. As I spoke with this man, one of his greatest concerns was not to secure more finances and more resources for his work as is with so many, but it was that the communities he was establishing throughout West Africa maintain a blameless reputation and testimony among the world. What an example for us in the West to follow! This genuine apostle was not chasing money and resources, popularity or fame, but was primarily concerned with keeping the work pure. Remember, when Jesus cleansed the temple, it signified that purity is priority.

What a contrast from some of the self-appointed apostles and prophets we see today! The apostle Paul would have gagged if he could see how some modern-day apostles profit from their downlines or how they require pampered treatment. Apostleship has nothing to do with privilege. In fact, Paul, at one time, made tents for a living and provided for others on his team in order to avoid the appearance of entitlement. How different things are in many circles and spheres of church and ministry today.

Suffering and sacrifice were such a part of the lives of the early apostles. This character trait would quickly sift out many false apostles today for their unwillingness to suffer for the Lord Jesus and His gospel. In the early Church, due to severe persecution, spiritual leadership had to count the cost and pay a high price to plant churches and oversee and lead God's people. True apostles push the boundaries of Christianity forward, into hostile territory — and as a result, they encounter more than their fair share of persecution and spiritual warfare, often fleeing personal attacks against their lives. They are never content to live in a comfort zone. Yet even in foreign prisons, they find joy and fulfillment. No wonder the larger percentage of Christian ministry takes place in the so-called "free world," while many of the harder places, where stronger persecution exists, remain unreached and in many cases, virtually untouched.

ANOTHER EXAMPLE OF A TRUE APOSTLE

As another example, I know of an apostle with a precious heart and ministry in India that has planted hundreds of churches in unreached tribal regions, along with building hospitals, schools, orphanages, homes for the aged and mentally ill, not to mention feeding the hungry day and night.

The tribal village pastors and missionaries this dear brother has raised up have been persecuted and beaten for their faith, and at least one of them has been martyred. Truly these men are sacrificial ser-vants.

For this Indian leader, apostleship is not about owning his own private jet (and I'm not opposed to ministers having jets), or having the largest television audience. It is about teaching his own leaders and people to remain faithful to Christ even when receiving death threats. And it's about sending those he trains into difficult regions, where they could face martyrdom.

As Western nations face a moral crisis and many powerless churches continue to operate in the wisdom of man, I pray that we will allow the Holy Spirit to shake the lust, greed, pride, and self-centered-ness out of our movement. False ministers and false apostles will al-ways prefer the primrose path of ease and convenience over the Cal-vary road of sacrifice and suffering and taking up their crosses and fol-lowing Jesus. May God grant us true apostolic anointing and character that is marked by New Testament courage, unquestionable integrity, and Christ-like humility.

Today people equate apostleship with entrepreneurship and the mere building of organizations. This is actually a non-Biblical concept, as they are worlds apart. Entrepreneurs are not apostles, for they will unabashedly turn the house of God into a place of business and a den of thieves in quick fashion. True ministers and apostles are broken, praying, suffering men. They are bold and strong in the Lord, but weak in themselves and exert a great dependency on the Lord.

The following verses from the life and example of Paul says it all:

"For I think that God hath set forth us the apostles last, as it were appointed to death: for we are made a spectacle unto the world, and to angels, and to men. We are fools for Christ's sake, but you are wise in Christ; we are weak, but you are strong; you are honorable, but we are

despised. Even unto this present hour we both hunger, and thirst, and are naked, and are buffeted, and have no certain dwelling place; and labour, working with our own hands: being reviled, we bless; being persecuted, we suffer it: Being defamed, we entreat: we are made as the filth of the world, and are the offscouring of all things unto this day" (1 Cor. 4:9-13).

And notice the tenderness of his father's heart for those he had begotten through the gospel, something so rare today.

"I write not these things to shame you, but as my beloved sons I warn you. For though ye have ten thousand instructors in Christ, yet have ye not many fathers: for in Christ Jesus I have begotten you through the gospel. Wherefore I beseech you, be ye followers of me" (1 Cor. 4:14-16).

Let us be followers of this stellar example of love and humility. Flee from haughty "ministers" and those who strut. Recognize that humility is one of the marks of a genuine apostle. And don't be fooled by the outward and mistake entrepreneurial ability for the true apostolic anointing. True ministers and apostles do not merely build organizations, purchase buildings, push movements, or promote agendas or causes. They preach Christ crucified and nurture new communities upon this holy foundation.

And with all the talk there is today about spiritual fathering, where are the fathers who travail in birth for sinners to be saved and for Christ to be formed in young converts?

"My little children, for whom I labor in birth again until Christ is formed in you..." (Gal. 4:19).

Why are we addressing the apostolic ministry? Because if the Church is going to be transformed from a house of merchandise and consumer-based ministry to a house of prayer, it must begin with this foundation of authentic apostolic ministry and true fathers of the faith.

CHAPTER FIVE

THE ORDER OF THE COMING RESTORATION:

PURITY, PRAYER, AND POWER

The Church must be cleansed and transformed from a house of merchandise to a house of prayer.

*And He said to those who sold doves, "Take these things away! Do not make My Father's house a **house of merchandise!**"* (Jn. 2:16).

*"Is it not written, 'My house shall be called a **house of prayer** for all nations'?"* (Mk. 11:17).

The love of money is the root of all evil (1 Tim. 6:10), and in fact, it is the only other god or master Jesus mentioned in His ministry that people serve — the god of mammon (Matt. 6:24). What "the root of all evil" means to me is that every evil is connected to the love of money — or what money can give you or make you. This is a giant force in the earth and what drives most of humanity. We will continue to see this more clearly in later chapters and how this has rendered much of the Church powerless.

But right now, I want to share some new insights that I believe the Holy Spirit revealed to me concerning the cleansing of His Church, particularly His judgments in Acts 5 with Ananias and Sapphira and Acts 8 with Simon the sorcerer. Without the judgments of the Lord in the Church, His holiness and fear will not be established in His people. Remember: these are two of the key scriptures the Spirit of God high-lighted to us that birthed this book.

ANANIAS AND SAPPHIRA AND THEIR HYPOCRISY

Ananias and Sapphira's sin was lying about the amount of money they contributed to the thriving church in Jerusalem. But the greater sin was the root of why they did it, which we will soon see. There was a great move of God going on during the inception of the early Church, which compelled many believers to sell their possessions and lay the proceeds at the apostles' feet (Acts 4:34-35). Ananias and Sapphira wanted to be a part of this great move but for the wrong reasons, so they conspired together to lie about the total amount they were giving.

The Church is referred to as the pillar and ground of truth. No lie could stand within it in its glorious beginnings.

*"I write so that you may know how you ought to conduct yourself in the house of God, which is the church of the living God, **the pillar and ground of the truth**"* (1 Tim. 3:15).

Have you ever thought of how the very first act of judgment in the early Church was concerning a lie? That is very significant. The lie represents a mask of religion and hypocrisy that fills many churches today and is diluting the glory of God. The early Church was cleansed and purged immediately from what Ananias and Sapphira were attempting to introduce into the local body in Jerusalem.

More than the love of money, hypocrisy was the main issue the Spirit of God put his finger on while I was studying this account of Ananias and Sapphira. Jesus called hypocrisy "...the leaven of the Pharisees."

"Beware of the leaven of the Pharisees, which is hypocrisy" (Lk. 12:1).

Leaven is yeast, and it has a fermenting effect on dough, which is what causes the bread to rise. And since it takes only a small amount of yeast to transform an entire lump of dough, Jesus is warning His disciples that it takes only a little bit of what the Pharisees have to ruin a person. Paul said that a little leaven leavens the whole lump (1 Cor. 5:8). In Christ's estimation, the conduct of these Pharisees had a leavening and corrupting effect upon those who followed their example. Just a tiny amount of the leaven of the Pharisees would be sufficient to turn a man into a bad and useless person.

In other words, what Ananias and Sapphira were introducing into the young body in Jerusalem had the potential to ruin what God was doing. Was there malicious intent on their part to ruin anything or hurt anyone? I don't believe so, but the glory was so pure and white hot in the early beginnings of the Church age that even a lie without presumed malicious intent could not stand. If it was allowed to stand and not be judged, it would have spread.

A lack of accountability and righteous judgment today is a huge problem in the Church, enabling the leaven of sin to spread like a cancer. Biblical discipline is sorely lacking. First and second admonitions to correct the unrepentant are uncommon and dis-fellowshipping from such is nearly unheard of.

"A man that is an heretic after the first and second admonition reject" (Titus 3:10 — KJV).

I don't want to excuse Ananias and Sapphira by telling you that there seemed to be no malicious intent to harm anyone. They did conspire together and agree together to tell this lie (Acts 5:9), and it was Satan that filled their heart to do this (Acts 5:3). That alone makes it evil and wicked.

If you'll go back and read the introductory chapter of this book, you'll find a long utterance where the Spirit of God put emphasis on masks of religion and veils of hypocrisy being a great stumbling block to the manifestation of His glory and power. God doesn't expect perfection, but He expects honesty and transparency. The lie, veiled in hypocrisy, that was told by Ananias and Sapphira was against the Holy Spirit, and it is representative of the leaven that fills much of the Church today.

The Greek word for hypocrite or hypocrisy is *hupokrisis*, which literally means "reply." The word came to denote a theatrical performance by one who spoke in dialogue. Then it was used of play-acting, role-playing, pretending, and, hence, acting insincerely — hypocrisy. A hypocrite conceals his true motives under a cloak of make-believe.

Today we have a generation of Ananiases and Sapphiras who would lie for the honor and glory of men rather than tell the truth for the honor and glory of God (Acts 5). Layers of lies and false projections and motives have produced veils of deception and masks of religion that have caused the glory to diminish and depart. If we learn to live in the sight of God instead of the sight of man, hypocrisy will be flushed out of our lives, and the glory of God would increase personally and collectively in the Church.

The early Church had just been birthed and was localized in Jerusalem only at this time. It was yet in an embryonic stage of development. Just as doctors can often detect something wrong in the early stages of a pregnancy, so did the apostle Peter by the revelation of the Holy Spirit detect a lie in the Church.

"But a certain man named Ananias, with Sapphira his wife, sold a possession. And he kept back part of the proceeds, his wife also being aware of it, and brought a certain part and laid it at the apostles' feet.

*But Peter said, "**Ananias, why has Satan filled your heart to lie to the Holy Spirit** and keep back part of the price of the land for yourself?"* (Acts 5:1-3)

When people sell everything and come and lay the money at the feet of genuine apostles in order to distribute it among the needy, that is a major move of God. The love of money had no hold on these early believers. It was not a requirement for anyone to sell their possessions. They did it willingly. The problem was that Ananias and Sapphira lied about the amount they gave for the insidious reason of wanting to be esteemed in the eyes of man. The root of their sin was not in what they did, but in why they did it.

Ananias and Sapphira avoided financial disclosure and tried to make the records appear as if they had given a larger percentage than what they actually gave. But the real motive connected to their lie had to do with pride and wanting to be highly esteemed in the church. It is one of the first teachings of Jesus in the Sermon on the Mount.

*"Take heed that you do not do your charitable deeds before men, to be seen by them. Otherwise you have no reward from your Father in heaven. Therefore, when you do a charitable deed, do not sound a trumpet before you as the hypocrites do in the synagogues and in the streets, **that they may have glory from men**"* (Matt. 6:1-2).

Ananias and Sapphira touched the glory of God with the desire for the glory of men. That was the root issue. In my humble opinion, this is also the root issue in the modern Church, and in every generation, it is the one thing that dilutes and diminishes the glory of God quicker than anything else. When there are strong moral convictions about honesty and purity in all areas of our lives, and a true humility among ministers and saints, there will be a greater glory in the Church. Much of the glory we've had in the modern-day Church has been the glory of man. The reason there's been so little judgment today like that which fell on Ananias and Sapphira is because of the absence of the true glory of God, for this level of severe judgment that produces death is always in proportion to the present level of glory.

Consecration to God in holiness and purity is vital to increasing the glory of God in the Church.

THE EFFECT THIS CLEANSING HAD ON THE EARLY CHURCH

*"In hearing these words, Ananias fell down and died. **And great fear came on all those who heard these things**"* (Acts 5:5).

*"At once she (Sapphira) fell down at his feet and died. Upon entering, the young men found her dead and carried her out and buried her beside her husband. **Great fear came on the entire church and on all those who heard these things. Many signs and wonders were performed among the people by the hands of the apostles.** And they were all together in Solomon's Porch. No one else dared join them, but the people respected them. **Believers were increasingly added to the Lord, crowds of both men and women**"* (Acts 5:10-14).

Can you see how this cleansing led to increased fear and power, with many believers being added to the Lord?

We often forget these portions of Scripture and how this judgment produced the component of the fear of the Lord, which stopped this lie and other impurities from gaining access into the early Church, thus preserving its white-hot purity and keeping it from being defiled. This miracle of judgment contributed to the glory, power, and growth of the early Church. Notice also the effect it had on the people:

"No one else dared join them (the disciples), but the people respected them" (Acts 5:13).

The Message Bible says it this way: *"But even though people admired them a lot, outsiders were wary about joining them. On the other hand, those who put their trust in the Master were added right and left, men and women both."*

Could these incidents of judgment in the early Church be a type and shadow of what we may expect in the last days' Church in both the coming judgment and glory?

- Could it be that preachers who have peddled the word of God for gain and fame have their ministries judged and some even be publicly humiliated and taken out of the way?

- Could churches and ministries that have been built on compromise and the wisdom of man see a mass exodus as people begin to seek pure truth and authenticity as well as the reality of the Holy Spirit and the power of God?

- Could we see organizations and companies who have used their power and wealth to persecute the righteous be shaken and some big CEOs even die? Could we also see the same type of judgement on leaders of nations who persecute the glorious Church and do not give glory to God (think of King Herod, Acts 12:23)?

I believe we will see these types of severe judgments again but only as the glory increases and is restored to the true Church.

POLARIZATION: ONE EFFECT OF GOD'S JUDGMENTS AND THE FEAR OF THE LORD

The judgment that fell on Ananias and Sapphira caused sinners to be leery of joining themselves to the apostles and the Church while at the same time gaining public respect and influence. This divided or polarized those who were not interested in genuine repentance and living wholeheartedly for the Lord from the multitudes who were being genuinely converted and being added to the church. Oh, how we need this work done today in this era of postmodern and so-called "progressive" Christianity! It would root out so much sin, hypocrisy, complacency, carnality, and compromise.

The dividing line was very distinct in the early Church. In a day when we are trying to include everyone into our sheepfolds by toning down on the demands of the gospel, there was a certain exclusivity that the judgments of God and the fear of the Lord produced in the Church's earliest beginnings. People couldn't enter in with sin in their lives. In many places today, it is difficult to tell the difference between the Christian and non-Christian, but not in the early Church. God wants to restore this polarization in the Church of today.

The great fear that came on the entire Church and those who heard of these events is a necessary component for the overall health of the Church, and it is also a precursor to actual revival and spiritual awakening in the nations. What many Christians don't understand is that these kinds of judgments in the Church are a manifestation of God's mercy to the masses, because when the Church is judged and cleansed, that is when we have the greatest impact on the world. Conversely, when there is lack of judgment in the Church, it means a widespread judgment to the masses, and mercy reserved for only a small righteous remnant.

"For the time is come that judgment must begin at the house of God: and if it first begin at us, what shall the end be of them that obey not the gospel of God? And if the righteous scarcely be saved, where shall the ungodly and the sinner appear?" (1 Pt. 4:17-18)

Imagine the impact of this judgment, not only upon that present early apostolic generation, but upon their children and grandchildren, and the ensuing generations who witnessed these things and/or heard them. When Ananias' and Sapphira's dead bodies were carried out by the young men, it was a dreadful object lesson of the fear of the Lord to future generations. *Don't touch God's glory* was the message. I'm sure this event was voiced abroad for years to come. This was, in fact, a judgment against counterfeit Christianity that greatly impacted the Church and the world. As I said, it was an act of mercy to the world in preserving the mighty influence, glory, and power of the Church from moral compromise and tainted motives enveloped in personal, selfish ambition and hypocrisy through Ananias and Sapphira. It was important to preserve the purity of the Church in the early days of its inception since it was located only in Jerusalem at that time.

Notice another result that the fear of the Lord contributed to the early Church.

*"Then the churches throughout all Judea and Galilee and Samaria had peace and were built up. **And walking in the fear of the Lord and in the comfort of the Holy Spirit, they were multiplied**"* (Acts 9:31, MEV).

Can you see how, as the polarization in the early Church increased, so did the power and impact increase simultaneously? There was a multiplication of new converts and new churches. The Lord Jesus was building His Church, and one of its greatest persecutors and opposers of the Church at that time, Saul, was mightily converted. This one miracle of conversion alone produced peace and edification in the churches because they were all previously afraid of him. When we remain a pure and prayerful people, God will often even convert His greatest opposers and persecutors, and will Himself provide divine protection and remove those things that once hindered the Church. Hallelujah!

POLARIZATION DEFINED

One of the definitions of polarization is a division into two oppo-sites. Polarization happens when people are divided into contesting groups. Polarization is a concept that comes from science, and it in-volves light, radiation, or magnetism moving in specific directions. Outside of this scientific concept, polarization usually refers to how people think, especially when two views emerge that drive people apart, sort of what occurs when one tries to bring together the north side of two magnets.

As an example, when Democrats and Republicans fight, it can cause polarization. A Civil War is also a serious form of polarization. Polarization involves people moving in two directions — becoming al-most as separate as the North and South Pole. In this postmodern day of superficial church growth, which tends to focus more on peripheral and demographic elements, these verses show us the importance of the inward character and holiness of believers, and how it relates to both true spiritual and numerical growth.

When we fail to include the judgments of God and the fear of the Lord in our doctrine, lifestyle, and practice, we are building with flim-sy materials of wood, hay, and stubble that will not stand up under the trials, pressures, and hardships of life and, more importantly, before the Judgment Seat of Christ (1 Cor. 3:12-15). The fear of the Lord, which is nurtured through the eternal judgments of God, is a great contributor and foundational to a healthy, growing church.

A heart seeking to truly obey Him is what the Lord has always looked for in His people. This heart is cultivated through our love for the Lord but also through holy fear. Once again, this fear is birthed in God's people primarily through a knowledge and manifestation of His judgments.

SECOND JUDGMENT INCIDENT IN THE EARLY CHURCH

The second incident the Holy Spirit highlighted to us that came under immediate judgment involving another form of hypocrisy and the desire for an honored reputation among men in the early Church is seen in Simon the sorcerer.

"But there was a certain man called Simon, who previously practiced sorcery in the city and **astonished** *the people of Samaria,* **claiming that he was someone great, to whom they all gave heed, from the least to the greatest,** *saying,* **"This man is the great power of God."** *And they heeded him because he had* **astonished** *them with his sorceries for a long time"* (Acts 8:9-11).

This is a character profile on Simon before his conversion. Notice that he used sorcery to astonish the people of Samaria. The word "astonished" is used twice in the above verses. He operated in a great realm of demonic power that caused everyone to listen to him, and he was known throughout that region as *"the great power of God."* But then he believed the things Philip preached concerning Jesus and the kingdom of God and was baptized with multitudes of other Samarians (v. 13). So, we could say that Simon was converted to Christ. The Bible says that he continued with Philip and was amazed at this new power he was witnessing through Philip's ministry, and then he witnessed the same power through Peter and John's ministry before deciding to make bids on it.

"And when Simon saw that through the laying on of the apostles' hands the Holy Spirit was given, **he offered them money,** *saying, "Give me this power also, that anyone on whom I lay hands may receive the Holy Spirit"* (Acts 8:18-19).

Simon was used to being the center of attention and having a reputation for being great. Apparently, this was the motive of his heart in offering money to have the same power Peter and John were anointed with. Here we see the love of appearance and a desire for an honored reputation among men working in Simon's heart as it did with Ananias and Sapphira. He wanted to be highly esteemed and remain great in the eyes of the people. While Ananias and Sapphira wanted to be known for their giving and generosity, Simon wanted to be known for his power.

God sees the motives of the heart that no one else can see (See author's book *Purity of Heart*). What does He see in the modern Church today? Think about all the pride, unforgiveness, animosity, jealousy, hypocrisy, envy, competition, and the countless other heart issues He sees. It is these issues that make up the totality of the impurities of the character of the Church. In the earliest beginnings of the Church age, these things were dealt with at the door. Today they are allowed to fester and grow and dilute the power and the glory of the Church. As God revealed to Peter the hidden issues in Ananias and Sapphira's heart, so He did again with Simon.

*But Peter said to him, "Your money perish with you, **because you thought that the gift of God could be purchased with money!** You have neither part nor portion in this matter, for your heart is not right in the sight of God. **Repent therefore of this your wickedness, and pray God if perhaps the thought of your heart may be forgiven you. For I see that you are poisoned by bitterness and bound by iniquity**" (Acts 8:20-23).*

To understand the magnitude and seriousness of this incident, notice how these verses read in another translation.

*But Peter said to him, "To hell with you and your money! **How dare you think you could buy the gift of God!** You can have no share or place in this ministry, **for your heart is not honest before***

God. *All you can do now is to repent of this wickedness of yours and pray earnestly to God that the evil intention of your heart may be forgiven.* **For I can see inside you, and I see a man bitter with jealousy** *and bound with his own sin!"* (Phillips)

What a rebuke! I'm gripped with holy fear just reading it. From this translation, we see that not only was Simon trying to buy the gift of God — not only was his heart not being honest with God (lying as Ananias and Sapphira did), but there was also a serious issue with jealousy in his heart. He wanted the same power and gift Peter and John had for his own personal glory, so he could be someone great as he had been as a sorcerer. The Church and ministry today is filled with such jealousy and competition, even among many pastors and ministers, that it would appall most Christians if they knew the extent of it. We've become a generation of Simon the sorcerers.

Here's another interesting insight I gained while studying these two accounts of Ananias and Sapphira in Acts 5 and Simon the sorcerer in Acts 8.

THE ONE WHO DISCERNED THE HYPOCRISY BECAME A HYPOCRITE

Peter was God's channel of discernment, judgment, and correction. Although money was involved, the big sin and issue was hypocrisy and a desire for an esteemed and honored reputation among men. But guess what? Later in his ministry, Peter gave place to the same sin and issue of hypocrisy.

"Now when Peter had come to Antioch, I withstood him to his face, because he was to be blamed; for before certain men came from James, he would eat with the Gentiles; but when they came, he withdrew and separated himself, fearing those who were of the circumcision. And the rest of the Jews also played the hypocrite with him, so

*that even Barnabas was carried away with their **hypocrisy*** (Gal. 2:11-13).

What does this tell us? It tells us that we are never as free as we may think we are from the very sins and issues God may use us in addressing and correcting in others. This teaches us the vital necessity of continually walking and ministering in the gentleness and meekness of Christ lest we be guilty of the same.

"Brethren, if a man is overtaken in any trespass, you who are spiritual restore such a one in a spirit of gentleness, considering yourself lest you also be tempted" (Gal. 6:1).

Here is another interesting gem of wisdom from this account: Why did the apostle Paul publicly rebuke Peter so sharply? Was it to validate his own ministry and authority? Was it to demonstrate the importance of public rebuke and show that even some of our greatest leaders can sin this way? Or, knowing that hypocrisy is a leaven, was it more to keep this leaven from spreading to the others who were present and to prevent Peter's error from being used by the Judaizing teachers to support their position? I believe the latter was the primary purpose of Paul's rebuke.

We do know that Peter received a great revelation from the Lord of the Gentiles' inclusion in the gospel. We do know he came to Antioch and labored among the brethren there without showing any prejudice toward the Gentiles (Acts 10:48; 11:2). But then later, when some Jewish brethren arrived from Jerusalem, he yielded to the fear of man and peer pressure and withdrew himself from associating with the Gentiles. In doing this, he stopped being straightforward with the gospel and influenced others to play the hypocrite along with him. What he was doing was teaching and practicing a double standard.

Peter allowed some character weaknesses from his past life to resurface. His problem was not what he truly believed, but what he was now practicing. Even Barnabas, who was a mature leader, was caught up in this hypocrisy. This is an example of the power of influence that can quickly spread like leaven.

LACK OF JUDGMENT — A BIG PROBLEM IN THE CHURCH

Paul's rebuke of these influential leaders, as Peter exercised in the beginning, is missing in much of Christendom today. The absence of this sort of accountability is producing unimaginable problems in the body of Christ. This lack of judgment in the modern Church today has caused the glory of the Lord to depart.

Here's an example. In recent times, in high-profile media interviews, some "celebrity" ministers have been guilty of blurring the lines between truth and error, and sin and righteousness. When put on the spot in a public platform and asked a direct and pointed question concerning the great moral issues of 21st-century America, such as homosexuality and abortion, ministers have turned cowardly and given some yellow-bellied, political response. This creates confusion, not only in the world, which is looking for a clear sound from preachers but also to believers, who have no discernment. It brings division to the Church.

For example, one very influential and popular minister who has millions of followers was asked if homosexuality was wrong, and his general response was that his views were evolving. Evolving? That's like saying the Bible is evolving.

Another well-known so-called "pastor" was asked if abortion was sinful, and he offered this half-baked response: "That's the kind of conversation we would have finding out your story, where you're from, what you believe. I mean, God is the judge," at which point the secular audience broke into raucous applause. When the world claps for you concerning your definition of abortion, I can tell you it was a bad job.

It grieves me to no end and God hates it, and His angels bristle at such namby-pamby minister masqueraders who will not walk in the Lord's truth and authority. But my point is this: these types of ministers need to be held accountable by someone in their network or eldership circle for misrepresenting the word of God and making abominable behavior sound so respectful. Either that, or they need to get out of the ministry and be a politician or find another occupation that fits their slick and flimflam demeanor.

When "ministers" compromise to prevailing world culture on a major media platform, I repeat, they need to be called out by someone in their network. Biblical church discipline needs to be applied. At least two admonitions should be given for repentance and if they remain unrepentant and without remorse, they should be rejected or excommunicated according to Scripture.

"If a man is a heretic, after the first and second admonition reject him" (Titus 3:10 - KJ21).

The majority of the body of Christ has no understanding of this sort of Biblical Church discipline because it is hardly ever practiced and sorely lacking in most of today's professing church.

This lack of accountability and do-nothingness is at the root of many of our problems in the body of Christ because of our failure to understand judgment. As one friend of mine said recently, you do not get to talk like a compromising politician about homosexuality and abortion in front of pagans and then act like Paul the apostle on Christian television. Some of these "Christian" talking heads need to grow a backbone, eat some spinach, or something. Forgive me, but we have too many cowards and frauds that are grossly misrepresenting the

Lord, and it's causing unimaginable damage to the body of Christ, and no one ever judges their actions and holds them accountable.

PETER, AN INTERESTING CASE STUDY

What we can learn from Peter's actions and the examples of the aforementioned ministers who failed to speak the truth is the inherent danger of following poor leadership — and to know that men even as good and respectable as Peter and Barnabas can miss it. There are many present-day leaders upholding positions that are bringing division and confusion to the body of Christ.

This beckons us to ask the question: What kind of influence are you having on those around you? We need to constantly be on guard concerning the influence we are having on others because our actions speak louder than our words. Inconsistencies in our character are signs of immaturity. Like many of us, including myself, Peter preached a better message than he actually was living.

It takes courage to obey the gospel and live out our convictions. It takes courage to oppose error and popular teachings and stand for truth. It takes courage to oppose even your friends who are practicing error and trying to influence you with it. It takes courage to live for the Lord in a very ungodly world and preach the gospel to them.

Peter's life and ministry is an interesting character study because of all his ups and downs. He is a leading figure and voice in the beginning years of the early Church, but then he is not heard from in the second part of the book of Acts, as Paul's life and ministry became more prominent. What happened to Peter? I will leave that to the reader to consider, but could it be that he came under the strong dealings of God again because of his hypocrisy and the fear of man? Could he have slipped back down the religious slope of the Pharisaical camp during a season of his life? It's possible, but without revelation we simply don't know.

Both of Peter's epistles, however, written later in his life, and church history, leave us good reason to believe he finished strong. When you read the tone of his first epistle, he seems to be a broken man who was now more acquainted with Christ's sufferings. Ancient church tradition suggests that he was martyred — and actually crucified upside down because he felt unworthy to die as the Master did.

CHURCHES AND MINISTERS MUST JUDGE THEMSELVES CONCERNING MONEY

Nevertheless, Peter was one of the key leaders and voices in the early Church and used by the Lord to address the pride and hypocrisy that was seeking access into the young body in Jerusalem and then in Samaria.

I believe the kind of judgment we see in Acts 5 with Ananias and Sapphira and in Acts 8 with Simon the sorcerer will also increase in the final hour churches who refuse to judge themselves in these last days, for judgment must begin in the house of God (1 Pt. 4:17). In context, the house of God must also be cleansed and purified through suffering (read 1 Pt. 4 in its entirety, and you'll see suffering is a theme), for purity is a prerequisite for the passing over of judgment and the preparation of the glorious Church (1 Cor. 11:31). What I'm saying is that, in the same way Jesus cleansed the temple, even so there will be another cleansing at the end of the Church age as there was at the beginning. Some of the cleansing in this hour has to do with the same issues that were found in Ananias and Sapphira and Simon the sorcerer. The strongest and most severe judgment will be on ministers who've become money-minded and served God with false motives and become worshipers of mammon.

In the case of Simon the sorcerer, I believe he also made money using sorcery, as is the case in many nations today where it is rampant. I lived in West Africa for many years, and it was common for the locals to pay money to a witch doctor to obtain healing and freedom for them or a close member of the family. Simon wanted to pay for the power of God, so he could not only be great in the eyes of the people but make money using it. Here we see another parallel in ministry today — using God and the ministry to make money. Simon had a lust for power, but he also had a lust for money as hinted by this verse in yet another translation.

"Ask the Master to forgive you for trying to use God to make money. I can see this is an old habit with you; you reek with money-lust" (Acts 8:22-23 — The Message).

Too many are profiting dishonorably from their ministry. Notice in the following three translations of 1 Peter 5:2 one of the great qualifications for ministers, especially shepherds and overseers:

"Tend (nurture, guard, guide, and fold) the flock of God that is [your responsibility], not by coercion or constraint, but willingly; **not dishonorably motivated by the advantages and profits [belonging to the office]**, *but eagerly and cheerfully..."* (AMPC).

"Just as shepherds watch over their sheep, you must watch over everyone God has placed in your care. Do it willingly in order to please God and not simply because you think you must. **Let it be something you want to do, instead of something you do merely to make money"** (CEV).

"Take care of the group of people you are responsible for. They are God's flock. Watch over that flock because you want to, not because you are forced to do it. That is how God wants it. **Do it because you are happy to serve, not because you want money"** (ERV).

Peter is addressing shepherds and dishonest gain, and their attitude and motive for serving the flock, but this applies to all ministers and not just shepherds or pastors.

A pastor friend of mine told me recently that he had a call from an itinerant preacher who wanted a meeting. This is common in churches today, of course. But this young preacher then had the audacity to tell the pastor that he usually received $2000 per meeting. The pastor told him that they were a smaller church and that he probably wouldn't receive that amount. The preacher persisted to emphasize that figure. I wouldn't have given that fellow the time of day except to bring him some stern correction to let him know that he wasn't qualified to minister. In this season of our lives, my wife and I are itinerant ministers, and we have never even hinted to pastors what we need or placed any kind of requirement on church offerings for our meetings. That young preacher was a hireling.

Ministers must judge themselves concerning money and their motives.

This is a severe judgment and must be so for the glory to reappear as strong and even stronger than it did at the beginning. If the weight of God's glory increased now, some would stand condemned and even die in judgment as Ananias and Sapphira did at the beginning (Acts 5), for many are living a lie. Christians are praying for revival and crying out for the glory of God, but if the Father answered their prayers, there would be many Ananiases and Sapphiras falling dead across this land, for the level of judgment is always in proportion to the level of glory.

Remember that their judgment was lying about money and wanting the recognition of being generous givers (hypocrisy). The love of appearance and reputation was working in their hearts. As I stated, Jesus taught us to give not to be seen of men (Matt. 6:1-4) and warned us of hypocrisy in it. We must judge ourselves in these areas.

"For if we would judge ourselves, we would not be judged. But when we are judged, we are chastened by the Lord, that we may not be condemned with the world" (1 Cor. 11:31-32).

AFTER PURITY COMES PRAYER: THE HIGH PLACE OF EFFECTUAL PRAYER

Once there is a cleansing in the Church, then there must be a greater consecration from God's people that leads to effectual, fervent prayer. In fact, when we are cleansed and purified of our hypocrisy and tainted motives of greed and covetousness and all that would de-file us, our prayers will be so much more effectual. When a spirit of re-pentance falls and prevails on a people, their first response is to begin to call on the Name of the Lord afresh and anew again and to pray fer-vently. Jesus said that His house will be called a house of prayer. The Spirit of God said this to my wife and me recently: *"If the body of Christ would press into the 'Could you not watch and pray with Me daily for one hour?' they'd see the book of Acts."*

True prayer always precedes the power of God. It releases divine activity and dispatches angels. It brings the provision of God. It births miracles, signs and wonders, and the gifts of the Holy Spirit. It deals with the enemies of the Church and seals her with divine protection.It brings the glory of God into manifestation. Oh, what we miss when we don't enter into true, effectual prayer and the communion of the Holy Ghost! But what I want you to see is this: it's prayer from a pure heart and a pure consecrated Church that will bring this kind of glory and power. Note this heart-stirring quote from Kenneth E. Hagin, written in the 1990s, on the importance of consecration:

"The consecration of believers was much deeper 50 years ago than it is now. Believers appreciation and reverence for the things of

God and the move of the Holy Spirit was much deeper, too. And as a result, God honored that depth of consecration and reverence by giving His people great manifestations of the Holy Spirit.

"Believers today need greater consecration and dedication to God. In the churches I pastored in the 1940s, we used to gather around the altar and pray at the end of nearly every service. We often sang the old hymn, 'Is Your All on the Altar of Sacrifice Laid?' We don't sing hymns like that much anymore, but folks today need to heed the message of some of those old scriptural hymns."

There's a connection between believers' consecration and the power of God. Paul prayed for the Church to know the *"exceeding greatness of His power"* (Eph. 1:19). This great power will come into manifestation through purity as a result of our consecration — and prayer. We've seen only a small measure of that power. When it comes into full manifestation, the Church will once again have the attention of the world.

Notice again another scripture of how purity, through the confession of our sins and faults, leads to effectual prayer and then power:

"Confess to one another therefore your faults (your slips, your false steps, your offenses, your sins) and pray [also] for one another, that you may be healed and restored [to a spiritual tone of mind and heart]. The earnest (heartfelt, continued) prayer of a righteous man makes tremendous power available [dynamic in its working]" (James 5:16 —Amp).

It is inferred in this scripture that the confession of our faults, offenses, and sins will release power to heal as we pray. The Spirit of God instructed my wife and me to admonish the pray-ers to pray fervently and effectually for the power of God to be made available to the Church today, but it must be done from a position of purity and cleansing. I don't think we realize how much sin and defiling heart issues there are in the modern-day Church. No wonder there is no glory and no power. Without the glory and power of God, the Church will continue to decline in her witness and effectiveness.

Why do you think the early apostles chose not to wait on tables but instead gave themselves to prayer and the Word (Acts 6:4)? In other words, what was their main reason and motivation for their unbending commitment?

The common answer would be that they had to pray and study, so they could stay in a place to minister to people. Of course, that's a part of it, but a more careful study would reveal an even deeper reason. With the unsettling miracle of judgment that killed Ananias and Sapphira and the fear it produced fresh on their minds, and then the present murmuring of the widows, the apostles realized quickly how critical it was for them to stay in the Spirit. They wanted to keep the glory of the Lord strong in the Church and maintain keen discernment. They wanted to stay out of the natural realm and live in the supernatural realm of God. It was vital that they stay in the Spirit, hearing from God, and contending, not only to keep the glory and power that they had gained from Jesus, but to thwart off the enemy and make new advances in God.

Isn't this what Jesus taught and exemplified for them in His earthly ministry? He stayed in the glory of the Father because He lived in abiding prayer and communion with Him. The early apostles learned that from Him—to stay in the Spirit and not initiate anything of their own reasoning or doing, and not to simply judge things from the seeing of the eye and hearing of the ear. All ministers are to live a life of prayer and to stay in the Word in order to gain and maintain the glory and continue to give birth to the things God wants to do. Of course, our motivation is simply out of a love for the Lord and our desire to know Him, but also to advance the glory of His work and keep it pure.

A SERIES OF THOUGHT-PROVOKING QUESTIONS

If the 120 had not waited on God, would they have received such a miraculous and spectacular outpouring of the Holy Spirit (Acts 2)?

If Peter and John had not participated in the daily hour of prayer, would the crippled man have been raised up at the gate called Beautiful (Acts 3)?

If Peter and John had not reported to their own company and prayed with them after they were severely threatened and beaten, would the building they assembled in have shook, and would they have been granted signs and wonders to continue preaching boldly (Acts 4)?

Would an angel have been sent to deliver Peter and the other apostles from prison if they had not been devoted and consecrated to the continued preaching of the gospel despite the persecution (Acts 5)?

Would the disciples have been multiplied in Jerusalem if the apostles had not given themselves to prayer and the Word (Acts 6)?

If Stephen had not consecrated his life to the Lord and prayed forgiveness for Saul, would there have ever been an apostle Paul (Saul — Acts 7)?

If Stephen's heart had not been so pure and full of love and forgiveness, would he have seen the glory of God and Jesus standing at the right hand of God (v. 55-56)?

If Ananias had not prayed, would Saul have ever been raised up in the way he was (Acts 9)?

If Cornelius had not waited on God in prayer and fasting, would he have received specific instructions from the angel of the Lord that led to the first glorious outpouring among the Gentiles (Acts 10)?

If Peter had not been sensitive to go up on the housetop to pray while lunch was being prepared, would he have received the men Cornelius sent to him, and would there have been a wide and effectual door opened to the Gentiles at that time (Acts 10)?

If the church had not been in constant prayer for Peter, would he have been delivered from prison (Acts 12)?

If the handful of prophets and teachers at Antioch hadn't taken the time to minister to the Lord and fast, would they have heard the direction of the Lord which gave birth to a missionary movement that changed the landscape of the early Church (Acts 13)?

As it was in the beginning, so it must be now. We are living in the time of the end. There is a famine for hearing the true wisdom and counsel of the Lord, and the pure works of the Father here in the West and in other nations are few. There's been a great decline of the power of God and a departure of His glory. There is an apostasy of the Word and the Spirit. We are nearer to the Lord's return than ever. If we as ministers are not examples in consecration and prayer, how do we expect others we lead to be consecrated and pray? And how do we expect to gain the same glory they had in the early Church? We must see and understand that consecration, purity, and prayer are connected to His glory.

It's going to take a deeper place in prayer to give birth to the move God wants to bring in this hour — prayer that is done in tongues with very little English or understood language. It's going to take deeper supplications and intercessions with groanings and travail. My wife,

Carolyn, uttered this phrase in prayer recently: *"His anointing is with me, and everywhere I see is bright, but I've got to go farther."*

When we pray mysteries from our hearts, there's so much divine power and light that is manifested and needs to be carried into the present darkness, but it takes faith and a greater yielded-ness to go farther into the Spirit and pray this way. Perseverance is an important element of praying like this (Eph. 6:18). If we really want a move of God, we must understand this aspect of prayer because every move of God starts like this and is maintained the same way. May God help us and anoint us to pray with all perseverance so that there can be a birthing of His power.

PRAYER IN THE SPIRIT GIVES BIRTH TO MOVES OF GOD AND HIS MIGHTY POWER

There is a book I have in my library that is a favorite of mine which I often refer to called, *Tongues: Beyond the Upper Room*, written by the man I just quoted, the late Kenneth E. Hagin. I attended Brother Hagin's Bible school back in the 1980s when there was a move of God on. He was a man of deep prayer, even on occasion saying that a few times he would get so far out in the realm of the Spirit in prayer he wasn't sure if he'd return. What?!! Yes, as a young student I had no idea what he meant when he said such things, but then when he compared it to an astronaut out in space who could be lost forever if disconnected from his tethers or anchors, I understood that he was speaking of a deeper spiritual realm in prayer that few have tapped into. He said the following in some of his final years on earth concerning prayer:

"The Lord told me that there is a depth of prayer and intercession in the Spirit that will be lost unless we who are experienced in prayer somehow get those truths over to this present generation of believers.

"I've known a few folks over the years who were great intercessors and who became experts in this deeper realm of praying in the Holy Ghost. But God wants more who can pray like those few. He must have more believers who know how to pray in that deeper realm, because there is a job to get done in these last days. If His plans and purposes are to be fulfilled in this late hour, more and more of His people must say no to their flesh and spend time praying out divine mysteries to God."

In this book, Brother Hagin emphasizes the value of praying in other tongues as the avenue into giving birth to greater moves of God. He also gives examples of supernatural testimonies that happened because believers "prayed through" in other tongues. He said if Spirit-filled Christians would start believing God for the move of His Spirit and pray in the Holy Ghost the way Pentecostal believers did in days of old, the mighty power of God that they experienced would come into manifestation again today.

What struck me most about this book and has stuck to me was when Brother Hagin compared the moves of God to waves of the ocean. He said that every wave that breaks forth close to the shore had its beginnings way out in the depths of the ocean. In other words, the potential energy and force of any wave begins long before you see the final result of it as it breaks forth on the seashore.

This is what praying in tongues accomplishes in the Spirit realm. When you pray in tongues at length, you give impetus to the next move of God's Spirit before that "wave" is visible to your sight. In other words, when you pray in tongues and make spiritual intercession, it's like you are helping to build up the power of that unseen wave that lies underneath the deep waters of the ocean. As you continue on in praying this way, you are aiding in the birth of the move of God that comes in waves.

Brother Hagin had a conviction that, before Jesus returns, there would be one last great and mighty "wave" or move of God's Spirit. Toward the end of his aforementioned book, he makes these statements:

"Oh, yes, we've seen the power of the Holy Ghost in a limited fashion, but a wave is coming that will bring His power on a higher level and in a far greater measure than we have ever seen heretofore. I can see that wave way out yonder in the deep waters. It's coming! The waves of Holy Ghost power are building higher. Keep on praying so you can ride that new wave as it builds and builds in divine power and glory. I'm convinced that this wave will be twice as high as the healing wave (1940s and '50s), the Charismatic wave (1960s and '70s), or the faith wave (these were moves of God that Bro. Hagin was a part of). In fact, it will be twice as high as all of them put together! I believe it is going to be the wave that sweeps us right on into the shores of the glory world!"

Glory to God!

WIGGLESWORTH PROPHECY

In 1939 in England when World War II was ready to break out, Smith Wigglesworth also prophesied of each of these moves in the presence of a young Lester Sumrall. But he saw something even greater that would come after these aforementioned moves of God that Hagin was involved in. Here is the totality of that word that he gave to Sumrall:

With tears rolling down his face Wigglesworth cried, saying, *"I probably won't see you again now. My job is almost finished."* As he continued to pray, he cried, *"I see it, I see it!"*

Brother Sumrall asked, *"What do you see, what do you see?"*

He said, *"I see a healing revival coming right after World War II. It'll be so easy to get people healed. I see it! I see it! I won't be here for it, but you will be."* And there was a healing revival right after the war in the later 1940s and '50s, one which the Lord also revealed to Brother Hagin after several hours of praying in the Spirit.

He continued to prophesy, *"I see another one; I see people of all different denominations being filled with the Holy Ghost."* That was the Charismatic revival or renewal. God raised up people during that era and many ministries, such as the Full Gospel Businessmen's Fellowship, among others.

Then Brother Wigglesworth continued, *"I see another move of God. I see auditoriums full of people, coming with notebooks. There will be a wave of teaching on faith and healing."* We did experience that wave he saw, and we called it the "Word of Faith movement."

Then he prophesied, and this is what I want you to see, *"After that, after the third wave* (this one is still in the future at this writing),*"* he started sobbing. *"I see the last-days revival that's going to usher in the precious fruit of the Earth. It will be the greatest revival this world has ever seen! It's going to be a wave of the gifts of the Spirit. The ministry gifts will be flowing on this planet Earth. I see hospitals being emptied out, and they will bring the sick to churches where they allow the Holy Ghost to move."*

Hallelujah! Glory to God!!!

May God anoint many more of us to pray effectually in this manner, so that this great move of God can manifest on the earth and the precious fruit of this last-days harvest of souls may be reaped.

SECTION II
THE WORSHIP OF MAMMON

CHAPTER SIX

MONEY IMPURITIES:

WRONGLY WIELDING THE POWER OF MONEY

The gross abuse of money has corrupted some of today's churches and ministries. Through ungodly counsel, ministers have given birth to Ishmaels that God never ordained, and then used manipulative tactics and gimmicks to persuade the people to pay for them. Men have built churches and ministries that have become machines that need to be kept running through excessive appeals and abuses of money.

As an example, one mega-church pastor got some of his minister friends to ride motorcycles into the church and on to the platform. People went crazy with the noise of the engines and the allurement of it all. Then a popular, larger-than-life television personality was flown in to take up a huge offering to pay off the mountain-sized mortgage debt the church owed on their building. Of course, with the people already in a heightened state of hysteria, it was easy to extract money from them, and the celebrity preacher, in all likelihood, probably received a healthy cut.

You may ask, "Is there anything wrong with raising money to pay off a church building?" Of course not. It's the method and the way it was done that makes it highly questionable. Hype is not a part of God's methodology. It is an impurity. It is almost equivalent to people throwing money at the preacher while he is preaching. Have you ever witnessed this and felt a disturbing unrest in your spirit? That is the grief of the Spirit of God within you.

I was in a meeting once where I observed a nationally known evangelist take up an offering under the influence of a seducing spirit. He gave a personal testimony of sowing a financial seed and attributed that seed to large amounts of financial provision that he reaped afterwards. It sounded so good that he enticed many people to come to the altar and sow the largest seed they could. My wife and I nearly got seduced by it as well, until the Spirit of God checked us. Many individuals gave $1000 in that one offering because the preacher highlighted that figure. That should've raised a red flag right there. A person ought to give as he purposes in his heart, not the amount the preacher entices them to give, which is quite common today. This evangelist walked away from a medium-sized church with hundreds of thousands of dollars. The pastor was greatly disappointed and regretted letting him use the church building for his meeting. Once again, he hyped up the people with a sales pitch that was hard to refuse. It was an impurity.

As we were praying one day, the Lord showed us that this man's ministry started off pure and right in his heart, but when his ministry got bigger and more organizational, his heart began turning and became corrupted in the same way that king Solomon's heart became corrupted. This happens to so many, especially as ministries and churches get bigger. My prayer is, "Lord, please help me keep my own heart pure in ministry, especially in the areas of pride, money, and sexual immorality."

We need to be careful when it comes to money, without being stingy or having a poverty mentality. A spirit of generosity must prevail in the Church, but let it be because God is moving on people's hearts and not because of a seducing spirit. When a minister becomes money minded, watch him, because he will eventually lose out with God. It's fine to fund-raise for building projects and mission projects as we sometimes have had to do, but be careful not to manipulate the people.

DON'T LET THE TAIL WAG THE DOG

What happens with pastors and ministry leaders today is they let the tail wag the dog instead of the dog wagging the tail. Let me explain.

As an example, if you gave a minister several million dollars to begin his adult life and ministry, in all likelihood he would squander it attempting to find the will and plan of God for himself. It seems reasonable that with the temptation of having access to all that money, he would base God's plan on trial-and-error and hit-or-miss methods. And even as good as his intentions may be, he would lapse into doing the "good" and what would benefit his own interests and never really find God's plan. In other words, without the dealings of God at work in his life, his motives would likely be corrupted by personal ambition (men must be tested and proven before being granted such authority, responsibility, and resources).

But if the same minister was stripped of pride, greed, and covetousness, and his motives purified through God's dealings and testings — and if he learned to pray and cultivate an ear to listen and be led by the Spirit of God, it would almost guarantee him following God's plan and purpose for his entire life and ministry. The blessing of the Lord and all the money and provision he would need to fulfill his calling would follow his obedience. This is true maturity. But with most men today in both life and ministry, the approach is upside down. Instead of the dog wagging the tail, the tail wags the dog — money being used as a means to an end and determining your own direction instead of being led by the Spirit of God. May the Lord give the reader understanding.

If you allow pride, greed, and covetousness, a desire for position, influence, and popularity to be greater than your desire for prayer and intimacy with God, you will always serve your own interests and disguise it as service to God. Remember that is what Ananias and Sapphira and Simon the sorcerer did. This will keep you out of the intimacy realm of prayer and communion with God, thus also keeping you from knowing and fulfilling His ultimate plan and purpose for your life and ministry. That's very sobering. If you're not prayerful and stay in the realm of revelation, you could live and die and never fulfill God's perfect plan for your life, or never even enter the first phase of it.

SERVICE OF MAMMON KEEPING THE CHURCH AND MINISTERS IN UNBELIEF

The service of mammon is keeping the Church in unbelief. Having riches (mammon) is not evil or wrong, but serving riches (mammon) is. This is manifested in leaders whose trust is more in men for money than God. Ministries have been guilty of using gimmicks and ungodly tactics to extract money from people. Pressure and manipulation are applied to people so they can give. Pastors will frequently check their church financial records to see who is giving and who is not, and then they wind up showing partiality to those who give more. These are forms of subtle unbelief and having your eyes on man. Are you truly trusting the Lord, or are you depending more on the strength of your flesh?

Now, I understand that, in appointing local church elders and deacons, pastors have to often check their giving records because it is an indication of where their heart is. If they are not giving to the local work, then their hearts are not there, and they should be disqualified for service in leadership. Where a man's treasure is, there will his heart be also (Matt. 6:21). Generosity is tied to the condition of a person's heart.

On the other hand, the circumstances and levels of faith are different in people's lives. You can't simply judge people by their financial contributions to a church. If they're prayerful, on fire for Jesus, and winning souls, their worth to the kingdom is invaluable, regardless of their financial giving, whereas oftentimes the lukewarm rich church members will manipulate and control a pastor through their giving, but their witness for Christ is lacking in their personal lives. Sometimes it's best never to look at the financial records, as a few wise pastors have chosen to do. Yet, of course, it is right and honorable to give and support the work of God and godly shepherds who lead you and feed you, and there is a great blessing in it. Although certain principles are timeless, God doesn't lead every pastor the same, exact way.

GODLY EXAMPLES OF TRUSTING THE LORD

In one partner church of ours, the people had to nearly plead with the pastor to receive offerings because the Lord told him not to receive conventional offerings due to the mistrust that people have today of ministers' questionable dealings with money. Sometimes you have to establish trust over a period of time and teach people Bible truths concerning money. This pastor found a healthy compromise with his people, and they decided to place an offering box or basket by the entrance of the church so people could give as they purposed in their hearts and according to how God was touching and blessing their spiritual lives. This church has never lacked. As a matter of fact, they've prospered. At times the Lord has even sent "ravens" (unexpected sources/people and channels of income) to this church that have blessed them financially. This pastor was truly putting all his trust in the Lord.

For example, since this church first leased a building in a strip mall, the empty buildings in that mall have filled up with new tenants. The millionaire who owns those buildings took note of the great provision that had come to him since the church had been there, and he started giving this church large donations for their work. And this millionaire is a sinner!

I have another dear pastor friend whose church has a great outreach to the children in the community, and another millionaire was touched by their love and heart for them. This man is not even a member of the church, but on two different occasions, he has donated one million dollars to this church. God has more than one way of bringing provision and paying for what He's ordered. Of course, it is not wrong to receive conventional offerings and to teach people the value of giving. The important thing is to let the Lord lead you and to put all your trust in Him and not man.

The same type of unbelief could be applied to traveling ministers/missionaries like we are at this writing. Many traveling ministers are interested only in going to larger churches and ministering in conferences, where they know the likelihood of receiving bigger offerings and selling more product are there. That's a wrong motive and another impurity. We've ministered in large, medium-sized, *and* many smaller churches. I can tell you from experience that the size of the crowd does not necessarily equate to the size of the offering. We've been overwhelmed at times with the generosity of numerically smaller churches. God is faithful and will take care of you if you will serve Him and not mammon. The needs and expenses of traveling ministers are real, just as the needs of pastors and churches are real, but once again, the key is to put all your trust in the Lord and do what He says.

Financial increase and spiritual multiplication will often come from obeying a word of wisdom God gives you. In the ministry of Jesus, He asked for a little boy's lunch to be brought to Him — a few loaves and two fish — and when He blessed them and broke them, there was great multiplication (Matt. 14:17-20). The same can be applied spiritually. When the apostles received a word of wisdom for seven men to care for the widows, so that they could devote themselves to prayer and the Word, there was great spiritual multiplication (Acts 6:1-7). This word of wisdom also stopped the murmuring that was coming from the widows, who were being neglected in the daily ministration. That murmuring alone could've killed the momentum of the early revival in Jerusalem.

So, on the one hand, in the earliest beginnings of the Church age, people were selling their houses and lands and bringing the proceeds to the apostles' feet (Acts 4:34-35). But on the other hand, there were poor widows who needed care who were being neglected (Acts 6), and distribution was made to them as they had need. Notice again the unbending commitment to prayer these early apostles had that even the initial neglect of the widows did not cause them to neglect their devotion to prayer and the Word. God gave them a word of wisdom to resolve this problem that was threatening to divide them and deter the apostles from prayer and the Word.

The legitimate needs of people and the pure religion of caring for widows (Jm. 1:27) would not pull them away from their primary responsibility. Today, pastors and ministers are quickly and easily knocked out of prayer, not necessarily by the legitimate needs of people, but by petty things, pet hobbies, and menial tasks, or simply by their own failure to delegate administrative duties to qualified men as the apostles did. This is another area the Spirit of God spoke strongly to us about.

Pastors and fellow ministers, we have a great responsibility before God to stay in prayer and the Word. Put all your trust in the Lord. Listen to Him, and do what He says. All the wisdom, grace, and provision you need is found in Him. It is when we return to this pattern that we will begin seeing radical change in the Church of today.

MONEY IS DECEITFUL, AND THE DESIRE FOR RICHES IS UNSCRIPTURAL

Not only does the Bible say that the *love* of money is the root of all evil (1 Tim. 6:10), but money in itself is also deceitful. The deceitfulness of riches is one kind of thorn that Jesus said chokes the Word and causes it to be unfruitful in one's life (Mk. 4:19). Of course, money by itself is not bad or evil; it's a tool, and we all need it; it is a tremendous source of power and influence and blessing, but it's deceitful.

Wasn't it deception that led Ananias and Sapphira to lie about the amount of money they gave? If they knew it would cost them their physical lives, they would've never considered lying about it. Undoubtedly, the example of Barnabas and the desire not to be outdone by his generosity led to their deception.

"And Joses, who was also named Barnabas by the apostles (which is translated 'Son of Encouragement'), a Levite of the country of Cyprus, having land, sold it, and brought the money and laid it at the apostles' feet" (Acts 4:36-37).

They were more conscious of their reputation and approval among men than the approval and judgment of God.

Due to the desire for reputation, Ananias and Sapphira were deceived into lying about it. Riches are associated with a certain reputation and prestige. This is one of the characteristics of riches that can engender bondage and deception.

Paul warned Timothy about it and told him not to fellowship with anyone who considered gain to be godliness. Sounds like what many preach today, doesn't it?

"...supposing that gain is godliness: from such withdraw thyself. But godliness with contentment is great gain. For we brought nothing

into this world, and it is certain we can carry nothing out. And having food and raiment let us be therewith content" (1 Tim. 6:5-8).

As I have repeatedly stated elsewhere in this book, in Bible days, the Jews equated wealth with godliness. That was what the Law taught them, and to them it was a sign of God's blessing. In other words, if you were blessed financially, it was because you were keeping the Law and you were good and upright and favored by God. So, you can readily see that from this doctrine and belief system of that day many rich Jews thought they would inherit eternal life and go to heaven solely based on their riches. That's the reason Jesus told the story of the rich man and Lazarus. This is not just an account of the reality of heaven and hell, but if you'll read that entire discourse in context, including the verses and chapters before and after, you'll see that the main subject is money (Lk. 16:19-31). That is why the rich man seemed surprised when he found himself in hell (v. 25). Riches had deceived him and mastered him, and he did not consider the poor like Lazarus.

"But Abraham said, 'Son, remember that in your lifetime you received your good things, and likewise Lazarus evil things; but now he is comforted and you are tormented' (v. 25)."

That is also the reason the disciples were greatly astonished when Jesus told them how hard it was for a rich man to enter the kingdom of heaven (Matt. 19:23-26). The backdrop to this teaching was when they heard Him tell the other rich young ruler to sell everything he had, give it to the poor, and then follow Jesus if he wanted to inherit eternal life (Matt. 19:16-22). The rich man wouldn't do it. As they say, money makes a great servant but a lousy master. Unless you become a bond servant to Jesus and can give it all away if He asked you to, money could just be more of a master to you than you think. Be careful. Recently the Lord dealt with my wife and me about being in a more fully consecrated position if He decided to bless us with large amounts of money. If you *desire* riches, you will fall into temptation and a snare or trap and into many foolish and hurtful lusts.

*"**But they that will be rich** fall into temptation and a snare, and into many foolish and hurtful lusts, which drown men in destruction and perdition. For the love of money is the root of all evil: which while some coveted after, they have erred from the faith, and pierced themselves through with many sorrows. But thou, O man of God, flee these things; and follow after righteousness, godliness, faith, love, patience, meekness"* (1 Tim. 6:9-11).

Notice the expression, *"but they that will be rich fall into temptation and a snare."*

Other translations read, *"But those who crave to be rich"* (AMPC).

"But people who are trying to get rich" (CEB).

"But they that are minded to be rich" (ASV).

"and those wishing to be rich" (YLT).

"But people who long to be rich" (NLT).

"But those who desire to be rich" (MEV).

Can it be any clearer than this? The modern "prosperity theology," if not mixed with these warnings that Paul gave Timothy, will lead the heart to desire money and earthly possessions until people begin to seek after them. After all, the flesh will not resist financial prosperity teachings that promise riches. The flesh enjoys feeding on that. This teaching is not cruciform but can feed the lusts of the flesh if not tempered with warnings of the many dangers that the desire for riches can bring.

THE LOST CHURCH OF THE LAODICEANS

The Church of the Laodiceans had the same problem. They trusted in their riches and believed they had favor with God because of it. They were rich, increased with goods, and had need of nothing (what an example of the deception that trusting in riches produces), but Jesus told them that they were wretched, miserable, poor, blind, and naked (Rev. 3:17). How deceived they were!

Many Bible scholars believe the Laodicean church is the apostate church of the last days just before the return of the Lord. Just like the two rich men, they equated wealth, riches, and possessions with the blessing of God. They weren't aware of their true spiritual condition. Yet all they needed to do was to know what the Scriptures really said instead of just believing what the spiritual leaders of their day taught them. If they had just gotten in touch with their own hearts on the matter by communing with God, the Lord would've revealed the true condition of their hearts.

Isn't that what we are seeing in our day? Many Christians believe more what the elevated teachers in our Christian culture say rather than what the Bible actually teaches. I can tell you right now that some of the most popular teachers and preachers in the marketplace of Christianity today are on their way to great loss of eternal reward, and in some cases even perdition, if they don't experience a rude awakening. Wealth and riches have become a snare to them, and they are falling into many foolish and hurtful lusts and erring from the faith, piercing themselves through with many sorrows. May God have mercy on their souls and help us all to be sober and alert concerning the love of money and deceitfulness of riches.

THE YOUNG DEMONIAC THAT I CAST THE DEVIL OUT OF

Several years ago, I cast the devil out of a 19-year-old boy while conducting meetings in the nation of Gambia, West Africa. We brought him to Jesus, got him filled with the Holy Spirit, and enrolled him in Bible school afterwards. Praise the Lord!

I was so intrigued with his testimony that, immediately following his deliverance, I interviewed him. I discovered that evil spirits had visited him since he was seven years of age and enticed him to enter into a covenant with them. For a dozen years or so, the devil would grant this boy pleasures and then inflict pain upon him and beat him, more pleasures and then more pain, until it became almost unbearable for him. I asked him if he had sought freedom and help from Christians and churches. He said he had, but none were strong enough to help him get free. In one incident, he recounted to me how the evil spirit in him ransacked the office of the pastor of a large Charismatic church and slapped him in the face when they tried to cast the evil spirit out of him. **Here's what the evil spirit spoke: "This church has no power because they don't live holy, and all they talk about is money!"** Can you believe a devil said that? Demons know churches. Demons know men.

"And the evil spirit answered and said, "Jesus I know, and Paul I know; but who are you?" (Acts 19:15)

This church had no power over the evil spirit in this boy because they were unholy and full of greed and covetousness. Their powerlessness was due to these impurities. Don't think that these things do not matter, because they do. A house divided against itself cannot stand (Matt. 12:25). I know that God's gifts and callings are irrevocable, and God may use churches, ministries, and individuals for a time even when they are living in sin and deception because He loves the people they minister to and wants to bless them, but soon judgment catches up with them if they don't repent. But when it comes to the corporate anointing and power in a church, money impurities and greed dilute it and make the church ineffective.

We've got to repent and drain the swamp in the church of dirty money before true restoration can come. God's house must be a house of prayer and not a house of merchandise or a den of thieves.

THE TWISTED DOCTRINE OF SOWING AND REAPING

Let's look at what has happened to the sowing-and-reaping doctrine. We've made it all about money. But do you realize that the following scripture that many preachers use is not even about reaping money?

"But this I say: He who sows sparingly will also reap sparingly, and he who sows bountifully will also reap bountifully. So let each one give as he purposes in his heart, not grudgingly or of necessity; for God loves a cheerful giver" (2 Cor. 9:6-7).

The problem has been that we've made these verses into a formula. This is a religious mindset that sees us as servants rather than sons. It's the difference between a sharecropper who works someone's field for a set percentage of wages versus true sons who are laboring in the field with the Father for a harvest of souls. As you will soon see, the reaping of souls is what these verses in fact emphasize, and not money. Let's read these verses in context.

The above verses and the entire chapter of 2 Corinthians 9 are written in the context of the famine in Jerusalem that took place during a time of great persecution. None of the Jews were helping the Jewish Christians. Instead they were proselytizing them and trying to get them back under the Law. The apostle Paul was collecting this money from the Gentile churches as a relief fund for the Jewish believers.

These new Jewish believers were having a difficult time, however, differentiating between the gospel of grace and the Law. They were also having difficulty understanding how God could include the Gentiles as joint heirs in His kingdom. They were not fully understanding how God could love the Gentiles as much as He loved the Jews. Paul saw this relief fund as a great opportunity to break down this barrier.

This relief fund love offering from the Gentile believers in a great time of persecution and famine would go a long way toward persuading the Jewish believers of the Gentiles' equal place in the kingdom of God. The Lord didn't want His Church divided between Jews and Gentiles. Paul was hoping that this large offering from the Gentile believers would melt the Jewish believers' hearts and unify the Church. That is what the Lord wanted. How far our understanding of these verses of Scripture has drifted from their original meaning!

God the Father is thinking of souls, and man is thinking of money. God desires souls, and we desire money. In this context, God desired a harvest of Jewish believers, and Paul is explaining to these Gentile believers that those who sow much toward helping these Jews will reap much, and those who sow little will reap little. In other words, those who sow much in finances will reap much in souls, but those who sow little in finances will reap little in souls. Can you see it?

These Gentile believers were to purpose in their own hearts how much of a participant they would be. The Father does not coerce His people into giving in the same way men often do. He does not demand or manipulate anyone to give but desires willing hearts and glad participation. Because the Gentile believers are sowing this large offering into their Jewish brethren in a time of need, these Jews will glorify

God for their loyalty and obedience to the gospel and for their love for them that matches their profession. These Jewish believers will acknowledge the salvation of the Gentiles and know for certain that they are true brethren. This was the harvest God was seeking.

Sowing into this offering produced a harvest of souls for the heavenly Father. The grace of the Lord Jesus Christ was what gave the Corinthians an abundance to sow — not their giving. Men have taught God's people that their provision from God is based on how much they sow. Do you realize that this was what the scribes and Pharisees taught the widows? Jesus commended the widow because she gave two mites (Mk. 12:41-44), which represented all she had, but have you ever wondered why she gave all she had? Look at verses 38-40, and you'll find a clue. Notice specifically these words: *"Beware of the scribes... who devour widows' houses."* Jesus told them to beware of the scribes who were devouring widows' houses. That's because the scribes taught these widows that God required them to give their all and that their provision came from what they gave, but nowhere in the Old Testament can you find such a requirement. These are all money impurities that have defiled the Church today, and God is calling us to forsake all practices that steal from His people.

Sowing and reaping is out of balance in today's Church. I am not denying that there is a law of sowing and reaping at work in our lives (Gal. 6:6-8), but it's not limited, nor is its main application to money. Are we sowing strictly for personal profit or to advance God's kingdom? That's the issue.

Let me make a statement that may stun some of you. Our personal provision does not depend on the law of sowing and reaping. In other words, it does not depend on our giving. If you grew up in a fairly stable home with a good father who provided for you, did he provide for you only when you did your share of chores around the house and faithfully performed all your duties? Were you allowed in the refrigerator or at the dinner table only if you had lived up to your father's expectations that day? How much better of a father is our heavenly Father? Can you see how we've made this sowing-and-reaping doctrine into a formula? We are part of our Father's family! His provision for us is not based on our performance or our sowing and reaping.

The birds of the air neither sow nor reap nor gather into barns, and yet the heavenly Father feeds them. Are we not much better than a bird? The lilies of the field grow and neither toil nor spin, and yet the heavenly Father gloriously clothes them. Are we not much better than lilies (Matt. 6:25-30)? Do we not have more value than the birds of the air and the lilies of the fields? We are children of God! These verses tell us that our provision is not based on anything we do or our performance. We sow, we give, we labor in the gospel because we are children who trust our Father and stewards who love our Master. Our performance is part of our faithful stewardship but does not determine our personal provision. How freeing that was to me the first time I learned it! This revelation brought me into a greater ability to understand and receive the love of the Father and inspired me to actually give more with the proper motive and attitude.

Now to qualify what I just said, although our stewardship and performance does not determine our personal provision, it does determine our rewards and the amount of responsibility God can entrust us with both in this life and the next. We will stand before God and give account of our lives and stewardship. Disobedience never pays, and in fact, can cost you dearly and cause you to forfeit the blessings of God. Stewardship and obedience are vital to our Christian life, but they don't feed us and clothe us and provide for our basic needs. God provides for us simply because we are His sons and daughters. In other words, He provides for us by grace and not by our works. This revelation will set you free, but it will also undermine the financial foundation and systems of many churches and ministries today that are based on this formula.

ANOTHER IMPURITY: MONEY AND CONTROL

When we served as missionaries in West Africa, we witnessed the corrupted power of money and the control and sway it can have over people. Of course, the world is corrupt in their use of money, for they are only behaving according to their sinful and unregenerate nature, but it should concern us when so many in Christendom operate the same way. Money is often wrongfully used to beguile and bewitch believers and ministers. Unfortunately, this is operative in the Church and its leadership today to a great extent.

In our early years of ministry as missionaries, God called and separated our apostolic team to a work of establishing Bible training centers for the many denominations we worked among. These training centers carried a threefold purpose: 1) to nurture doctrinal order and unity in the body of Christ; 2) to meet a spiritual need in a region through evangelism, discipleship, and the equipping of ministry gifts; 3) to accelerate divine activity and the move of God in a region. We were divinely commissioned and received strategic wisdom to help the body of Christ come into order in the nations God called us to.

As we opened these training centers, many would come from their various churches and denominations. Excitement and momentum would build, and great change would come to the spiritual body in these nations. However, there was also opposition. Local pastors rose up against these training centers, and some began to use the power of money to dissuade some of their key members or promising young church leaders from attending, or to resign from the training center to take paid positions within their churches. Some of our students succumbed to this temptation and missed a great opportunity to be thoroughly equipped and trained outside of the religious establishment or traditional church system they were a part of. The behavior of these pastors was rooted in pride and envy, similar to the attitude the chief priests and Pharisees demonstrated toward Jesus and His popularity with the people through the display of His power and meeting the people's needs.

"Then the chief priests and the Pharisees gathered a council and said, "What shall we do? For this Man works many signs. If we let Him alone like this, everyone will believe in Him, and the Romans will come and take away both our place and nation" (Jn. 11:47-48).

When these pastors saw that they were losing their influence over some of their members, they used the power of money and position to sway them back into their denominational and traditional churches. That's a wrong spirit. It's control. True leaders want God's will for their people, not their *own* will for them.

PERSONAL EXAMPLE

Some years ago, this happened to me on a personal level, when a senior pastor asked me to dissolve our own ministry in order to work under another ministry for which he was an influential advisor. We were struggling financially and ministerially at this time, and it could've been a real temptation for me because it offered me a position and some financial security, but I knew it wasn't God's will for us. This senior pastor probably meant no harm and was perhaps only trying to help us, but even good people with good intentions can get you off track from the perfect will of God. When someone offers you a good position with money and some sense of security attached to it, it can be a real temptation to take it against what your heart may be telling you, especially if you've been struggling financially. But I can tell you now in hindsight, if I had accepted this offer, my wife and I would've been miserable today — confined and spiritually shackled from fulfilling God's true calling and vision for our lives and ministry, for we would've been placed under the ministry of another.

There is a time and season to work under the authority and ministry of another, for it is good for a young man to be under discipline so that he can be proven, learn, and mature. But when the Lord separates someone to his own ministry, it is vital that our freedom to operate according to the will of God be unhindered by the policies, procedures, and traditions of men, and trying to fit in under the vision of another when God is separating you to your own. Here is the word of wisdom God spoke to us during this season of our lives:

"You have not been equally yoked with leadership for many years now. You can no longer be yoked with men who do not think or walk according to My higher kingdom ways. You can no longer be unequally yoked, for it will slow you down and abort your calling. But now you must no longer look back, but I will place you on fast forward as you walk in agreement with those of like-precious faith. When you're equally yoked, it's easy to move with no confinement. It is time for equal yokes."

This word produced freedom in us to move with God. We went from treading water to swimming in a free-flowing river. There is power in being like-minded. There is power in being equally yoked with others. Agreement in the Spirit with those of like-precious faith is vital to our success in advancing the kingdom of God.

How many young ministry gifts are under the spirit of control of another? What would've happened to John the Baptist and his calling as a forerunner to Christ had he submitted himself to the religious traditional system that his father and lineage came up in? He wouldn't even have been called John (Lk. 1:59-63). It was a tradition for him to be named after his father, Zacharias, but God broke this tradition, as He often does to birth a new movement. And yet it was Jesus Himself who affirmed John and encouraged him in his calling and ministry (Matt. 3:13-15).

CONTROL CAN HURT AND SLOW DOWN MINISTERS

Recently we met an evangelist who was having great success in getting many people saved and healed, but his senior pastor asked him and his wife to stop conducting evangelistic crusades and sit down in their local church services to learn. In his pastor's own estimation, this evangelist's character did not match his calling, so he needed to lay his ministry down and grow and mature. This, however, was not the witness of other ministers who knew him. This young evangelist was not rebellious or un-submissive in any way and was actually a very kind and loving man who wanted to stay at his church and work things out. But the fact was, there were jealousies and envies that were working in this pastor and the church, so after much consternation, prayer, and counsel from others, this evangelist and his family chose to leave the church. I applaud him.

The Lord spoke to us concerning this situation and told us that, in our own ministry, we had walked on a similar tightrope for many years and learned not to compromise, while still walking in our authority as ministers and maintaining a love for those who did not see what the Lord had put in us or called us to. Because of our experience in this type of situation, the Lord asked us to help others who are struggling with the same. Here's what the Lord said:

"So now this wisdom will come forth and be seen and help those who are stuck in ruts, but are called, for there will be pastors — yes, I have pastors who understand kingdom business, and you must reiter-

ate *to them the need for them to understand how to work with the other gifts in a local body and not to be jealous or envious (or overly protective or controlling), but to help build their ministries, for it will only help them and their local churches.*

"For in every place I have set gifts and callings of those who can witness to the lost, who carry a fire for the lost, and those who pray and carry the spirit of prayer, and I've even called some to go forth like apostles and prophets and teachers.

"I bring these things to your remembrance now of how you walked this out in your own lives, how hard it was, and the struggles you went through, and the understanding you gained of the importance of keeping your heart right. But look now and see how you walked that tightrope with Me and how I never let you fall, and how I spoke to you and prayed through you, and how I opened doors and made relationships available to you. These things will now help you in helping My body.

"And even that evangelist must be encouraged, and prophecies will be released to help him, for he has to come out of that rejection now, as he is seeing the other side of jealousy and envy, and it's hurting him. He's also feeling bad and doubting himself — pondering whether he missed it and went wrong somewhere. So, know that his gift must be solidified and protected, and he must walk in love for him to succeed in the next place."

Can you see how the spirit of control can hurt, divert, and oppress ministers? I don't know to what extent money played a role in this evangelist's challenges with his home church, but it may have been a factor, as it is often the tool used to manipulate and control people. This happens on a large scale in churches and ministries. This is the reason oppressive leadership have a constant turnover in staff and employees. There's no joy or liberty working under someone who is heavy-handed or confining in their leadership style. Thus, it is often difficult for maturing believers who have functioning ministries to fit themselves into an existing church organization. Often, doctrinal differences and suspicions of "sheep-stealing" can emerge for an already-fruitful ministry. This is a common problem with displaced itinerate ministry gifts.

Our topic in this chapter is still money, but can you see how it also relates to the move of God? This young evangelist could've continued to be such a blessing to his local church and helped them grow spiritually and numerically, but because of a jealous and heavy-handed pastor, he was forced to leave. This book is about restoring the glory and power of God to the Church, and properly utilizing, mobilizing, and working alongside other ministry gifts is a big part of that.

This young evangelist had about 20 people from this church who helped him with his ministry and crusades in such areas as prayer and administration. These people were told that the evangelist was in error and rebellion, and thus he lost much of that volunteer help. And often with such discarded and falsely accused ministries, it becomes difficult to find another church with values similar to his own to fellowship with.

But there is also another side to releasing younger ministers in their gifts and callings. Many need to be proven faithful. What many label as "control" is often protection. Older, more-seasoned ministers and fathers in the faith will wisely place restrictions on younger ministers in order to protect them from their own immaturities and also to test their hearts, for many are driven by selfish ambition and their own agendas. God Himself uses these things to test us. Study the life of Joshua, David, and Elisha in the Old Testament and those like Timothy, whom Paul mentored, in the New Testament, and you'll clearly see this principle at work.

In this chapter, I've done my best to try to outline the many impurities and forms of control that are rooted in money. Careful study and review of these should help us in staying free from these impurities and abuses. As we do, the power and glory of God will increase in our personal lives, ministries, and churches through the humility, love, and honor found in the body.

CHAPTER SEVEN

THE GREAT GODDESSES OF MONEY AND NUMBERS

"You cannot serve God and money" (Matt. 6:24).

This chapter serves to warn us of ministers with excessive financial prosperity teachings and lifestyles of extreme luxury and extravagance. I've thought long and hard about these things for many years and have received some light from the Scriptures on the perilous fate of some of these ministers.

This is a solemn warning against those who are walking in the error of Balaam.

"Woe to them! For they have gone in the way of Cain, **have run greedily in the error of Balaam for profit***, and perished in the rebellion of Korah"* (Jude 11).

Jude uses strong terms when he compares false teachers to *"spots in your love feasts,"* *"clouds without water,"* *"autumn trees without fruit, twice dead,"* *"raging waves of the sea,"* and *"wandering stars for whom is reserved the blackness of darkness forever."*

These were men who *"crept in among them"* and even ate at their love feasts, which were fellowship meals. In other words, they were part of the church.

Peter also writes in eerily similar language warning of false teachers given to covetousness.

*"***And in their greed they will exploit you with deceptive words***. Their judgment, made long ago, does not linger, and their destruction does not slumber"* (2 Pet. 2:3).

He speaks of the doom and depravity of these false teachers, using terms such as, *"spots and blemishes," "carousing in their own deceptions," "having eyes full of adultery," "enticing unstable souls," "a heart trained in covetous practices,"* and *"accursed children"* (2 Pet. 2). And notice the comparison to Balaam again:

"They have forsaken the right way and have gone astray. They follow the way of Balaam the son of Beor, **who loved the wages of wickedness, but who was rebuked for his iniquity**. *The mute donkey speaking with a man's voice constrained the madness of the prophet"* (2 Pet. 2:15-16).

A dumb donkey had to speak what the Lord was really saying because Balaam had gone astray after the wages of unrighteousness. Too many today are speaking what the Lord is *not* saying, and *not* speaking what He *is* saying. They, too, may need dumb donkeys to speak on their behalf and constrain them. Some have given over to familiar spirits and other voices, and still believe God is speaking to them — but He's not. They are deceived.

Please understand that Balaam was a genuine prophet. The Spirit of God would come upon him, and he would hear from the Lord (Num. 22:8-9, 24:2), but money ruined him. Covetousness led to his downfall. God warned him, but he didn't listen (Num. 22:12-13). The Scriptures list him as an example of one whose heart was not right toward money. How many false prophets, slick televangelists, and carnal-prosperity preachers does this apply to today? Some have received genuine callings and anointings from the Lord, but they have been caught in the error of Balaam.

Perhaps the greatest error of these carnal-prosperity preachers is that they *"suppose that godliness is a means of gain"* (1 Tim. 6:5, NKJV), as already mentioned. They equate their millions and their excessive materialistic lifestyles with spirituality — even telling the public that they are rewards for preaching the gospel. The apostle Paul uses the strongest of terms as to how we should respond to them:

"From such withdraw yourself" (1 Tim. 6:5).

Without discernment, you can be in the presence of a minister of God but not realize they have corrupted themselves. Once spiritual things have a "For Sale" sign on them, you just might find yourself in the presence of a modern-day Balaam.

How many wrong things must a minister do before you stop being mesmerized by his gifts? These things are all written for our benefit. You can avoid the error of Balaam as well as the error of deceit in any minister. God gave us the Word so we don't have to be ignorant of spiritual matters. He gave us his Spirit so we may discern truth from error.

"Beloved, do not believe every spirit, but test the spirits, whether they are of God; because many false prophets have gone out into the world. We are of God. He who knows God hears us; he who is not of God does not hear us. By this we know the spirit of truth and the spirit of error" (1 Jn. 4:1, 6).

In defense of many of these carnal-prosperity preachers, people will be quick to say that they also give away far more than most people ever will in a lifetime. So does George Soros. So does Bill Gates. So does Warren Buffet, and many others of the world's wealthy. That is not proof of their spirituality or godliness. The fact that a prosperity preacher is generous does not justify his message. It simply indicates that he practices what he preaches. Some of the rich in the world do that. All it does is testify to the fact that some of these carnal-prosperity preachers are rich and generous.

"But they give to the gospel," some might argue, whereas the rich in the world usually don't. The issue is: Are they serving God or mammon?

I realize the poor can be covetous, too, but in my humble opinion, this sin is far more often associated with the rich. The scriptures mainly use the rich as examples of covetousness, not the poor.

This is a warning against carnal-prosperity preachers who lead unstable and gullible souls into covetousness by preaching a message that gain is godliness, that financial prosperity equates to spirituality, and who encourage everyone to receive the material prosperity and riches Jesus supposedly purchased for them at the cross. It is also a warning to those who follow such preachers and make much of this materialistic message. That is not the gospel, my friends.

UNDERSTANDING THE SEVERITY OF COVETOUSNESS

The word "covetousness" in the Greek is *pleonektes*, and it regresses from good to bad. It's a greed so strong that it will even defraud and manipulate others and forge ahead at their expense. The root word, *pleon*, is the basic word for "more" — more in quantity, in quality, and numerically. Here are other offshoots of this word:

Pleonekteo: to overreach

Pleonexia: avarice; extreme greed for wealth or material gain; excessive or inordinate desire for gain.

This word is grouped in the same category as fornication, lascivious living, and immorality (Eph. 5:3, Col. 3:5-6). Those who desire to increase in material wealth, worth, and the things of this world are classified as idolaters at heart in God's sight. The Word tells us to be free of covetous conduct and from desiring the things of this world (1 John 2:15-17) and to be content with such things as we have (1 Tim.

6:8, Heb. 13:5). Come on, now! How many believers, especially in Charismatic circles, do you really know who are content with food and clothing and such things as they have?

Have we forgotten that an idolater has no inheritance in the kingdom of God? (Eph. 5:5, 1 Cor. 6:10)

TO JUDGE OR NOT TO JUDGE

And for those who are already holding up their God-card of "Thou shalt not judge," I'll offer the contrary and what Paul said about judgment.

"Do you not know that the saints will judge the world? If the world will be judged by you, are you unworthy to judge the smallest matters? Do you not know that we shall judge angels? How much more the things that pertain to this life?" (1 Cor. 6:2-3, MEV).

We are not only to judge matters that pertain to this life and the church, but we are to dis-fellowship and even expose all unfruitful works of darkness. Covetousness and idolatry are among these unfruitful works (Eph. 5:5). We must expose them. That's part of righteous judgment.

"Let no one deceive you with empty words, for because of these things the wrath of God is coming upon the sons of disobedience. ... And do not have fellowship with the unfruitful works of darkness; instead, expose them. For it is shameful even to speak of those things which are done by them in secret. But all things are exposed when they are revealed by the light, for everything that becomes visible is light" (Eph. 5:6, 11-13).

This carnal-prosperity gospel bred in the West is a false gospel with a false Jesus, which can result only in a false salvation (refer to author's books *The Real Gospel, The Real Jesus,* and *The Real Salvation*).

There are even those who will argue that Jesus was rich from His carpentry business, lived in a luxurious home, and wore the designer clothes of that day, and, of course, died so we could have all this and more. Oh, beloved — run from those who teach such things!

Think of the examples in Scripture, some of which I've already listed, concerning the deceitfulness of riches and the covetousness attached to it, and how many have fallen into temptation and the snare of these things. This is my solemn warning, and as the Lord witnessed to me — that some of these carnal-prosperity preachers have not only fallen into a snare but are in danger of drowning in destruction and perdition.

In recent years there has been much controversy in the body of Christ concerning ministers purchasing multi-million dollar jets and living in very large multi-million dollar mansions, with some even owning several mansions in different locations. With all the contention and the wrangling over this issue, I believe we've missed the central point. What is this really about? What is the main issue here?

I see the general public falling into three main categories. There are those who will criticize these rich ministers and cast them off as complete reprobates — even referring to them as "agents of Satan." Honestly, that is simply a knee-jerk reaction. Then on the other extreme end, there are those who idolize these ministers and their jets and will even defend their luxurious and extravagant lifestyles, calling them a "blessing from God." The majority, however, are probably somewhere in the middle of these two extremes, with most just remaining silent about it lest they appear judgmental.

Certainly, we can't judge their hearts, but we are to judge all things in the light of God's Word. We can judge their doctrine, and we can judge their character and their fruit. The Word is clear on that.

"Beware of false prophets who come to you in sheep's clothing, but inwardly they are ravenous wolves. You will know them by their fruits" (Matt. 7:15-16a).

Twice Jesus said that we'd know false prophets by their fruit (v. 20). Here's the mistake we often make. We judge them by the fruit of their ministry (their platform and popularity or supposed number of people they are reaching, which actually is a suspect and superficial way of judging) instead of the fruit of their personal lives (Matt. 7:21-23).

RULES CHANGE FOR MINISTERS

We need to understand that the rules change for ministers. We've been entrusted with the lives of people. We're under a stricter judgment (James 3:1). To whom much is given, much is required (Luke 12:48). We live in a glass house. Because of our position, our example impacts more people than the average believer. It's true that only God knows the heart and only God sees men's true motives. But again, the Word is clear. Even the appearance of evil must be avoided (1 Thess. 5:22). Ministers can't give people any grounds for accusation.

"Now a bishop (superintendent, overseer) must give no grounds for accusation but must be above reproach" (1 Tim. 3:2a, AMPC).

"For a pastor must be a good man whose life cannot be spoken against" (1 Tim. 3:2a, TLB).

Peter says it this way when it comes to a minster's relationship to money:

"Tend (nurture, guard, guide, and fold) the flock of God that is [your responsibility], not by coercion or constraint, but willingly; **not dishonorably motivated by the advantages and profits [belonging to the office]** *..."* (1 Pet. 5:2, AMPC).

There are many advantages and profits that are obtainable from ministry today. It is much easier in this day of poor accountability to get rich through the gospel and to be motivated by that advantage. Getting rich off the ministry is the bigger issue here. And a minister has no grounds to justify it and say that it's nobody's business. Ministry is a public trust.

The example ministers set speaks the loudest. This is the reason there are qualifications for ministers to function as a leader or in an office in the church. We must be able to say "No" to many things that would be permitted in the lives of others. We must resolve not to be a stumbling block to the weak, thus sinning against Christ (1 Cor. 8:9, 12).

GOD IS NOT OPPOSED TO HIS PEOPLE BEING RICH

Yet, in all this, I'm not saying that it is wrong to be rich and have this world's goods — as long as *they* don't have *you*. However, I believe the more balanced view of financial prosperity is to have a full supply where there is no lack, and you have more than enough to be a channel of blessing to others. Part of a minister's testimony is to avoid excessive and extreme doctrines or a lifestyle that could potentially bring reproach to the gospel.

It's not that the Lord doesn't want us to enjoy His financial and material blessings. He is not opposed to His children being rich and owning a nice home or driving a nice vehicle. God Himself has no problem with money. For heaven's sake, He walks on streets of gold! God is not short of money. It's just that He doesn't want those things to *own us* to the point that we display an inordinate desire for them, which is often manifested through a luxurious lifestyle and poor stewardship.

Again, please hear me clearly: God is not opposed to His people having riches and being blessed, for the Word tells us that God *"richly gives us all things to enjoy"* (1 Tim. 6:17, MEV). There are also financial blessings that come from our obedience, and we are to enjoy them without guilt and condemnation. Many have prospered abundantly through successful businesses and financial investments, but the rules are different for ministers, and caution and discretion must be exercised. Did you notice the separate instructions Paul gave to Timothy concerning riches?

First, to ministers, he told Timothy in no uncertain terms to flee the desire and love of money:

"For the love of money is a root of all kinds of evil, for which some have strayed from the faith in their greediness, and pierced themselves through with many sorrows. But you, O man of God, flee these things..." (1 Tim. 6:10-11).

If this instruction applies to Timothy, then it's also applicable to all ministers. "Flee" is a strong word. "Run from it!" Paul is telling Timothy to flee the love of money and its destructive results.

Secondly, he told Timothy to warn the rich (non-ministers who do not stand in an office or a position of church leadership/oversight):

"Command those who are rich in this world that they not be conceited, nor trust in uncertain riches, but in the living God, who richly gives us all things to enjoy. Command that they do good, that they be rich in good works, generous, willing to share, and laying up in store for themselves a good foundation for the coming age, so that they may take hold of eternal life" (1 Tim. 6:17-19).

Notice that ministers are to command the rich in this world — especially those who are part of their congregations — not to be conceited or high-minded or trust in uncertain riches ("uncertain riches" means that they will soon be gone) but to be generous and rich in good works, knowing their eternal return on their investments is great (and will never be gone or fade away). Question: How can any minister stand in the Lord's authority and command the rich in this world not to be conceited or trust in uncertain riches if he is rich and living in extravagance and luxury himself? How can he even preach the real gospel with any authority? Answer: They usually don't. Instead, because of their own lifestyle, they compromise and resort to preaching the "gain is godliness" message. That's the "American Gospel." That's the way a large segment of the American Church has wandered in the last few decades.

I believe the Lord's true ministers should be well taken care of. I guard my heart diligently against begrudging anyone whom God has blessed in any way. I know of one very godly minister who was given seven different homes throughout his lifetime of ministry. I rejoice in that. And if men want to use their personal money to build a million-dollar home and drive a luxury car, God is their judge, not me. But this creates room to be scrutinized by the public and can hurt the cause of Christ. That's my point. Some may call it a form of persecution for having been blessed by God, but be careful you don't find your identity in these material and monetary blessings.

My warning here is solely against the covetousness and the poor stewardship that is so glaring in many circles of the body of Christ today, which derives mainly from the teaching that "gain is godliness." Paul denounced this perverted teaching in the strongest of terms (1 Tim. 6). On the other hand, being rich doesn't mean you're sinful and carnal, just as being poor doesn't mean you're holy and spiritual.

The bigger questions we should be asking are these: Do preachers who live in extravagance and luxury bring reproach to the gospel?

Does it play into the image of the self-serving, manipulative televangelist? Does it make it more difficult for other Christian leaders to raise funds for their work? Does it feed their own desire and that of others to be rich, thus endangering their spiritual lives and even leading to destruction and perdition? I would answer a definitive and resounding "Yes" to each of those questions.

IS IT RIGHT FOR A MINISTER TO LIVE IN A MANSION?

It is rather prevalent, especially in America, for mega-church pastors and mega-ministers to live in luxury. I could name a few names, but that is not the purpose of this book, nor is it my business. God is the judge of every man and every minister. However, it is common knowledge that there are ministers today who own multi-million-dollar homes, with some having multiple homes in different places, while living a life fit for kings. Is this right? Is it godly? What does Scripture say about it?

The apostle Paul may be our best example. In 1 Corinthians 9, he writes that his apostolic office entitled him to certain privileges but that he renounced them for the sake of reaching the Corinthians and the lost world with the gospel. Nonetheless, the rights he renounced were not to live in a mansion or to lounge in luxury, but simply to be compensated for preaching the gospel. Think about that in contrast to some of today's ministers, who will actually defend their right to be rich, to indulge in extravagance, and own a multi-million-dollar mansion.

We should understand that Paul had a right to financial support, and it was perfectly reasonable for him to be compensated for his labor in ministry. In fact, he lists three reasons that justify receiving such support. First, he wrote that society dictates that those who render a service, such as soldiers, farmers, and shepherds, ought to receive compensation for their work (1 Cor. 9:7). Second, he writes that the Mosaic Law prescribed a just recompense for those rendering a service — a principle which is applied to even working animals like an ox that treads out the corn (1 Cor. 9:8-13). And third, Paul states that the Lord Himself commands the principle of financial support for those who preach the gospel (1 Cor. 9:14). Yet in spite of all these scriptural reasons to receive financial compensation, Paul still did not insist on these rights.

Remember, this was not a sin issue. He would not have been out of favor with God if he decided differently. He simply renounced this right for the sake of the people. If he had insisted on the right to compensation, his motives could have been questioned, and the work of the gospel might have been hindered (For more on dealing with the motives of the heart, refer again to *Purity of Heart*).

After Paul makes his case for receiving financial support, ironically, he lists three other reasons for giving up his rights. First, his unique calling as an apostle and the necessity and stewardship of that office caused him to surrender that right (1 Cor. 9:15-18). Second, his evangelistic motivations to reach Jew and Gentile alike caused him to be a servant to all (1 Cor. 9:19-23). He was constrained by the weaknesses of others that he might win them to Christ. And third, Paul lays out a case for self-discipline, so that after he'd preached to others, he would not be disqualified (1 Cor. 9:24-27). It was vitally important to him not to lose his place with God and his crown and reward. Where is this mindset among ministers today?

The apostle Paul went to great lengths to enter the world of others and lead them to salvation. I believe one of the reasons for the American Church's ineffectiveness today in reaching our own nation with the gospel is that there is a great mistrust of ministers among the general public. The world is not stupid. They see the wealth of many of these big ministers and the luxury they live in. They are also aware of the many scandals that have come to light in recent years concerning some of these ministers. They see the glaring hypocrisy. They see the superficiality. This lack of holiness and true character has eroded the honor and respect that the world might otherwise have for ministers.

I believe one of the greatest needs in the church today is for ministers to regain the trust of the world. The world needs to see integrity, humility, servanthood, sacrifice, and suffering. They need to see authenticity and the highest form of love. To be candid, the ministry in the West has been contaminated. The church world is defiled. It is a travesty — and much worse than many within the Church have even thought.

Although the apostle Paul justified his apostleship and his right to be compensated for his ministry, he takes the higher road of humility, servanthood, and sacrifice and illustrates the way of love. Love will go to extremes to reach others with the gospel without charge and to make sure the Word of God is not made void in people's lives.

In essence, Paul made a vow of poverty in order to reach the world with the gospel. "A vow of poverty?" you say. "Poverty is a curse! We've been redeemed from the curse (Gal. 3:13)! You are preaching heresy!" I can hear the screams already — proof, perhaps, that this topic is a giant sacred cow that many will defend to the death. Please hear me out, and learn one of the great secrets of the effectiveness of Paul's ministry.

THE BIGGEST LESSON A TRUE MODERN APOSTLE TAUGHT ME ABOUT MONEY

When the elder board of the late Lester Sumrall made several attempts to persuade him to upgrade his ministry image by purchasing a luxury car, he gruffly responded by saying: *"I like my Chevrolet, and I'll keep my Chevrolet!"*

When I was a Bible-school student, one of the first guest speakers we had was Brother Sumrall. In his introduction to a week-long seminar, he said that when he and his wife got married, they made a vow of poverty. As soon as he said that, the students gasped because we were taught that poverty was a curse. Recognizing that the air had gone out of the room and that he now had every student's attention, Sumrall explained himself. *"I believe in prosperity, but not for my back pocket!"* Boom! A big mental stronghold was knocked out of our minds, and balance was restored.

To me, this is the godliest and most admirable position on financial prosperity. I'm glad I learned it early. We are blessed to be a blessing.

Sumrall saw millions of dollars flow through his hands, and, as far as I know, all without altering his own lifestyle. He built churches and schools, purchased radio and television stations, and even had his own ship and airplane that he used for transporting food, goods, and supplies to help the poor and needy around the world. I believe he also had his own ministry airplane, but when he came to the nation of Liberia to minister in our annual convention at 76 years of age, he and his wife traveled coach on a commercial airline.

I'm not saying it is sinful, carnal, or in any way wrong to travel First Class or Business. Actually, it can be a blessing and keep you refreshed on long trips so you can minister more effectively. I'm just saying that Sumrall stuck to the vow of poverty he made in his younger days all for the sake of the gospel. He was being a good steward, and he walked in a measure of spiritual authority that is rare today. That is the greatest example for anyone to follow. I'm sure his reward is great.

Although I most assuredly believe that God prospers and blesses His people, and there are plenty of Scriptures to make a case for that end of things, we as ministers and people of God, for the sake of others who are weak and do not possess this knowledge, must surrender that right. That's the whole point.

Let me explain further. I used the word "poverty" to get your attention. I do believe poverty is a curse and not a blessing, but the poverty I am speaking of is where you will not abuse the rights of being compensated for the gospel and use it for personal luxury. You will not abuse the public trust and financial support you receive from your donors for your own extravagance.

It is not my purpose here to delve into the theology of money but into the heart of it. After all, money is not evil, but the love of it is the root of all evil (see 1 Tim. 6:10). There are many facets of truths and schools of thought concerning money, and there is plenty of content given to it in Jesus' ministry.

Much of what I hear taught today, however, is on God's will to prosper us and how financial prosperity is a part of the gospel. Undoubtedly, some of the more extreme and excessive teachings have done more harm than good to the cause of Christ.

What I'm not hearing much of today is this: What about stewardship and sacrifice? What about doing without a certain desire or pleasure, so others can be blessed? What about living to give?

Jesus chose not to call on the Father for twelve legions of angels to deliver Him from a sure death (Matt. 26:53) and our redemption. He chose not to heap up riches for Himself. He chose not to accumulate this world's wealth. But He emptied Himself of everything for us. This is the lifestyle Jesus exemplified before His disciples. This is also the example Paul set for the church and its ministers.

It's time for ministers to do the same and to regain the trust we've lost.

COMPARING ATTITUDES TOWARD MONEY NOW TO THEN

Compare these extreme quotes on money from our day's most popular preachers to those of centuries past.

"The Bible says that He has left us an example that we should follow His steps. That's the reason I drive a Rolls Royce. I'm following in Jesus' steps." Anonymous

I've chosen to refrain from naming the said preacher. I don't want to discredit all the good he may have done. As I've stated, blowing out someone else's candle does not make mine shine any brighter. Besides, the point here is to keep the main point the main point, and not go off on a tangent on how some preachers are just after your money. Not all preachers are that way. Two wrongs don't make a right. Thank God for the many pure-hearted preachers in the land today who've not been tainted by greed and the love of money. Thank God for the extreme generosity of so many who support the gospel and the work of the local church, and who contribute great financial support to projects that help the poor and needy.

Nevertheless, how can such a careless and erroneous statement come out of this popular preacher's mouth? So, following Jesus has been reduced to driving a Rolls Royce? But what does the Bible say?

"For to this you were called, because Christ also suffered for us, leaving us an example, that you should follow His steps: 'Who committed no sin, nor was deceit found in His mouth'?" (1 Pt. 2:21-22).

One of the greatest examples given in Scripture for following in Jesus' steps has to do with suffering wrongfully. That is the example we are to follow. (See also Matt. 10:25 and Jn. 15:20, among many others, that teach us how we are to follow our Master.)

Here's another quote from a popular preacher:

"Give $10 and receive $1000. Give $1000 and receive $100,000. Give one house and receive one hundred houses or a house worth one hundred times as much. Give one airplane and receive one hundred times the value of the airplane . . . in short, Mark 10:30 is a very good deal."

So Mark 10:30 has been reduced to "...a very good deal"? How pathetic! What was meant to be a Scripture to forsake all for the gospel and suffer persecution for that kind of godly, consecrated lifestyle has been reduced to a money-and-materialism Scripture. What an example of corrupted motives! Once again, I refrain from naming the source of this erroneous quote; suffice it to say that this ministry is one of the most popular ministries in America today, with a very large following.

Does Mark 10:30 really mean that kind of hundredfold return on all your giving? Let's read that verse in context. First of all, this entire statement spoken by Jesus starts with verse 29.

So Jesus answered and said, "Assuredly, I say to you, there is no one who has left house or brothers or sisters or father or mother or wife or children or lands, for My sake and the gospel's, who shall not receive a hundredfold now in this time — houses and brothers and sisters and mothers and children and lands, with persecutions — and in the age to come, eternal life" (Mk. 10:29-30).

There is nothing in this verse that is in context with this popular preacher's quote. This has nothing to do with sowing money, houses, and airplanes in order to reap one hundred times more. These verses have nothing to do with money. Period. This preacher's interpretation is the product of the Western gospel of riches and materialism. The real meaning of these verses is in the context of leaving all to follow Jesus.

I was a missionary for many years and left houses, family, and lands to follow Jesus and serve overseas. I'm not 100 times richer now than I was then. What I have received is that I've gained at least 100 more brothers, sisters, mothers, and children. Due to my travels to preach the gospel, I've lived and slept in 100 more houses than the one I left to follow Jesus, and never paid for most of them. I've been to and visited many more lands than I left. And I've received a little persecution with it all. Notice in the preacher's careless interpretation of this text that nothing is mentioned about receiving persecutions. They don't want to claim that part.

Once again, the Bible teaches us that a desire to be rich is dangerous.

"But those who desire to be rich fall into temptation and a snare and into many foolish and harmful lusts, which drown men in ruin and destruction" (1 Tim. 6:9—MEV).

Unless money is indeed your servant, and you are a non-profit bond-slave of Jesus Christ, money could eventually ruin you.

VERY BAD TEACHING ON MONEY

Here are a couple of more modern-day quotes on money taken from this much-maligned verse of Scripture:

"For you know the grace of our Lord Jesus Christ, that though He was rich, yet for your sakes He became poor, that you through His poverty might become rich" (2 Cor. 8:9).

"It is just as much God's will for us to be rich (financially and ma-terially) as it is for us to saved." — Anonymous

"It is disrespectful to the work of redemption not to receive the fi-nancial wealth Jesus provided for us at the cross." — Anonymous

Many preachers today have so misinterpreted the aforementioned verse and have turned it into economics — saying that Jesus was made economically poor so that we might be economically rich. How ab-surd! I used to believe this myself until I studied the message God gave me for this book, and I allowed Him to deal with my own heart. The gospel of salvation cannot be equated with the financial situation of Je-sus on the Earth. That is not the issue. It isn't about Jesus becoming poor materially that we might be rich materially. It is that God became a man in the incarnation — that's the impoverishing. That's how He, being rich, became poor.

He was born of a woman (Gal. 4:4), was made in the likeness of sinful flesh (Rom. 8:3), and went to the cross (Col. 1:20). He laid aside the free exercise of all of His divine attributes. He left being face to face with the Father and took on human form (Phil 2:5-8).

He emptied Himself, *"taking on the form of a servant and being made in the likeness of men."* That's the poverty of Jesus.

There's no salvation through the economic sacrifices of Jesus. In fact, if that were the case, we would've expected Him to be a lot poorer than He was. I cannot find any evidence He was even classified in any sense among those in His society as "poor." There's nothing to indicate in the life of Jesus that He was poor. He lived a common, ordinary life, like many other people did in His day.

Notice the expression *"for your sakes He became poor... that you might be rich."* Is this talking about being materially and economically rich? No, but to make poor sinners rich. Spiritually and eternally rich? Yes. Rich with the same riches that He possessed and still possesses. Rich in salvation, forgiveness, joy, peace, life, light, glory; rich in honor and rich in majesty. We are so rich that we are called joint heirs with Christ and kings and priests. We are promised an inheritance incorruptible and undefiled that fades not away, laid up for us in heaven (1 Pt. 1:4). We were really poor, but now we are rich as He is rich.

"For all things are yours" (1 Cor. 3:21). All things are yours in the world or life or death or the present or the future — all are yours, and you are Christ's and Christ is God's (v. 22-23). Everything is ours. We are the rich. We are rich in position, and, as joint heirs seated in heavenly places, we reign with Him. We are rich in privilege. We are rich in relationship. We are blessed with all spiritual blessings in the heavenly places in Christ Jesus. Everything there is that could bless us, we were given.

When you're talking about Jesus becoming "poor," you don't want to get off into this material realm. It's not talking about Him giving up material things but giving up immaterial things. He's referring to rich and poor in the spiritual sense, as Paul did in 2 Cor. 6:10, where he says this of himself: *"As poor yet making many rich."*

He's not talking economically or materially but spiritually. Paul is speaking about the terrible deprivations that he had to suffer and endure to get the gospel to people, which made them spiritually rich. Paul had to also descend from the status of his high education and his great leadership ability, that he became a scourge and an offscouring of the earth to get the riches of the gospel to other people. And that was the "poverty" he speaks of regarding Jesus.

In verse 9 he begins by saying, *"For you know."* The word *"for"* links us up with the prior verse. In verse 8, he says, *"I speak not by commandment, but I am testing the sincerity of your love by the diligence of others."* In other words, Paul is saying, "I don't need to command you to do this, because you know how Christ gave. I don't need to command you to give graciously, because you have an example that supersedes any command I could give. Rather than doing it because I command you, do it because you see Christ exemplified in it. In other words, the giving of Jesus Christ provides a greater incentive and motivation than the command of the apostle Paul. Every Christian knows Christ came down and gave His life, and that should be the single greatest motivation, even more motivating than the model Paul gave of the Macedonians.

How shameful that some have made 2 Cor. 8:9 all about financial and material riches.

A DIFFERENT ATTITUDE ON MONEY FROM ANOTHER ERA

Now let's look at how diametrically different preachers from another era thought about money.

In 1744 John Wesley had written: *"When people spend money on things they do not need, they begin to want more of what they do not need. Instead of satisfying their desires, they only increase them."* Daily experience with his parishioners showed him that, the more they indulged their flesh, the more they wanted. Oh, how we need to understand this uncommon wisdom and exercise solemn vigilance today concerning the covetous nature of riches.

Wesley especially warned against buying too much for children. People who would never waste money on themselves might be more indulgent with their children. On the principle that gratifying a desire needlessly only tends to increase it, he asked these well-intentioned parents: *"Why should you purchase for them more pride or lust, more vanity or foolish and hurtful desires? Why should you be at further expense to increase their temptations and snares and to pierce them through with more sorrows? Would you send your spoiled children to hell?"*

John Wesley taught to give all you can and not to set your heart upon uncertain riches. He gave this warning: *"You have undoubtedly set your heart upon gold, and it will eat your flesh as fire."*

And then he added this: *"When I have money, I get rid of it quickly, lest it find a way into my heart."*

What a radical contrast from what carnal-prosperity preachers teach today!

Now here are some other quotes from men of old who have also gone on to their reward. Notice how careful they were about their attitude toward money.

"I continually find it necessary to guard against the natural love of wealth and grandeur which prompts us always, when we come to apply our general doctrine to our own case, to claim an exception." — William Wilberforce

"Shun as you would the plague a cleric who from being poor has become wealthy, or who, from being nobody has become a celebrity." — St. Jerome

"You have reached the pinnacle of success as soon as you become uninterested in money, compliments, or publicity." — Thomas Wolfe

"Nothing that is God's is obtainable by money." — Tertullian

Quite a contrast between the "now" and "then" schools of thought on money. Men and ministers of old were much more careful when it came to money. They understood the inherent danger of it leading to temptation and being a snare, as the apostle Paul warned. They saw money almost as a god or goddess, which is one of the identities of mammon — being a deity.

The Lord highlighted the worship of mammon because it is a major stumbling block and sin in the Church today, and one of the main reasons for the Church's lack of power. He also used it to warn us personally as we come into more favor and increase in our own lives and ministry, for as I've stated, many of the Lord's ministers have become money-minded and lost the anointing.

Let us repent from serving the goddess of money (mammon).

THE GODDESS OF NUMBERS

"Yes, I know the feeling...it took us about a year to find a church that truly loved people, not just numbers." — A common churchgoer

"...it may be that the Lord will work for us. For nothing restrains the Lord from saving by many or by few" (1 Sam. 14:6).

In the first portion of this chapter, we wrote about the dangers and deceitfulness of riches (money). Now we will discuss the dangers and deceitfulness of measuring our success by numbers. Money and numbers are somehow tied together and represent the pinnacle of success for many people, especially in ministry today. People know that money and numbers mean power, significance, and influence. But the question we must ask is this: What kind of power, significance, and influence is it breeding? Here's a truth that will minister peace to many:

Effective leadership does not mean numbers. You can be a great leader and not have a numerically large church, ministry, or following.

Although numbers represent people, and it is worthy to reach as many as we can, we can no longer be impressed and driven by mere numbers. Numbers represent success only if a person is obeying God.

Otherwise, they can actually be a cover-up and a façade for failure in real fruit, character, and ethics. Numbers of people can represent resources and funds, and the logical reasoning of many church leaders and ministers is that, with more resources and funds, we can do so much more for the kingdom. That can be true, but it can also be false, as you will soon see.

The question that is often asked at many ministers' conferences when interfacing with other pastors is, "How big is your church?" or "How many are you running?" as if the numbers determine how successful the pastor or the church is. Both the question and response are extremely shallow and are a superficial measuring gauge of the spiritual health of a church. It's like asking me, "How many children do you have?" to determine how successful a father I am. I have only one son, so I guess I'm not very successful, while other men who have more children are considered successful. Strange way of measuring success, isn't it?

A church high in numbers and attendance is not necessarily a healthy church any more than a big family is a sign of a healthy family, and it may not be a sign of effective leadership any more than a big family is a sign of effective parenting.

Our personal and ministerial leadership is determined by disciples we are making — mature and responsible people who adhere to the commands of Jesus and are being conformed into His image, and who themselves are reproducing other disciples in the community. Whether or not our leadership is effective is determined more by what happens in our daily lives outside the church assembly than by what happens inside the assembly place one or two or even three days a week.

Numbers should not be a goal, lest they become a god, but the goal should be the lasting fruit of transformed lives. Let's not forget that Jesus changed the world with twelve disciples — and one didn't make it.

HERE'S WHAT REAL GROWTH LOOKS LIKE

The most effective churches that I know of are those who are transforming their community person by person and family by family. The most effective disciples I know are those who have learned to leave the ninety-nine who are doing well and love the one who is not. You don't need big numbers and big money to do that. You need kingdom values and the heart of God. You need a willingness to focus on the person in front to you, and to be inconvenienced, when necessary, for others' sake.

Do you know why so many churches are failing in truly transforming their communities? Here is the simple Scriptural answer:

"For the others all seek [to advance] their own interests, not those of Jesus Christ (the Messiah)" (Phil. 2:21 —Amp).

There it is! When I was a young missionary, I wrote a book called *Soulish Leadership*, from a burden I received that came from all the pastoral "turf wars" I witnessed in every city and nation we were in. The envy, jealousy, strife, division, and personal-kingdom-building mentality was nauseating. I realized over time that men are primarily interested in advancing their own cause and agenda, and not the kingdom's. It takes a man full of the mind and heart of God to endorse another. For example, I have a dear friend who pastors a very healthy church and buys newspaper ads for new pastors who come into the area to start another church. That is what you call kingdom values. Would to God that all pastors followed this example!

What would happen in your community if it didn't matter who received the credit for advancing the kingdom? What is required from disciples of Jesus is not numerical growth of any particular group or church, but rather, growth of Christ's kingdom, free of personal agendas, financial gain, and personal-ownership issues.

Until we stop caring about the numerical "results" of our churches, or of people and individuals we're reaching out to personally but leave the fruit to God's workings and care, we are really not in a position to be the judge of what true growth is. What if kingdom growth meant the end of everything you are involved in? Could you let go of what is dear to yourself so that another might succeed? Would you be willing to be nothing for the greater good? Would you give away your time, talents, and treasury for no other reason than the good it causes others? That is the kind of genuine love of God that will transform a community.

These are called the true values of the kingdom of God. When our values are aligned with God's great heart, and His meek and lowly nature, true kingdom growth will take care of itself. It is a rarity today, but there are some small churches that are growing in numbers and in fruit who are not even trying to grow. They are growing this way because there's been a transformation in their thinking — not necessarily in their methodology or philosophy of ministry but in their values. When our actions spring forth from transformed Christ-like thinking and kingdom values, there is fruitfulness, but not always how we expect it in significant numerical growth.

DO NUMBERS MEAN AS MUCH TO GOD AS THEY MEAN TO US?

"So the churches were strengthened in the faith, and increased in number daily" (Acts 16:5). Churches can supernaturally increase in numbers, without relying on carnal and manipulative methods, but

numbers can also be a deceiving thing. The crowd may indicate a man's popularity but not necessarily his spiritual credibility.

Please hear my heart. I am not suggesting that numbers do not ever represent godly kingdom success, but they are not to be the primary driving force. If they are, then it becomes as a god that you worship, although to many that seems ludicrous. Of course, I am not at all opposed to big numbers. Jesus and the early Church ministered to multitudes. I am talking about our value system and the motive and foundation from which we serve and live.

One anonymous writer offers this compelling quote:

"The apostasy of the early Church came as a result of a greater desire to see the spread of its power and rule than to see new natures given to individual members (people being genuinely converted; [emphasis mine]). The moment we covet a large following and rejoice in the crowd that is attracted by our presentation of what we consider truth and have not a greater desire to see the natures of individuals changed according to the divine plan, we start to travel the same road of apostasy that leads to Rome and her daughters." Anonymous

What a compelling and convicting truth! When a person is genuinely converted and born again, his sinful nature is transformed into the very nature of God. His spirit is translated from the kingdom of darkness to the kingdom of light and of God's dear Son (Col. 1:13). There's a big difference between a lust for numbers and a true love for people and for them to be born again and become a disciple of Jesus. When the disciples returned from their mission in Luke 10, they rejoiced that even the demons were subject to the Name of Jesus. Jesus, however, redirected their focus and told them to rejoice instead that their names were written in heaven. In other words, rejoice in your salvation and not in your authority over demons. Rejoice in souls, not in power and success. Rejoice in souls, not in money or numbers.

Our Lord Jesus fed thousands of people but focused His primary efforts on raising up twelve men. One of His hard teachings on eating His flesh and drinking His blood scared away those thousands and even a few of His own, but He did not chase them (Jn. 6:41-69). Yet He was the example of the good Shepherd who left the ninety-nine to go after the one who strayed, and He taught us to do the same (Lk. 15:4-7).

And let's not forget our Old Testament examples of how the Lord cut down Gideon's army from 32,000 to 300 able men (Jud. 7); or of the battle Jehoshaphat won when his armies were outnumbered three to one (2 Chr. 20); or of Elijah's victory over the 450 prophets of Baal (1 Kings 18); or of the time the Lord's anger was stirred against David for counting his army and trusting in his own military strength instead of the power of God (2 Sam. 24).

Numbers can be very deceiving and misleading. Thank God that large numbers of people are being reached, hopefully for the good, but don't make the mistake of evaluating a man's success and spiritual credibility by those large numbers. As I said, those numbers may be a sign only of a man's popularity. God rewards faithfulness, not ability or popularity. If God has called you to shepherd only a few families, then love them and nurture them faithfully, and you will receive the same reward as any mega-pastor who did the same from a pure heart.

We cannot measure true success by a church's or ministry's popularity, or by the size of their mailing list or their annual budget, or numbers of people who attend their meetings. We must bring to an end this type of mentality that has turned the gospel into a business or enterprise which is evaluated by these false measures of success. Western Christianity has become what a young evangelist friend of mine called "a shell game." In a recent exchange, he offered these observations and thoughts:

"I'm noticing that a lot of big ministry is like a shell game. It looks like there is something of value, but in reality it's really only an appearance of it. For example, most of American Christianity has so glorified teaching that a big teacher can amass a following and wealth from it. The problem is that people don't necessarily need more teaching, but they need transformation.

"It's the same way with most televangelists. You never see them say, 'Here is this young man I ministered to at the restaurant we went to before the meeting.' There is often no tangible fruit.

"So, the reason I mention this bigger ministry is because they are a multi-million-dollar ministry, and I don't think they can pull one testimony of someone that they have brought to Christ, baptized in water or the Holy Spirit, or trained to do evangelism.

"So, the issue with all of these big ministers is that they really have no ground game, and the ground game of changed lives is what really counts. If I had one million people, I know I could turn a city upside down pretty drastically and pretty quickly. These guys got 30 million dollars and no true fruit to show for it. Teaching Christians who have been around for 20-30 years doesn't necessarily count as fruit. Transformed lives do. We live in an oversaturated teaching culture. I know people who have been taught for 30 years, and they still can't seem to learn, but they think everything is totally fine. The same wounds from 30 years ago in their lives are still deeply rooted.

"For example, when a persecuted church ministry that has a 90% rating on charity watch takes in only 1.5 million a year, even though they go and help the families of martyrs, provide Bibles, training, etc.,

while a televangelist ministry can take in 30 million a year and have no real evidence of using the money, there is a real problem there that needs to be called out." -David Hoffman

You may or may not agree with my young friend, but when someone is giving an opinion, I look for the mind of Christ in what he is saying. My friend's observation comes from his frustration of doing large grassroots evangelistic events without the benefit of a lot of financial support. He's anointed. His character is impeccable. He produces much fruit of changed lives, but the financial support is minimal. When he measures and evaluates the fruit of his efforts against these million-dollar ministries who conduct popular teaching conferences, he sees an imbalance and inequality in the distribution of wealth for ministry purposes. He makes a valid point.

POOR STEWARDSHIP

I paid attention to his reasoning because this is actually something the Lord has spoken to my wife and me about in the past. He told us that many of the big-budget ministries, in comparison to the huge amounts of money spent on their conferences and events, were not making a calculable or qualitative impact on people's spiritual lives. Believe it or not, the Lord used ministries that own multi-million-dollar jets as an example of the amount of money that is spent compared to the actual impact and lasting fruit of what is done. He was relating it all to poor stewardship and the wrong measuring gauge we use to judge popular churches and ministries. God often sees things much differently. Some people might say, as I have said, that God is not short of money, but He is also not a poor steward, for even Jesus exemplified good stewardship when He instructed His disciples to pick up twelve baskets of leftover food from the miracle of the multiplication of loaves and fishes (Jn. 6:12-13).

As an example of poor stewardship, a number of years ago, I was part of a small ministerial planning committee that hosted regional conferences in the northeast part of America. Collectively, we chose the conference speakers and determined the budget for these conferences. It was always the decision of the majority to bring in a well-known speaker because they would draw the bigger crowds. I never felt comfortable with this line of reasoning and planning, feeling that our motives were questionable, but the majority ruled.

Some of the invited ministers owned or leased their own jets, and the cost for the fuel alone was $5000. This led to the committee spiking up the registration fee to adequately cover the cost. Once again, to me, this was now two wrongs, and two wrongs never make a right. After the conference was over, I always found the actual fruit and impact to be wanting in comparison to the amount spent. And of course, some people wouldn't even consider attending such a conference because of the high registration fees. That means lower-income people who may have wanted to attend were excluded. I'm sorry, dear friends, but that just doesn't pass the Jesus test. In my humble opinion, this is the reason these conferences never had the fullness of God's favor on them.

Unfortunately, most people are fooled by the hype, professionalism, and presentation of such big ministries and big events, and often success is evaluated by the sheer numbers in attendance. But in this superficial age of consumerism, we need to unplug our minds from this sort of thinking and plug ourselves into the mind of Christ, which is mainly concerned with meeting the real needs of people — the first of these being salvation and real heart transformation and, second, their practical needs. In the judgment of the sheep and goat nations, this much is clear (Matt. 25:31-45). We will discuss the meeting of people's practical needs in a later chapter.

Here is a grand piece by A.W. Tozer that speaks volumes and stirs me deeply:

FAILURE AND SUCCESS: THE GREAT GODDESS OF NUMBERS

"Now if anyone builds on this foundation with gold, silver, precious stones, wood, hay, straw, each one's work will become clear; for the Day will declare it, because it will be revealed by fire; and the fire will test each one's work, of what sort it is (1 Cor. 3:12-13).

"The emphasis today in Christian circles appears to be on quantity, with a corresponding lack of emphasis on quality. Numbers, size and amount seem to be very nearly all that matters, even among evangelicals; size of the crowd, the number of converts, the size of the budget, and the amount of the weekly collections. If these look good, the church is prospering and the pastor is thought to be a success. The church that can show an impressive quantitative growth is frankly envied and imitated by other ambitious churches.

"This is the age of the Laodiceans. The great goddess Numbers is worshiped with fervent devotion, and all things religious are brought before her for examination. Her Old Testament is the financial report and her New Testament is the membership roll. To these she appeals as arbiters of all questions, the test of spiritual growth, and the proof of success or failure in every Christian endeavor.

"A little acquaintance with the Bible should show this up for the heresy it is. To judge anything spiritual by statistics is to judge by other than scriptural judgment. It is to admit the validity of externalism and to deny the value our Lord places upon the soul over and against the body. It is to mistake the old creation for the new and to confuse things eternal with things temporal. Yet it is being done every day by ministers, church boards, and denominational leaders. And hardly

anyone notices the deep and dangerous error." (Tozer, *The Set of the Sail*, 153)

Oh, Lord — convict us! Forgive us! Deliver us from the goddess of Numbers! Amen.

CHAPTER EIGHT

THE MYSTERY OF INIQUITY:

WHY THE LOVE OF MONEY IS THE ROOT OF ALL EVIL

"But what things were gain to me, these I have counted loss for Christ. Yet indeed I also count all things loss for the excellence of the knowledge of Christ Jesus my Lord, for whom I have suffered the loss of all things, and count them as rubbish, that I may gain Christ..." (Phil. 3:7-8).

The apostle Paul saw something deep in the Spirit. It fueled him to know the Lord in a much more intimate dimension than most of his ministry peers who more closely fit this description: *"For all seek their own, not the things which are of Christ Jesus"* (Phil. 2:21).

Moreover, his profound and weighty speech to the Ephesian elders at Miletus unveils the eternal axis of this man's heart.

"For I know this, that after my departure savage wolves will come in among you, not sparing the flock. Also from among yourselves men will rise up, speaking perverse things, to draw away the disciples after themselves" (Acts 20:29-30).

What is it in a man that causes him to desire man's approval more than the approval of God that he would even draw people away from God to himself? What is in the heart of a minister who desires to minister in their public gifting more than they desire to minister privately to the Lord? To twist doctrine in order to develop a personal following? Surely it is because they've not seen Christ or known His heart in the way Paul saw Him and knew Him.

Why would these Ephesian elders, after hearing Paul admonish and warn them with tears from the depths of his heart, still go on in the future to speak perverse things to draw away disciples after themselves? Why do ministers seek popularity and a large audience more than the audience of One? Numbers more than real fruit? Public reputation more than private reputation? Earth's approval more than heaven's?

I propose this piercing truth to you: Is it not because the mystery of iniquity is at work in their hearts?

If so, will it not take a miracle of major proportions pertaining to the transformation of our character to deliver us from this sort of flesh and soul dominance?

After sitting under the ministry of Paul and witnessing his impeccable character and his purpose and manner of life, how could these Ephesian elders fail to heed his warnings and soon depart from his example and teaching?

Paul had come to many visions and revelations of the Lord (2 Cor. 12:1) and the inexpressible words he heard in paradise, unlawful to utter (v. 4), placed this beloved man in a dimension most of humanity, including some of the godliest ministers, never reach. He received much grace for the eternal Church that has served her for centuries of time — then and now. Although still an imperfect man, we'd better pay attention to the admonitions and warnings of Paul.

Among the hundreds and thousands he ministered and preached to, how was it that only Timothy was trustworthy?

Like his Master, Paul knew what was in man (Jn. 2:24-25). He understood the mystery of iniquity (2 Thes. 2:7). He understood that, even among ministers, this iniquity was at work.

*"Many will say to me in that day, Lord, Lord, have we not prophesied in thy name? And in thy name have cast out devils? And in thy name done many wonderful works? And then will I profess unto them, I never knew you: depart from me, **ye that work iniquity**"* (Matt. 7:22-23 — KJV).

What a fearful verse of Scripture that even applies to one of the Lord's own!

How could someone like Judas, who spent three years with Jesus, betray Him for the wages of iniquity (Acts 1:18)?

And how could Lucifer, who knew the glories of heaven and dwelt in the presence of God, have iniquity found in him? How could he yield to pride and fall from such a high and holy state of creation (Ez. 28:11-19)?

Such is the mystery of iniquity. The love of money or mammon is the mother of all iniquity. For this reason, it is the root of all evil.

YOU CANNOT SERVE GOD AND MAMMON

Now notice these next fascinating and revealing verses, particularly the boldfaced phrases, and you'll receive further revelation of the mystery of iniquity.

*"Now the Pharisees, who were **lovers of money**, also heard all these things, and they derided Him. And He said to them, "You are those who justify yourselves before men, but God knows your hearts. **For what is highly esteemed among men is an abomination in the sight of God**. The law and the prophets were until John. Since that time the kingdom of God has been preached, and everyone is pressing into it. And it is easier for heaven and earth to pass away than for one tittle of the law to fail. **Whoever divorces his wife and marries an-***

other commits adultery; and whoever marries her who is divorced from her husband commits adultery" (Lk. 16:14-18).

From Luke 15 to the first part of Luke 17, the central theme of Jesus' discourse and teaching is on money. In Luke 15, when the Pharisees criticized Jesus for eating with sinners, He tells the parable of the lost sheep, the parable of the lost coin, and the parable of the lost son to contrast the value of people to money. One of the great lessons in these parables is that it's people that are eternal and have great value, not money in itself. Obviously the Pharisees did not believe sinners had any value, but they believed that sheep and coins did.

In Luke 16, Jesus continues talking about money as he begins the chapter by telling the parable of the unjust steward (v. 1-13). The steward used the rich man's money to cancel other men's debts. Jesus does not approve of the steward's fraud but illustrates his stewardship and commends his prudence in using present opportunities for his future welfare. Symbolically, Jesus is our rich man, and we are to tell men that the price for their sin has been paid and their debt has been cancelled. The big lesson here is to use money or mammon for the benefit of others and to win souls (Lk. 16:9). Money is very beneficial when it's your *servant* and used for eternal purposes, but it's evil when it's your *master* and used only for temporal and selfish purposes.

Another lesson to learn from this parable is the reward we gain from our good stewardship of money. The way we handle money is the way we will handle the true riches, which are people. And the way you handle another man's riches will determine the measure that God will bless you with your own (v. 11).

How you handle money reveals volumes about how you'd handle people. Is a person's soul more important to you than your money? If

God sees that it is, and you prove it out, then you are in line for God's promotion.

The following verse is the central theme of all Jesus is teaching in these middle chapters of Luke's gospel and one of the purposes of this book.

"No servant can serve two masters; for either he will hate the one and love the other, or else he will be loyal to the one and despise the other. You cannot serve God and mammon" (Lk. 16:13).

Much like it is today, the Pharisees used religion to steal from the people. Notice how they were referred to as *"lovers of money,"* which translates better in the original Greek as, *"lovers of silver."* This is the most accurate definition of covetousness.

"Now the Pharisees, who were lovers of money, also heard all these things, and **they derided Him**" (Lk. 16:14).

At this point in Jesus' discourse, the Pharisees began to get very upset because they realized He was talking about them. The word "deride" means to stick one's nose up at or scoff at. As the Pharisees scoffed at Him, Jesus said this: *"You are those who justify yourselves before men, but God knows your hearts.* **For what is highly esteemed among men is an abomination in the sight of God** (v. 15)."

What is it that the scribes and Pharisees esteemed highly? What is it that men esteem highly in every generation? These verses unveil a great secret.

"Beware of the scribes, who desire to go around in long robes, love greetings in the marketplaces, the best seats in the synagogues, and the best places at feasts, who devour widows' houses, and for a pretense make long prayers. These will receive greater condemnation" (Lk. 20:46-47).

Here again is the mystery of iniquity working in the hearts of these religious leaders.

These attitudes of the heart and love for position and the honor of man are an abomination to God. What God esteems is humility, obedience, and a love and value for people — to do justly and love mercy.

"He has shown you, O man, what is good; and what does the Lord require of you but to do justly, to love mercy, and to walk humbly with your God?" (Micah 6:8)

Here is what the Spirit of God wants to work in every man and minister's heart embodied in the Person of Jesus Christ: *"I receive not glory from men [I crave no human honor, I look for no mortal fame] ..."* (Jn. 5:41). When you can say the same, you've reached a place of heart transformation very few ever do.

HAVE YOU DIVORCED GOD TO MARRY MONEY?

For years I could never make sense of Jesus' comments on marriage and divorce (v. 18) and how it applies to the subject at hand.

"Whoever divorces his wife and marries another commits adultery; and whoever marries her who is divorced from her husband commits adultery."

Jesus is teaching on money and suddenly makes a statement on marriage and divorce. This seems to be a startling and abrupt interruption to all Jesus is saying, and at first glance, it appears terribly disconnected to the subject at hand. Some commentaries even doubt that this verse of scripture should be here at all. They misinterpret it as a scornful interruption of rebuke to the Pharisaical listeners.

How does that fit in with everything Jesus is teaching on money and stewardship? Here it is: **God was married to Israel by the Law,**

but the Pharisees divorced Him when they married money or sil-ver. That is very sobering, but it lines up with the truth that we cannot serve God *and* mammon. Like the Pharisees, many in ministry leadership today are married to mammon.

Jesus further elaborates on this problem in Luke 16 in the account of the rich man and Lazarus. I've used this story for evangelistic purposes, and it will preach, but in context, Jesus is continuing to teach on the same theme of stewardship and the built-in cultural system of the Jews who believed gain to be godliness—or better said in today's church world, financial success equates to spirituality. In essence, Jesus teaches that the poor stewardship of the rich man and his love for money doomed him to hell. And if the Pharisees didn't repent and change also, that is where they would end up.

Measuring your life by what money can buy you or make you and using it as a happy substitute for your relationship with God is the iniquity of all mankind. It is covetousness and proof that you are serving mammon.

"Take heed and beware of covetousness, for one's life does not consist in the abundance of the things he possesses" (Lk. 12:15).

One of the big reasons Jesus told His disciples to beware of the scribes and Pharisees is because they were covetous. This is a big issue and problem in today's Church that God wants to address and cleanse.

I've purposely placed this chapter in the middle of this book because it is the nucleus of much of what we are discussing, and it ties everything together regarding all I've said about money. I trust your spiritual eyes are being enlightened to the central truth encompassed within these chapters. I also trust that you are understanding how Satan once again has woven his hand of manipulation and deception into the Church, using the love of money and covetousness to defile it of its true character, glory, and power. Examine yourselves to see if you are truly in the faith under the Lordship of Jesus Christ, or if you have subtly placed your trust in mammon and uncertain riches. Can the Lord fully manifest His glory in the Church today, when so many are serving mammon?

THE TREND IN CHARISMATIC CIRCLES

There has been a trend in recent years in Charismatic circles that is eerily close to the Jewish belief system of identifying gain with godliness. At the core of this belief system is the belief that the more materially and financially blessed you are, the more favor you've obtained with God, and the more you've received what His redemption purchased for you at the cross — as if *"Jesus being made poor so we could be rich"* (2 Cor. 8:9) is the proof of our spiritual salvation. We are commanded to withdraw from men of corrupt minds and destitute of the truth *"who suppose that godliness is a means of gain"* (1 Tim. 6:5).

My wife and I were in a meeting once where some Charismatic high falutin' preachers were adamantly preaching that it's as much God's will for us to be rich as it is to be saved. We immediately discerned that these men were operating with the wrong spirit. This is the extreme of this teaching. Both Jesus and Paul addressed this erroneous belief system. This was such a grave matter that Paul warned Timothy not to be associated with these men and commanded him to flee this dangerous teaching and the fallout associated with it. He told him that those who believe this doctrine and preach it are in danger of destruction and perdition. Let me refresh your memory again of this concept found in Jewish culture, using a couple of examples from Jesus' ministry.

After Jesus' encounter and exchange with the rich young ruler, He turned to His disciples and said this:

"Then Jesus looked around and said to His disciples, "How hard it is for those who have riches to enter the kingdom of God!" And the disciples were **astonished** *at His words. But Jesus answered again and said to them, "Children,* **how hard it is for those who trust in riches to enter the kingdom of God**! *It is easier for a camel to go through the eye of a needle than for a rich man to enter the kingdom of God." And they were* **greatly astonished***, saying among themselves, "Who then can be saved?"* (Mk. 10:23-26)

Notice the disciples went from being "astonished" to being "*greatly* astonished" — the reason being because this belief system that gain is godliness was so ingrained into the mindset of the Jewish culture that it jeopardized their salvation and eternal standing with God.

Additionally, as I stated, when Jesus gave the account of the rich man and Lazarus (Lk. 16:19-31), He was highlighting the same issue. The entire context is concerning the corrupting power money can wield over a person.

Of course, money in itself is not evil, but the desire to be rich leads to many foolish and hurtful lusts, and the love of it is the root of all evil, which leads to many sorrows.

"But they that will (desire) to be rich fall into temptation and a snare, and into **many** *foolish and hurtful lusts, which drown men in destruction and perdition.* **For the love of money is the root of all evil***: which while some coveted after, they have erred from the faith, and pierced themselves through with* **many** *sorrows"* (1 Tim. 6:9-10).

Again, in context, what Paul is addressing here is what Jesus also addressed having to do with the strong Jewish belief system that taught them that gain is godliness (1 Tim. 6:5) — the belief that obedience to the Law produces financial prosperity and disobedience results in poverty. God certainly blesses our obedience to His Word, but it's been twisted and corrupted by covetousness, which feeds a desire for more and more while equating it to godliness and spirituality. We have this same type of teaching today in various forms.

Paul is tracing the cause of these *"many foolish and hurtful lusts"* back to the love of money as the root of *"all evil."* The love of money is the root of vastly more than we usually think it is. It is the first step to sinning more. It is a slippery slope and the root of all evils that men do and live by. How is this so?

Although "money" is of no value in and of itself (the actual paper currency, or coin), it is necessary to meet our basic needs, and is a godly means of giving to others and blessing the work of God. But it is also a cultural symbol which can be traded for the many desires/lusts that we may have. Therefore, the love of money in Paul's mind corresponds to the root longing for the things money can buy and the status it can give you without God. That is why all these many desires/lusts *"plunge men into ruin and destruction."*

For example, my wife and I knew of a fine young Christian couple with several children who relocated to a large American city with vast wealth from the booming industry and commerce that was in that city. They were very godly and consecrated people, but the mammon spirit in that city got a hold of the husband until he became obsessed with starting businesses and making profits. His motives became tainted by greed and covetousness. Over time their marriage, home life, and children began to crumble due to the husband's incessant desire to be rich and purchase the finer things that money can buy. He traded a godly marriage and family for wealth. He became covetous, strayed from the faith, and it pierced him and his family through with many sorrows.

Money is constantly being exchanged and traded for something else, whether it be materialism, social status, prestige, influence, pleasure, etc., and the results can be devastating. The root is covetousness or the love of money. This is what Paul is saying. In other words, finding your identity in what money can make you or give you outside of God is the root of all evil. That is the personification of serving mammon. Our deepest and most wholesome identity should solely be grounded in having our names written in the Lamb's book of life, being adopted into the family of God and becoming a child of God, being loved by the Father, and worshipping Him now and for all of eternity. Any substitute for that can become a subtle form of pride and self-importance and the working of iniquity. Self-importance is a big one.

"Often Satan injects pride into the believer's spirit, evoking in him an attitude of self-importance and of self-conceit. He causes him to esteem himself a very outstanding person, one who is indispensable in God's work. Such a spirit constitutes one of the major reasons for the fall of believers." Watchman Nee

SATAN IS THE AUTHOR OF THE LOVE OF MONEY

"You were perfect in your ways from the day you were created, till **iniquity** *was found in you"* (Ez. 28:15).

Lucifer's fall from heaven was the result of the iniquity that was found in him. Iniquity is evil and includes anything that is outside of God's original will and plan. Iniquity distorts the origin of what God created and ordained for the life of man and will eventually culminate in the failure to fulfill God's ultimate purpose for our lives.

"Nevertheless, the solid foundation of God stands, having this seal: "The Lord knows those who are His," and "Let everyone who names the name of Christ depart from **iniquity***"* (2 Tim. 2:19).

Wherever iniquity is present, the glory is absent. They cannot co-exist. The glory has departed from much of the Church today because of iniquity. Too many are serving the root system of mammon and materialism, not God. The seal of the foundation of God is upon those who have departed from iniquity and worship Christ alone.

This mindset and philosophy originally found in Lucifer can be seen not only in the temptation of what he offered to Adam and Eve of a higher status as gods, but also in the wilderness temptations of Jesus Christ. Satan tried to get Jesus to find His identity in what He could do or in his performance, and in what He could be outside of God's original plan and purpose.

Now when the tempter came to Him, he said, "If You are the Son of God, command that these stones become bread" (Matt. 4:3).

Let's understand that the love of money in a Christian is much more subtle than that which is in the world. It is actually a love or friendship with anything you consider to be evidence that you are favored and blessed by God. The Jews measured the blessing of God by wealth and riches. Many are doing the same today. Can you see the subtlety and deceitfulness of that? In like manner, Satan was tempting Jesus to produce evidence that He was the Son of God. In other words, by performing a miracle, Jesus would prove His identity and confirm who He really was. But Jesus had already received His true identity as it was confirmed by the heavenly Father following His water baptism in the Jordan.

And suddenly a voice came from heaven, saying, "This is My beloved Son, in whom I am well pleased" (Matt. 3:17).

Jesus' identity was found in the love and affirmation of His heavenly Father. Nothing else could ever substitute for that.

The wilderness temptations were to test Jesus of finding His identity in anything else except His relationship to the Father. Think about this: in the wilderness, Jesus was alone. He did not have any food or fellowship with people. No one followed Him, and He did not meet anyone's needs. There was nothing to affirm His place or position in life and ministry. Even the identity with ministry based on performance, so common today, He overcame, so that He could be our standard. His total dependence on the heavenly Father was tested in the wilderness.

Many Christians' identity is never complete without some sign of God's blessings, which usually centers around financial and material possessions, or the anointing and ability God may give them, or their status in life and ministry. The truth of Jesus' life was not in the ability or the power and status God gave Him, but it was solely rooted in the fact that God was His Father and obedience to the Father's will was His meat (Jn. 4:34). Eventually He was killed for declaring His Sonship to the religious leaders of that day. His continual fellowship with the Father and the love He received from being His Son and doing His will was Jesus' constant delight and should always be ours.

Yet today we have televangelists and big prosperity preachers telling us that their 30,000-square-foot home is the blessing of God in their lives for preaching the gospel. In other words, their gain is because of their godliness. To them financial and material gain means the favor of God. This type of gain is often equated with spirituality and seeming obedience. It implies that if you're not extremely wealthy like they are, then perhaps you haven't been as obedient to God as they have. Again, there's nothing wrong with having riches, influence, significance, power, anointing, or a successful business as long as those things are not your *identity* and do not dictate who you are *in your heart* or who anyone else is. Class distinctions based on these things are not a part of kingdom thinking. When they are, you have entered into mammon worship.

At the point where Jesus overcame temptation in the wilderness is the point where Adam and Even failed. They believed Satan's lie that they would be as gods if they ate the forbidden fruit. It's also the point where Lucifer fell from heaven and failed. He based his life and point of reference on his beauty and the abundance of his possessions, and not on God. Lucifer's heart was lifted up in his beauty, and his wisdom was corrupted, which resulted in his fall.

"Your heart was lifted up because of your beauty; you corrupted your wisdom for the sake of your splendor; I cast you to the ground, I laid you before kings, that they might gaze at you" (Ez. 28:17).

Conversely, Jesus was perfect from the day He was born. He was sinless and possessed all the power and wisdom of God. If Jesus would've had a change of heart and found His identity in what the Father gave Him instead of His Sonship, He would've fallen just as Lucifer (Satan) did. His wisdom would've also been corrupted. If He would've turned the stone into bread or jumped off the top of the temple, His identity would've been in His performance or the power He possessed.

"Then the devil took Him up into the holy city, set Him on the pinnacle of the temple, and said to Him, 'If You are the Son of God, throw Yourself down'" (Matt. 4:5-6).

Satan was tempting Jesus with a message that promoted the same iniquity he'd succumbed to. This is Satan's belief system that is rooted in all evil. The wisdom he was given had been corrupted. Many today have corrupted the wisdom that God originally gave them. When we walk *outside* of God's original design for us in simply rejoicing that we are His children and our names are written in the Lamb's book of life, and finding our complete satisfaction in simply doing the will of God for our lives, we start entering into darkness and a form of iniquity. All evil began in the heart of Lucifer, and this same evil system is what pulls us away from not only our sonship, but from being God's true bond-slave that serves Him and not mammon.

Remember that the author of pride and covetousness is Satan himself. The love of money originated with him. He was the first one who began trading what he possessed for something else. He is the author of all evil and is very familiar with the root of it.

CHAPTER NINE

MERCHANDISING THE ANOINTING

AND MARKETING THE MATERIALISTIC GOSPEL

There will be some repetition in this chapter as we continue to gain further insight into the mystery of iniquity. We will discuss some of the same verses of scripture and expound on them.

Once again, all covetousness and the love of money, which is the root of all evil, originated with Lucifer. Iniquity was first found in his heart. In heaven. In the presence of God. In His glory. Let that sink in.

"*Thou wast perfect in thy ways from the day that thou wast created, till* **iniquity** *was found in thee.* **By the multitude of thy merchandise** *they have filled the midst of thee (center of your being) with violence, and thou hast sinned...*" (Ez. 28:15-16 — KJV).

Here's how these verses read in the Online Bible:

"*You were blameless in your ways from the day you were created till wickedness (iniquity) was found in you.* **Through your widespread trade** *you were filled with violence, and you sinned*" (OLB).

How could iniquity enter into Lucifer's heart? The above verses tell us. "*By the multitude of thy merchandise*" or "*Through your widespread trade.*"

The word **"widespread"** is the translation of the Hebrew word **"rob."** The word **"trade"** is the translation of the Hebrew "**rakullah**," which the printed *Strong's Concordance* translates as "to peddle." "To peddle" is to be translated as sell, deal in, hawk, or sell from house to house.

Lucifer's "trade" is therefore not to be understood as if he had some kind of sales shop or trading company in heaven, but in essence he went "selling" from "door to door." He started to "peddle" and "hawk" in heaven. Lucifer fell into sin and violence through his widespread peddling and his abundant hawking (Online Bible Commentary).

Lucifer found an audience with one third of the angels in heaven, and as a result, they were banned from heaven. He fell into sin through "the multitude of his merchandise" or "widespread trade," and through his "abundant hawking," and he became the adversary of God.

MERCHANDISE

In other Bible versions, the word "merchandise" is translated as "trading" or "commerce." There is often a double meaning and application in many passages of Scripture, especially in the Old Testament. There is a literal and a spiritual application here both to King Tyre and Lucifer (Satan).

*"By the multitude of thy **merchandise** they have filled the midst of thee with violence, and thou hast sinned: therefore I will cast thee as profane out of the mountain of God: and I will destroy thee, O covering cherub, from the midst of the stones of fire"* (Ez. 28:16 — KJV).

Interestingly, this word "merchandise" was also used by Jesus when He cleansed the temple.

*"And He said to those who sold doves, "Take these things away! Do not make My Father's house a house of **merchandise!**"* (Jn. 2:16).

There are actually two separate accounts of Jesus cleansing the temple — once at the beginning of his ministry here in John's gospel, and the other toward the end of his ministry (Matt. 21:12-14, Mk.

11:15-17; Lk. 19:45-46). It's interesting to me that He started and finished His ministry this way.

In the first account, he rebuked the moneychangers and those who were buying and selling and making the temple a house of merchandise, but in the second cleansing, He was much more severe and called it a *"den of thieves."* Among the differences between the first and second cleansings is that, in the first, the Lord ordered them to stop such practices. At the second cleansing, it was too late to command them to stop, and at that time, they were denounced as "thieves and robbers." Their day of visitation and grace had passed.

Seducers today are waxing worse and worse, and many churches either ignorantly or by way of training, association, and imitation have become places of business, entertainment centers, consumer-based models of religious enterprises, social clubs, or even charitable organizations — all moving away from God's original design and amounting in some way to dens of thieves where merchandising and consumerism are king.

EXAMPLE OF MERCHANDISING USING MADISON AVENUE TACTICS

In his article on *Unholy Hype*, Dr. Anthony G. Payne writes:

"Few reading these words are unaware of the absurd level of promotional hype that exists in the church world today. You can't miss it because the jingles, slogans, branding language, and public relations output of so many ministries parallels that of secular organizations and especially product manufacturers and marketers. Indeed, it almost goes without saying that growth-minded churches and organizations must aggressively bumper-thump or promote themselves.

"However, what churches and other religious establishments have discovered is that highly effective advertising, public relations, and

marketing require that they bring something to the table that "out-classes" or "outmaneuvers" their "competition" or at least tends to make them stand out as especially worthy of a prospective parishioner or follower's time (and, hopefully, financial support). Instead of asking, "How do we best communicate the gospel and get people saved and then living lives that please God and bear fruit?" church leaders find themselves asking, "What program, music, music group, event, books, films, DVDs, or presentations can we introduce or sponsor which will draw in the unchurched, especially Millennials?"

Dr. Payne makes a great point and paints a clear picture of the promotional hype that has infiltrated many churches and ministries today. It is a form of merchandising. He continues:

"Those ministries, churches, and religious organizations which work PR well typically grow, and, as a result, their leaders naturally assume this is something God approves of and has blessed. So they invest more dollars in promoting themselves, including hiring a PR firm or creating their own in-house version, and even shifting their focus to sermons and books and such that focus not on sin, repentance, and changing one's ways and growing in holiness, but instead extol God's promises and blessings and how to more surely exploit these using faith and perhaps (verbal) confessions with little or no sacrifice, obedience, or even the right motives."

Dr. Payne speaks from experience. For the past 30 years, he has done promotional writing and handled PR strategy and outreach for various healthcare professionals and some celebrity physicians, as well as helping churches and ministers. He has also tracked the explosive growth of church bodies and associations from using marketing methods and PR campaigns. He has experience in such areas and was even instrumental in turning a southern California firm from potential bankruptcy to a very profitable company. But he has witnessed these same secular methods used in many churches and ministries today.

Read carefully as Dr. Payne continues to expound on these excesses of promotional hype in ministry today.

"Let me take you a little further into what I see being played out, especially in many mega-churches and in the lives and preaching of more than a few televangelists. What many of these PR virtuosos have done is bait the hook with something people find as irresistible as lotteries, horse races, and mega-prize contests: namely, "prosperity theology," which is to say, the prosperity gospel. And it is so, well, utterly true-blue American because it cherry picks God's promises and marries them to entrenched American capitalist sentiments and practices. Of course, what I see happening is believers buying into a species of wishful and magical thinking which turns God into a faith-activated Cosmic ATM Machine or Father Slot Machine.

"This in my opinion has turned many ministries into religious Ponzi schemes in which believers give more and more in the hope or fervent belief that God will bless them steadily up the proverbial material pyramid until they are as prosperous as their favorite preacher pitch person. These hype-bewitched folks appear to be oblivious to the fact that these prosperity preachers and teachers have transformed Yeshua HaMashiach ("Jesus the Messiah") and his message from that of an itinerant rabbi who spoke unceasingly of how the rich will have a very hard time making it to heaven — into a prosperous Potentate who wants every believer to get stinking rich.

"Is it any wonder that some mega-churches and evangelical organizations have devolved into personality cults whose leaders are seduced by their own egos and base desires?

"Many Americans, including believers, have been seduced by those who adroitly combine hype (including language that borders on or is outright deceptive), fear, manipulation, and exploitation (both subtle and crass) with appeals to greed, ego, and so-called 'enlightened self-interest.' In my opinion, they do far more harm than their secular counterparts because their words and deeds can leave people not only poorer materially, but also spiritually."

Is this promotional hype not an example of merchandising the anointing of God and turning His house into a den of thieves?

BURNING UP THE GREED

As aforementioned, in three of the gospels (Matt. 21:12-13; Mk. 11:15-17; and Lk. 19:45-46) Jesus rebuked the religious leaders for turning His Father's house into a den of thieves, but in John's gospel, which is the less common and more distinct gospel (only 8% of John's content is found in the other gospels), He calls it "...a house of merchandise." In the first cleansing, recorded by John, they were doing business, but in the second cleansing, they were now thieves. About three years had passed between the two cleansings, which teaches us the solemn lesson that unless the heart of man is changed and the insatiable desire for money, influence, power, and significance is uprooted, and the mammon god is put asunder, outward reformation and external changes are of little value. For in three years, or perhaps less, the abuse that the Messiah corrected in the beginning of His ministry had returned in full force.

Even after Pentecost, when the Holy Spirit had invaded the temple (body) of man during the days of the early Church, the love of appearance and an honored reputation among men tried to find a place in the hearts of Ananias and Sapphira (Acts 5), whom we referred to in earlier chapters. Their root issue was hypocrisy wrapped in a lie, rooted in covetousness, so they could be esteemed in the eyes of the people for giving more than they actually gave. Remember, the love of money and covetousness entails much more than money. It includes an inordinate driving desire for position, power, influence, and the honor and esteem of man. Through the apostle Peter, the Spirit of the Lord dealt with this leaven in Ananias and Sapphira, but just three chapters later (Acts 8) the devil is seeking entrance yet again into the life of the Church through Simon the sorcerer, whom we've also already mentioned and discussed.

Satan knows that, if he can keep the root of all evil actively working in the Church, it will corrupt the nature of the tree, the work of God. The best thing we can do is allow our greed and love of money or covetousness to be burned up as the magic books were burned, which symbolized iniquity and evil profit, during a move of God in Ephesus.

"And many who had believed came confessing and telling their deeds. Also, many of those who had practiced magic brought their books together and burned them in the sight of all. And they counted up the value of them, and it totaled fifty thousand pieces of silver" (Acts 19:18-19).

I'm including this seemingly forgotten scripture because the Lord highlighted it along with Acts 5 and Acts 8 in the birthing of this book. This act of the burning of the magic books represented genuine repentance and deliverance at Ephesus from the love of money or the mammon spirit.

HAS THE CARNAL-PROSPERITY THEOLOGY FED INTO THE LOVE OF MONEY?

I want to highlight something Dr. Payne stated concerning *"prosperity theology"* in the aforementioned excerpt of his succinct article. I believe in true Biblical prosperity, and so I'm going to reword the term he used and call it *"carnal prosperity theology."* Here's his quote with my rewording:

> *"Let me take you a little further into what I see being played out, especially in many mega-churches and in the lives and preaching of more than a few televangelists. What many of these PR virtuosos have done is bait the hook with something people find as irresistible as lotteries, horse races, and mega-prize contests: namely,* **"carnal-prosperity theology,"** *which is to say, the* **carnal-prosperity gospel***. And it is so, well, utterly true-blue American because it cherry picks God's promises and marries them to entrenched American capitalist sentiments and practices. Of course, what I see happening is believers buying into a species of wishful and magical thinking which turns God into a faith-activated Cosmic ATM Machine or Father Slot Machine."*

The late Kenneth E. Hagin, called the Father of the Faith Movement, summoned a number of Charismatic preachers to Tulsa a few years before he died to warn them of the extreme teachings of the prosperity message that every one of them were guilty of. I've heard from some who were close to him that it broke his heart that his counsel was not received well and that these leading men stubbornly continued in the error of their ways.

Why wouldn't they heed the counsel of this General in the Faith? More than likely, it was because they had built much of their ministries on a wrong financial foundation, and it would cost too much to admit fault and reverse their steps. It would undermine much of what they had taught and done. This is the pride and iniquity that the Lord is putting His finger on in this hour, and it's what He showed my wife and me about Ananias and Sapphira and Simon the sorcerer. Actually, one of the Hebrew words for the word "labor," as in "vain labor," used in Psalms 127:1, is "iniquity." In other words, building God's house wrongly can be rooted in a form of iniquity.

"Unless the Lord builds the house, they labor (iniquity) in vain who build it..."

We need men today who are willing to lose their entire ministry, or crucify it and rebuild it if need be, rather than lose their place with God and their eternal reward.

Following is an article written by J. Lee Grady summarizing the book Brother Hagin wrote, *The Midas Touch*, which served to bring balance to Biblical prosperity.

Recent bizarre donation schemes and preachers asking their donors for tens of millions of dollars to buy the finest jets has brought the prosperity gospel back under the nation's microscope. It's time to revisit Brother Hagin's concerns and find a Biblical balance. Here is the article.

BEFORE HE DIED, KENNETH HAGIN WARNED AGAINST A MATERIALISTIC GOSPEL

By J. Lee Grady

Charismatic Bible teacher Kenneth Hagin, Sr. is considered the father of the so-called prosperity gospel. The folksy, self-trained "Dad Hagin" started a grassroots movement in Oklahoma that produced a Bible college and a crop of famous preachers — all of whom teach that Christians who give generously should expect financial rewards on this side of heaven.

Hagin taught that God was not glorified by poverty and that preachers do not have to be poor. But before he died in 2003 and left his Rhema Bible Training Center in the hands of his son, Kenneth Hagin Jr., he summoned many of his colleagues to Tulsa to rebuke them for distorting his message. He was not happy that some of his followers were manipulating the Bible to support what he viewed as greed and selfish indulgence.

Those who were close to Hagin Sr. say he was passionate about correcting these abuses before he died. In fact, he wrote a brutally honest book to address his concerns, which was published in 2000, a year after the infamous Tulsa meeting.

Many Word-Faith ministers ignored the book. But in light of the recent controversy over the prosperity doctrine, it might be a good idea to dust it off and read it again.

Here are a few of the points Hagin made in The *Midas Touch:*

1. Financial prosperity is not a sign of God's blessing. Hagin wrote: "If wealth alone were a sign of spirituality, then drug traffickers and crime bosses would be spiritual giants. Material wealth can be connected to the blessings of God, or it can be totally disconnected from the blessings of God."

2. People should never give in order to get. Hagin was critical of those who "try to make the offering plate some kind of heavenly vending machine." He denounced those who link giving to getting, especially those who give cars to get new cars or who give suits to get new suits. He wrote: "There is no spiritual formula to sow a Ford and reap a Mercedes."

3. It is not Biblical to "name your seed" in an offering. Hagin was horrified by this practice, which was popularized in faith conferences during the 1980s. Faith preachers sometimes tell donors that, when they give in an offering, they should claim a specific benefit to get a blessing in return. Hagin rejected this idea and said that focusing on what you are going to receive "corrupts the very attitude of our giving nature."

4. The "hundredfold return" is not a Biblical concept. Hagin did the math and figured out that if this bizarre notion were true, "we would have Christians walking around with not billions or trillions of dollars, but quadrillions of dollars!" He rejected the popular teaching that a believer should claim a specific monetary payback rate.

5. Preachers who claim to have a "debt-breaking" anointing should not be trusted. Hagin was perplexed by ministers who promise "supernatural debt cancellation" to those who give in certain offerings. He wrote in The *Midas Touch*: "There is not one bit of Scripture I know about that validates such a practice. I'm afraid it is simply a scheme to raise money for the preacher, and ultimately it can turn out to be dangerous and destructive for all involved."

(Many evangelists who appear on Christian television today use this bogus claim. Usually they insist that the miraculous debt cancellation will occur only if a person "gives right now," as if the anointing for this miracle suddenly evaporates after the prime-time viewing hour. This manipulative claim is more akin to witchcraft or hucksterism than Christian belief.)

Hagin condemned other harebrained gimmicks designed to trick audiences into emptying their wallets. He was especially incensed when a preacher told his radio listeners that he would take their prayer requests to Jesus' empty tomb in Jerusalem and pray over them there — if donors included a special love gift. "What that radio preacher really wanted was more people to send in offerings," Hagin wrote.

Hagin told his followers: "Overemphasizing or adding to what the Bible actually teaches invariably does more harm than good." If the man who pioneered the modern concept of Biblical prosperity blew the whistle on his own movement, wouldn't it make sense for us to listen to his admonition?

Can you see by these two articles how segments of the body of Christ have used the carnal-prosperity message to feed and fuel the love of money? Can you also see how unholy hype has been used to merchandise and market the anointing?

We have adopted the ways of the world to merchandise the sacred things of God. We've copied and Christianized worldly methods to reach the world (more on this in a later chapter on the wisdom of man *vs.* the wisdom of God). Why and how have we stooped so low? Do we realize how all this could negatively impact the ensuing generations of young believers?

We use worldly methods on Christian media to hype up what we think is the anointing, and we slap Jesus on it, and unbeknownst to many of us, He vomits it out. What Jesus vomits out, however, the immature swallow like little birds, and it breeds more immaturity. And once a generation passes, you have new leaders who wallow in carnality and compromise, thinking all the time it's the Lord. These are the things that kill ministries and steal their eternal fruit and rewards and affect future generations. The answer to all this hyper-spirituality is allowing mature fathers who understand the ways of God, the true anointing, and kingdom culture to lead us.

The problem is trust has been breached because of too many fallen leaders in mainstream pulpits. Meanwhile, frauds who have not yet fallen keep pushing their ministerial empires and personal mini-kingdoms. If you listen to them long enough with the ear of the Lord, you will discern that they are no better than manipulative car salesmen whose main purpose is to recruit more followers for their carnal and hyped-up agenda. Sadly, church and ministry growth-ism and popularity have trumped kingdom ways and kingdom culture.

DYSFUNCTIONAL AND FLAWED

We are dangerously dysfunctional and fatally flawed.

A ministry calling is not a career calling. True fathers in the faith are not interested in building your career. They're primarily interested in you being conformed to the image of Christ and helping you build character and a prayer life that will sustain you all the days of your life. Anything short of that is being fathered by lies and deception that are attached to a carnal and hireling agenda.

We've been guilty of taking the principles of the seven mountains (government, business, education, media, arts and entertainment, religion, and family) and canalizing them with the wisdom of the world.

But the Word says, love not the world or the things that are in the world (1 Jn. 2:15).

Don Lynch has it right again:

"Brand yourself, and promote your brand! Use the system to make more money for yourself and ministry at the expense of principles, processes, and protocols of kingdom culture. If you got it, flaunt it." Nope.

"Listen, some of you younger pioneers are being fed some garbage-dump slop about pioneering what is coming next. It is not even pioneering at all. It is just another personality-driven "Me, Myself, and I" show built with the same old tired system that promotes the frauds alongside the authentic.

"Get in. Get your part. Cash in on your anointing, prophetic revelations, and build your brand. Nope.

"Zero Bible on that stuff, my friends. Run far away fast, and find something that at least sounds like Jesus, Paul, John, Jude, and Timothy?"

Since when is ministry function done like social media marketing?

We need to re-examine our motives and priorities, and those people we've so blindly pledged our allegiance to follow. The Lord is truly wanting to move but only according to our oneness with Him and His ways — all for His glory and honor, which will also benefit us for all of eternity.

Not only have we been guilty of using worldly methods to merchandise the anointing and market a materialistic gospel, but, to further complicate matters, the Jewish message and mindset that both Jesus and Paul refuted has come back into view in the past century, which is the "gain is godliness" message.

EQUATING GAIN TO GODLINESS PRODUCES THE WRONG SPIRIT

Again, the root of all evil is covetousness or measuring your life by what money can buy you or make you — finding your identity in what you do and what you possess. And yes, even the kind of car you drive or house you live in. In many Christians' minds, these things are equated with spirituality and the blessing and favor of God. And to them it is proof or evidence of their godliness.

Jesus told the church at Smyrna that they were poor, yet rich (Rev. 2:9), and then he told the church of Laodicea, who prided themselves in their riches and wealth, that they were poor (Rev. 3:17).

I remember having a roommate in Bible school who was ashamed of me for driving an old beat-up car. It had a good functional engine and served me well during those years. He actually talked to me about it, telling me that it wasn't a good witness of God's blessings on his people. This is a small example of equating gain, such as a nice car, to godliness and spirituality — as if the proof of my salvation and sanctification is in the financial prosperity I possess, or in this case, the type of car I drive.

There is great insecurity and instability produced in people who measure themselves and others according to their status in life. Those who equate gain with godliness, much like the Jews did in the days of Jesus and the early Church, will develop a craving for more and more money, possessions, position, social status, and power, and will be enticed into pursuing it. They will be filled with unrest and inner turmoil as Lucifer was. True life and contentment will elude these people for the rest of their days on Earth until they return to the true Source of all life, Jesus Christ.

It's not wrong to be rich and have wealth, for God Himself gives us the ability to obtain wealth (Dt. 8:18), and, indeed, it can be a result of the fear of the Lord in one's life (Ps. 112:1-3), but notice again the instructions Paul gave to Timothy concerning the rich.

"Command those who are rich in this present age not to be haughty, nor to trust in uncertain riches but in the living God, who gives us richly all things to enjoy. Let them do good, that they be rich in good works, ready to give, willing to share, storing up for themselves a good foundation for the time to come, that they may lay hold on eternal life" (1 Tim. 6:17-19).

Paul is saying here that the rich should not go back to Judaism, where they trusted in their riches, thinking that they were righteous and approved by God because of their wealth. Instead, he admonishes them to be rich in good works, sharing and giving what God has given them.

In reality, *"the love of money"* has nothing to do with money, as such, but what money can be exchanged or traded for. It is difficult to define the problem outside of money, as the Jews understood it and as much of the Church understands it today.

A commentary of mine tells me that the Jewish worldview is that the entire universe, including man, is created in such a way that people climb the ladder of perfection systematically. They believe that, as man nears perfection, through his own efforts, God will help him attain a level that transcends his own limitations. Being set free from any nation that oppressed Jews and prevented them from attaining this so-called "prosperity" is, by the Jewish system, defined as "salvation" according to the Law, or the way to inherit the kingdom.

The Jews believed that poverty was uncivilized and a sign of disobedience to the Law. Poor people were considered sinners and despised and looked down on. Once again, as we've already previously noted, this is the reason the disciples were greatly astonished and confused when Jesus spoke of the difficulty rich men will have entering heaven and of the fate of the rich man in hell, while Lazarus, the poor beggar, went to heaven (Abraham's bosom). In the Jewish mindset, it was supposed to be the opposite: the rich man should be in Abraham's bosom and the poor beggar in hell. Again, this is because they believed that gain was godliness and that riches were proof of their spirituality. This doctrine has returned to a segment of the Church today in subtle form.

Imagine the lot of the poor in that day and how their life of absolute misery was seen as a public declaration of being rejected by God for not keeping the Law and achieving the righteousness it demanded. Also ingrained within the Jewish belief system was that the poor would go to hell and suffer for 12 months for their purification. When we understand this Jewish mindset toward wealth, riches, and poverty, we will be able to peer deeper into this mystery of iniquity and have a greater understanding of what the love of money produces.

THE "GAIN IS GODLINESS" MESSAGE HAS SPREAD TO THE NATIONS

The "gain is godliness" message has spread into other nations via America. For example, we've ministered in Africa for many years in several impoverished nations, and many of the poor Christians are now following their wealthy bishops' teaching and example of living a prosperous life. They are equating their wealth and possessions with God's favor, and many of them are striving to attain that in their own lives. This causes great pain and turmoil in many of them when they fail to attain these things, and it conjures up questions of why God is not blessing them with financial prosperity. This usually also produces an insensitivity to the poor around them as they seek to climb the prosperity ladder. This mindset and these excessive teachings on financial prosperity has done more harm than good in many ways and in many places. It has nurtured the worship of mammon. Like the Jews in Jesus' day, it can cause us to favor the rich and look down on the poor with disdain.

On one hand, we must remember the poor and teach them about the goodness of the Father to provide for them and bless them, but, on the other hand, they must also be careful not to equate it with godliness and being favored by God above those who may be even poorer. When my wife and I lived in one of these African nations, I remember sitting in a church service one Sunday morning and observing a well-dressed businessman not being able to find a seat after the service had already started. I watched the pastor remove a poor man from a chair in the front row so this rich man could sit there. Immediately in my spirit, James 2 was quickened to me.

"For if there should come into your assembly a man with gold rings, in fine apparel, and there should also come in a poor man in filthy clothes, and you pay attention to the one wearing the fine clothes and say to him, "You sit here in a good place," and say to the

poor man, "You stand there," or, "Sit here at my footstool," have you not shown partiality among yourselves, and become judges with evil thoughts?" (v. 2-4)

The Christians in that church probably thought nothing of this, since it was so ingrained into their culture, but in truth and fact, the leadership of that church had become judges with evil thoughts. I watched this church veer off from their pure, original calling as the spirit of mammon got hold of them. They grew in numbers and in finances, while congratulating themselves, but in reality, they had forsaken the true heart and worship of God.

Determining the true value of a person by worldly standards is showing partiality and having evil thoughts. This attitude abounds in Charismatic circles, where the carnal-prosperity message is taught. It fosters a cliquish exclusivity and class distinction.

THE RICH IN CORINTH

This was also the attitude in Corinth when the rich people refused to eat with the poor, so they ate in their homes before coming to their church gathering to partake of the Lord's supper (1 Cor. 11:17-31). Being European, they drank wine with their meal, and a few even got drunk before coming to the meeting. There was a class distinction threatening to divide them, and Paul was calling out the rich for bringing shame to the poor.

"What! Do you not have houses to eat and drink in? Or do you despise the church of God and shame those who have nothing?" (v. 22)

This kind of pride and arrogance displayed by the rich was causing cliques and strife and division within the Corinthian church. They were despising instead of discerning the body of Christ, which was made up of members from every background and walk of life. Paul concluded that this was the cause of illness and weakness among them and even of premature death. They were admonished to judge/examine themselves (1 Cor. 11:30-31) and repent of their partiality and evil thoughts.

The examining of themselves did not have to do with some secret sin they were engaged in or getting their slate wiped clean so they could partake of the Lord's supper. It had more to do with the rich, who refused to eat with the poor. They were not valuing and honoring the body of Christ and counting everyone as equal in the sense that Jesus died for them all. They were not esteeming their gathering as holy and sacred.

Paul quoted Jesus at the Last Supper by saying, *"Do this in remembrance of Me."* *Vine's Dictionary* interprets this to mean "an affectionate calling of the Person of Jesus Christ" that included every member who was sitting before them. Each member is a vital part of the body of Christ, and these Corinthians were to affectionately remember His body, who now were sitting among them in flesh and blood.

Isn't this what Ananias and Sapphira failed to do in the beginning when they introduced hypocrisy into the purity of the body of Christ? Outwardly they appeared to be someone of reputation, but inwardly, they were someone else. They did not value the purity and love that was saturating the body of Christ at that time. Surrounded by miracles and multitudes coming to the Lord, Ananias and Sapphira valued none of it but thought only of themselves.

Self-centered people cannot esteem the body of Christ as sacred in their hearts because they esteem themselves as sacred. If you esteem Christ, you will esteem His people. These rich Corinthian Christians proved that their hearts were closer to Ananias and Sapphira than they were to Jesus. Paul had to correct them lest they further divide the local body and be judged.

The love of money is the root of all evil because it causes us to evaluate ourselves according to what money can give us or make us. It is the head of the serpent, the root of all that is wrong in this world. If you stripped everyone of their riches and what riches had given them and made them, all that would be left would be their standing with God. We came into this world naked and with nothing, and we will leave naked and with nothing (1 Tim. 6:7). If we are not rooted in Christ, the true Source of life, we have nothing and are nothing, though we be rich.

Beware of the carnal-prosperity gospel and merchandising holy things, and of measuring yourself by what money has purchased for you or made you.

CHAPTER TEN

NEW THOUGHTS TO CONSIDER AND OLD THOUGHTS TO REVIEW ON THE WORSHIP OF MAMMON

"Now as He drew near, He saw the city and wept over it, saying, "If you had known, even you, especially in this your day, the things that make for your peace! But now they are hidden from your eyes. For days will come upon you when your enemies will build an embankment around you, surround you and close you in on every side, and level you, and your children within you, to the ground; and they will not leave in you one stone upon another, because you did not know the time of your visitation. Then He went into the temple and began to drive out those who bought and sold in it, saying to them, "It is written, 'My house is a house of prayer,' but you have made it a 'den of thieves.' And He was teaching daily in the temple. But the chief priests, the scribes, and the leaders of the people sought to destroy Him and were unable to do anything; for all the people were very attentive to hear Him" (Lk. 19:41-48).

Thus, judgment came to Jerusalem because they did not know their time of visitation. They did not receive their Messiah. He arrived in a package they failed to recognize. Jesus wept over Jerusalem for the tragic consequences that would be coming upon them.

In my studies and from reading several commentaries, the crooks in the temple enraged Jesus the most. Up to 4 million pilgrims flocked annually to Jerusalem to celebrate the Passover Feast. Each person or family was required to offer a sacrifice. Traveling with domestic animals was difficult, plus, if the priests found any blemishes, they were deemed unclean or unworthy. Thus, many people purchased lambs or doves in the temple at inflated prices.

Another requirement for Jewish males 20 years and older was the half-shekel temple tax (Ex. 30:12-16). Many males needed to exchange their money, since Roman coins were banned from the temple site because they bore Caesar's image, a violation of the second commandment concerning graven images. Money changers exploited the exchange rates to make bigger profits. Jesus' objection was not the selling of sacrificial animals or the necessary changing of money; it was the price gouging and the blatant fleecing of God's people. The fleecing of the sheep and failure to meet their deepest needs is at the center of many of the Church's problems today and are very personal to the Lord.

This practice had degenerated into a money-making scam. Dead formalism had replaced the sincere worship of God. Furious that people were being ripped off, Jesus wove a whip, and in anger and with shouting, drove the greedy merchants from the temple. One moment Jesus was weeping over Jerusalem, and then, shortly after, He was displaying His anger and fierce displeasure over the practices in the temple. Can you see the connection? What a great display of love and holiness, and of kindness and severity in the perfect blend of the Almighty.

Thieves are lurking near our temples today as well — filled with carnal thoughts, worldly attitudes, bitter envies and jealousies, selfish motives, and evil spirits trying to steal our passion and priority for prayer, intimacy with God, and for spiritual things. We, like Jesus, should use the whip of God's Word to cleanse our own personal temples.

The first-century money changers were in the temple, but they didn't have the spirit of the temple. Much as in a large segment of today's Church, they were preferring financial prosperity and profiting over prayer, trading holiness for hype, and probably preaching and practicing a "gain is godliness" message and a "God will bless you with riches" gospel. They loved money and materialism for what it could make them and do for them more than the honor of God alone.

Ministers today who are in the ministry for the esteem and honor of men will often use money to advance that motive. They quickly become a business with machinery, marketing, and organization having preeminence, and they default on being a true ministry built on prayer and the great commission. This attitude is prevalent and is the root cause of the evil system that has entangled a significant segment of today's church.

The Pharisees, in particular, were totally out of sync with the whole purpose of the Father's house. The Father's house is not a place to conduct business and make a buck. It is a house for calling on the Name of the Lord. It is also where the blind and lame come and are healed by the power of God and the deepest needs of people are met (Matt. 21:14).

The atmosphere in the Father's house is to be one of reverential prayer. The aroma from the incense on the golden altar before the throne of God is that of the saints on the Earth opening their hearts in worship, intercession, and supplication (Rev. 5:8, 8:3-5). It is this incense that produces holy fire in the hearts of men for the honor and glory of God alone. It is the great desire of God that this fire of intimacy would never go out. This alone will reduce and even eliminate human activity on the Earth and release divine activity through surrendered vessels.

THE DECEPTION OF EQUATING WEALTH WITH BLESSEDNESS

The problem and subtle deception today is when popular, self--seeking preachers equate their wealth and influence to their blessedness and favor with God and find their identity therein. This is a grave deception that has infected millions of people who follow these celebrity preachers and this doctrine. It is a crafty kind of darkness that originated in the Garden of Eden from the sensual wisdom of Satan. *"This wisdom does not descend from above, but is earthly, sensual, demonic"* (Jam. 3:15).

Again there is nothing wrong with having wealth, a prosperous business, or an influential church or ministry, as long as these things are sanctified and you do not use them as an identity and a measuring stick for true success. The moment you see them as evidence of your blessedness and favor with God, you have entered the realm of mammon worship and the subtle covetousness the Scriptures warn us about. This is usually the beginning of deception. God calls it "iniquity," and, for this reason, Jesus refers to some ministers as *"workers of iniquity"* (Matt. 7:22-23).

Let's remember again that this iniquity was first found in Lucifer and ultimately led to his fall.

"Thou wast perfect in thy ways from the day that thou wast created, **till iniquity was found in thee***"* (Ez. 28:15).

There are many hirelings and misguided ministers who preach the carnal-prosperity message, who manipulate the Scriptures on tithing and sowing and reaping, and who use gimmicks to extract money from people. They prophesy to gullible souls for a fee, twist the Word for selfish gain, and wrongly require seed offerings in exchange for the anointing. These preachers' practices steal from God's sheep and stem from their incessant desire for position and power and an honored reputation among men. They are a part of the modern-day den of thieves Jesus spoke of when He cleansed the temple. These impurities are rooted in the motives of the heart; they are defiling today's Church and diluting the real power and glory of God.

How is it that we have strayed so far from what Jesus and Paul preached, warning men of covetousness and the desire to be rich and refuting the "gain is godliness" message? How did we arrive at entertaining and receiving seducing spirits and doctrines of demons that string together a few obscure Scriptures to make up a be-all, end-all "gospel of riches"? To these false teachers, it seems disrespectful *not* to want to become extremely wealthy, since Jesus died so that we could all have wealth. They say that Jesus was made poor so we could be rich — as if deliverance from poverty was the proof of our spiritual salvation. Is that really the sum of what the Bible teaches?

This is a big part of what is defiling the Western gospel, my friends, and God has shown me that much of the excess and covetousness so common in the West today is rooted in this evil system. Let's remember that Jesus did not say, "Without money, you can do nothing." He said, *"Without Me you can do nothing* (Jn. 15:5)..."

To be clear, I am a holiness preacher who believes that it is God's will to prosper us and give us good success financially and otherwise (Jos. 1:8; Ps. 1:3), and I despise a poverty mentality. However, true Biblical prosperity has been perverted in much of today's Charismatic Church to serve the interests and idolatries of men, and this perversion is keeping the Church from experiencing the true glory of God.

The devil will fight to keep this dangerous doctrine from being fully exposed, or he will have people take it into the other ditch and develop a poverty mentality. I've already received some flak for this type of content I've written, as people fight for their *desire* to be rich, which has already been shown that the Bible condemns (1 Tim. 6:9). This verse is quite compelling to read in different translations, as I stated in an earlier chapter, when you realize the popularity of the desire for riches today.

The "gain is godliness" message that feeds the pride of man for position, influence, and power is not only defiling the Western Church but has spread like a plague to other nations as well.

THE DAMAGE OF THE CARNAL-PROSPERITY MESSAGE

I realize that there are many godly Christians, consecrated ministers, and great churches in the world today, but the extreme teachings and practices of some have brought much reproach to the name of the Lord and defiled His holiness. The carnal-prosperity message, the self-indulgent extravagant lifestyle of some who profess Christ, the focus on money, numbers, popularity, and influence, and the ministerial practices that take advantage of God's people, have diluted the impact and power of the gospel.

I have a good friend who ministers nearly every year in India for a large national apostolic organization that is making a tremendous impact on the poor and needy, planting hundreds of churches and training many to take the gospel into persecuted areas and thousands of unreached villages. Truly it is a sacrificial ministry, with many suffering for the gospel's sake. My friend asked the leading apostle and founder of this ministry what the greatest challenge was to the Charismatic church of India. Immediately and surprisingly, he told him that it was the carnal-prosperity gospel. Perhaps many Christians do not fully realize the extent of the harm and damage this carnal gospel has done.

This message that claims Jesus died to make us financially rich, that equates gain with godliness and spirituality, that encourages us to focus on our material prosperity and increase our earthly possessions is an utter perversion of the real apostolic gospel. Sadly, much of it has been exported from America to not only nations like India, but it has spread like a plague throughout Africa and other continents and nations as well.

To be perfectly clear once again, I believe in financial prosperity but not as a principal focus or foundational teaching in the New Testament. I also believe that God entrusts great Earthly riches to some of His people. I even believe that there are some God calls and anoints to be so-called "gospel entrepreneurs," who channel large amounts of money toward the work of God and larger projects to bless the poor and needy. But I also believe that there is probably not a more dangerous calling that requires such a holy consecration.

At the same time, I totally and completely refute the carnal-prosperity message, which deviates greatly from the message of the cross: death to the world and the flesh, and the call to forsake all to follow Jesus. The prosperity-gospel message makes Jesus our primrose path to financial and material success. This message, which some have peddled along with other questionable financial ploys and practices, has turned God's house into a house of merchandise and den of thieves.

Some of these celebrity ministers demand a certain guarantee of money before they can even minister in certain places. How can any minister in good conscience do this? Where is the Scriptural example and practice of it? A friend of mine who has a much-larger ministry than I do and who occasionally speaks in these circles told me some horrifying practices of a few of these big Charismatic personalities. Not only do they demand a certain size offering, but some of their requests range from being chauffeured in a Rolls-Royce to staying in a 5-star hotel, to hiring their own audio team to run their meetings, and then footing the bill to the church. One other minister I know of who owns a jet sent a medium-sized church his bill for the fuel, which was $10,000. The pastor was stunned, as this was not a part of the original agreement to minister and speak at his church. I will refrain from telling you how the host pastor responded and what he said, but it wasn't sweet, to say the least.

We could also place contemporary "Christian" bands and so-called "Christian" concerts in the same category. Most of them also make unreasonable demands to perform, and they operate much like these celebrity ministers. The problem is most of these ministries are not ministries at all — they're performers, and they function as a business and not a ministry. There's a big difference. They fall short of ministering the heart of the Lord. Jim Cymbala, one of the few mega-church pastors known for transforming the church he leads in Brooklyn, New York, into a true house of prayer, had this to say about musical groups who make merchandise of God's house and turn it into a den of thieves.

"I am dismayed by the contracts required by some contemporary musical groups. To perform a concert at your church, the stated fee will be so much (in either four or five figures) plus round-trip airfare — often First Class, not Coach. Every detail of the accommodations is spelled out, down to 'sushi for twenty persons' waiting at the hotel, in one case. All this is done so that the group can stand before an inner-city audience and exhort the people to 'Just trust the Lord for all your needs.'"

What hypocrisy! In this age of mega-churches, mega-ministries, mega-egos, and mega-money-making messages, we need a real wake-up call to get us back to the fabric of the real gospel and the apostolic message Jesus and the apostles preached and lived.

Here's a riveting quote, excerpted from an earlier passage in this book, that describes the extremes of this carnal gospel (with my own tweaks):

"What amazes me, and has for decades, are those carnal-prosperity preachers and teachers who try to transform Yeshua HaMashiach (The Anointed One Who Saves and Delivers) and His message from that of an itinerant rabbi, who warned His hearers against covetousness and spoke unceasingly of how the rich will have a very hard time making it to heaven — into a prosperous Potentate who wants every believer to get stinking rich." [Thank you, Dr. Anthony G. Payne. Well spoken.]

FACTS TO CONSIDER

Jesus said no one can serve God and mammon. He even said it would be very hard for servants of mammon and those who trust in riches to enter the kingdom of heaven (Matt. 6:24, Mk. 10:23-24).

Paul said to withdraw from those who preach that gain is godliness. He told Timothy to flee the troubles, sorrows, and dangers that derive from this deceptive teaching (1 Tim. 6:5-10). He even warns against the *desire* or the *longing* to be rich.

Have we forgotten that Lucifer was once a perfect being? He was very rich, existing in the same domain as God, and having everything he could ever desire. According to Ezekiel 31, he was the greatest tree in the garden of God. However, when his heart was lifted up in his stature, iniquity flooded his inner being, and it corrupted him; thus, he fell from his holy position and his heavenly abode. The iniquity found in him speaks of the envy and jealously that was in his heart for position and power. He wanted to be number one in hell instead of number two in heaven.

Since money did not exist in the Garden of Eden, we can substitute for "money" anything that would take the place of our marriage and union with God. The belief that something outside of God can replace our oneness with Him is the iniquity mentioned here in Lucifer, expressed as the *love of* money or merchandise.

Jesus said to those who sold doves in the temple, *"Take these things away! Do not make My Father's house a house of merchandise!"* (Jn. 2:16). The house of prayer, meant to provide the satisfaction of intimate communion with God, had been traded or substituted for something else — all for the glory of man.

Here are some more facts to review and consider:

Judas made a practice of stealing money from the treasury, giving access for Satan to enter his heart and betray Jesus for even more money (Jn. 13:2). A covetous heart will always prefer money and power more than intimacy with the Master. What a compelling contrast to Judas John the Beloved was as he leaned his head on Jesus' breast at the last supper, signifying his desire for intimacy with his Lord (Jn. 13:23-25).

Satan filled Ananias and Sapphira's heart to lie about money so they could be esteemed in the eyes of men (Acts 5).

Simon the sorcerer offered money in exchange for the power of God for the same demonic reason (Acts 8).

Lucifer was perfectly created and beautiful in every way and moved in and out of the presence of God. Judas walked with Jesus for three years. But they both allowed the love of money to destroy their eternal destiny. What makes you think that *you* will not succumb to the same evil and covetousness that comes from serving mammon and not God?

If Ananias and Sapphira as well as Simon the sorcerer, who in the midst of powerful and glorious moves of God, allowed jealousy and iniquity into their hearts because of a desire for prestige and an honored reputation among men, who do we think we are to be immune to such? As with every generation, God will deal with the pride, greed, and covetousness in man.

SECTION III

THE PURGING AND REFINING

OF CHARACTER

CHAPTER ELEVEN

THE REFINER'S FIRE

"Behold, I send My messenger, and he will prepare the way before Me. **And the Lord, whom you seek, will suddenly come to His temple,** *even the Messenger of the covenant, in whom you delight. Behold, He is coming, says the Lord of hosts. But who can endure the day of His coming? And who can stand when He appears? For He is like a* **refiner's fire** *and like launderers' soap. He will sit as a refiner and a purifier of silver; He will purify the sons of Levi, and purge them as gold and silver, that they may offer to the Lord an offering in righteousness"* (Mal 3:1-3).

The first messenger the above verses refer to is John the Baptist. Through the message of repentance, he prepared the way for the first coming of the Lord Jesus Christ. Similarly, there will be a company of John the Baptist-like preachers of righteousness who will prepare the way for the Lord's second coming.

The second Messenger, which is capitalized in most versions of the Bible, is the Lord Jesus Christ Himself, who will suddenly come to His temple. This phrase *"the Lord will suddenly come to His temple"* has a twofold application. The first temple was the one He cleansed at the beginning (Jn. 2) and near the end of His public ministry (Matt. 21, Mk. 11, Lk. 19). The second temple was the body of man that would house the mighty Holy Spirit subsequent to Christ's resurrection. Believers today are His temple or house.

"Know ye not that ye are the temple of God, and that the Spirit of God dwelleth in you?" (1 Cor. 3:16 — KJV)

"In whom all the building fitly framed together groweth unto an holy temple in the Lord..." (Eph. 2:21 — KJV).

"Ye also, as lively stones, are built up a spiritual house, an holy priesthood, to offer up spiritual sacrifices, acceptable to God by Jesus Christ" (1 Pt. 2:5 — KJV).

After waiting on God for a number of days, the Lord suddenly came to His new temple in the power of the Holy Spirit and filled 120 vessels (bodies of men and women).

*"And **suddenly** there came a sound from heaven as of a rushing mighty wind, and it filled the whole house where they were sitting. Then there appeared to them divided tongues, as of **fire**, and one sat upon each of them. **And they were all filled with the Holy Spirit** and began to speak with other tongues, as the Spirit gave them utterance...."* (Acts 2:2-4).

The cleansing of the temple toward the end of Jesus' public ministry was a preparation for His crucifixion and the finishing of an old-covenant, fruitless religious system. It was also a preparation for the resurrection and ascension of the Lord Jesus Christ as well as the initial outpouring of the Holy Spirit. In other words, the old temple, made of gold and silver and other man-made materials, and the fruitless system it represented, would be permanently destroyed, and God would now dwell in man. God is preparing His people in the same way in this hour — dealing with the carnal and fruitless religious systems of our day and calling His people out.

In the above passage of Scripture, the Lord Jesus Christ is likened to a **Refiner's Fire**. This fire is also symbolic of one of the Holy Spirit's functions. John the Baptist made this statement:

"I indeed baptize you with water unto repentance, but He who is coming after me is mightier than I, whose sandals I am not worthy to carry. He will baptize you with the Holy Spirit and fire. His winnowing fan is in His hand, and He will thoroughly clean out His threshing floor, and gather His wheat into the barn; but He will burn up the chaff with unquenchable fire" (Matt. 3:11-12).

Fire is a refiner and purifier. We are now in a very critical time in the body of Christ — when the **Refiner's Fire** must do its work. There must be a thorough cleansing in the Church today in preparation for the return of the Lord and the glory that is yet to come.

A NEW SPIRITUAL DOOR IS OPENING

A few years ago, as my wife and I were praying, she saw a very large door and heard a distinct squeaking sound as it turned on its hinges. It was an ancient spiritual door that had not been opened in a long time. We believe it is similar to the spiritual door that opened in the time of Jesus' birth. After 400 years of silence, with no prophetic vision or revelation, since the days of the prophet Malachi, a large door began to open, and God finally began to speak through certain consecrated individuals.

"And behold, there was a man in Jerusalem whose name was Simeon, and this man was just and devout, waiting for the Consolation of Israel, and the Holy Spirit was upon him. And it had been revealed to him by the Holy Spirit that he would not see death before he had seen the Lord's Christ. So he came by the Spirit into the temple" (Lk. 2:25-27).

This old man, Simeon, was waiting for the Consolation of Israel. The phrase "Consolation of Israel" is linked to the redemption of Israel that some in Jerusalem were looking for (Lk. 2:38) and of the kingdom of God (Lk. 23:51). Prior to the time of Jesus' birth, there was a "remnant" in Israel who had revelation of what was coming, and they were waiting. The Consolation of Israel involved the coming of the Messiah and the revealing of salvation for all nations (Lk. 2:29-32). Simeon even knew by revelation that the Gentiles would be offered salvation as well (v. 32). This was unheard of in those days, as the Jews had been God's chosen people for centuries of time. Many Jews never received this revelation of the salvation of the Gentiles, even when it came through Jesus and the apostles.

Anna was another old woman, a prophetess, who received revelation by the Spirit of God concerning the coming Messiah.

"Now there was one, Anna, a prophetess, the daughter of Phanuel, of the tribe of Asher. She was of a great age, and had lived with a husband seven years from her virginity; and this woman was a widow of about eighty-four years, who did not depart from the temple, but served God with fastings and prayers night and day. And coming in that instant she gave thanks to the Lord, and spoke of Him to all those who looked for redemption in Jerusalem" (Lk. 2:36-38).

Notice how Anna spoke of Christ to *"all those who looked for redemption in Israel."* A large spiritual door had now opened.

WITH EVERY OPEN DOOR COMES THE RELEASE OF DIVINE ACTIVITY AND ALSO ADVERSARIES

Try to imagine the divine activity that was suddenly happening in Israel during the time of Jesus' birth. Besides this revelation that was given to Simeon and Anna, there were warnings and direction given in dreams to the wise men and Joseph (Matt. 1:20; 2:12-13, 19-20, 22). There were angelic visitations granted to Zacharias, father to John the Baptist (Lk. 1:11-20), the virgin Mary (Lk. 1:26-38), and the shepherds (Lk. 2:9-15). There were in-fillings of the Holy Spirit (Lk. 1:41, 67) and prophecies (Lk. 1:42-55, 67-79). Remember, this kind of divine activity had not happened in about 400 years.

As it was in the time of Jesus' birth when a huge door was opened that resulted in all this divine activity — as it was when Jesus began and fulfilled His public ministry about 30 years later, as it was in the days just prior to and after His crucifixion and resurrection, as it was in the days of the initial outpouring of the Holy Spirit, and as it was in the time of the early Church, so will it be in the last days, just prior to the second coming of the Lord. But as it was during the time of these events 2,000 years ago, when only a remnant knew and understood these things, and there were also many adversaries, much opposition, and demonic activity, so will it be in the last days just before Jesus' return. Many will not be ready, and the opposition will be great as Satan's lease on the Earth shortens.

And as the Lord prepared His remnant and revealed to them the time of His birth, so He is preparing His people today for that which is yet to come. Isn't it interesting that nearly a generation later after the birth of Jesus, many still did not receive Him as the Messiah? Many did not receive their time of visitation (Lk. 19:41-44), and it resulted in their judgment. Interestingly, it was immediately after Jesus pronounced judgment on Jerusalem that He cleansed the temple for a second time, as Luke records it (Lk. 19:45-46). But it was the chief priests, the scribes, and the leaders of the people who vehemently opposed Jesus and sought to destroy Him (v. 47-48). And so it is today as the time of Jesus' return draws nearer.

We are now in a time of preparation for the coming crisis of last days events, especially as it pertains to the judgment of the world, the final harvest, and also the glory that is to come. There are a company of John the Baptist-like messengers who are of the spirit and power of Elijah (Lk. 1:17), and who function as a **Refiner's Fire** by the power of the Holy Spirit, which will cleanse and purify those who receive their words and ministry.

Let me say it another way: Before the worst shall come and the day of darkness encompasses us about, there will be those who shall be sent by the Lord, who shall carry the fullness of His truth and fire, not only to America but to other nations. For there is a work that must be done — first and foremost spiritually — before the Lord returns. This work has already begun.

THE REFINER'S FIRE

Notice the expression, *"He will purify the sons of Levi, and purge them as gold and silver, that they may offer to the Lord an offering in righteousness"* (Mal. 3:3). This is a very important word, especially for ministers. Lives and destinies are at stake, and a new spiritual door has been opened, but we cannot walk through it unless we are willing to yield to the **Refiner's Fire**.

As my wife and I were praying for a sick minister recently, the Holy Spirit cut in. He began to teach us by revelation the reason ministers often don't enter into the fullness of their callings and why sometimes even their lives are cut short. This is what He said: " *There are reasons why men were limited and didn't enter into the times and seasons of their lives. There are limitations through character. Over and over again, I deal with men, but until they're put under the* **Refiner's Fire** *and My dealings, they cannot go into that new season, and walk in that new place."*

What a word.

The Lord has turned up His **Refiner's Fire** on our own personal lives and ministry. He has spoken to us more thoroughly and more urgently about our love walk, our words, our lifestyle, and our diet.

These things do matter, friends, if we want to fulfill the call of God on our lives and enter into the fullness of our ministry. These things are important if we want to run our race and finish our course with joy.

When you allow the **Refiner's Fire** to deal with your soul, fleshly strongholds, attitudes, and emotions, then the devil cannot have a handle on you. Actually, it is because of God's mercy and protection that ministers often don't receive a greater anointing and glory on their lives and ministries, for with it comes a greater judgment. To whom much is given much will be required, and ministers receive a greater condemnation (Lk. 12:48; Jam. 3:1). History is littered with casualties of mightily anointed men who left this Earth prematurely and whose callings were aborted for lack of the **Refiner's Fire**. God was merciful in taking some of them home early so their fruits could be saved and their works could follow them.

Let me give you an example of God's dealings with us from our own lives, so you can learn from it. A few years ago, when we were ministering in another nation, two ministers asked my wife and me how a certain mutual minister friend of ours was doing. We told them that we had heard he was now divorced and that his adult children had backslid. In the past, this divorced minister preached frequently and had a platform in the nation we were in. The Lord told us our comments could rob him of favor and future opportunities to minister in that nation.

We didn't know the details of the divorce, nor did we know if the minister was at fault, or if he was, whether he had repented. You are siding with Satan, the accuser of the brethren, when you accuse others after they've repented. Many ministers would think nothing of making comments like this, but the Lord does. We repented before the Lord and apologized to those two ministers the next day.

Some may not think of this as a big deal, but our attitudes, words, offenses, and dealings with other ministers and the body of Christ in general are important in determining our health and whether we enter into the fullness of what God has planned for our own lives and ministries. Yielding to the **Refiner's Fire** will take us into our next assignments, open doors, and new levels of blessing and glory that God has ordained for us.

The gifts and callings of God are without repentance — meaning God will not change His mind about your calling and purpose in Him, but the fullness cannot be seen in a man's life until he goes through the **Refiner's Fire**. Ministers need to go to the altar again and live from there. In order for ministers to go through certain doors of utterance of greater glory, they have to be refined, not easily offended, and not given to any carnal appetite. It's the Lord's protection for your life and ministry.

Years ago, in an extended time of prayer and fasting, the Father told me that He had not opened certain doors for me because of His protection. Then I wept when He said that I would've ceased to be a man after His own heart had He opened those doors when I wanted Him to (I share a little more about this in the next chapter and more in my book *The Journal of My Journey to His Holiness*). He is a good Father. He will not give us instructions that He knows we cannot obey through our insufficient character, thus giving access to the enemy to legally attack us. Parents do not give their elementary-school children instructions fit for a college student. Lack of maturity of character limits what they are able to do and obey.

Moses was a great example of a minister who moved in the flesh, killing a man to deliver his brethren from bondage, and as a result he spent 40 years in the **Refiner's Fire** on the backside of the desert. God had big plans and a high calling for Moses, but he could not fulfill it until the **Refiner's Fire** had done its work in his life. There is a difference in how God deals with us in the New Covenant versus the Old Covenant, but the principle remains the same. In the Old, God trained His people through frustration and hardship in the flesh, but in the New, it's through the Spirit in the new creation, although tests and trials certainly play a part.

Let's not judge other men, but let us judge ourselves (1 Cor. 11:31).

THE REFINER'S FIRE DEALS WITH THE HEART

"I counsel you to buy from Me gold refined in the fire..." (Rev 3:18).

What I'm saying is that there is a **Refiner's Fire** for the Master's use. This authentic fire deals with the heart. It removes veils of blindness and deception and brings awareness of where the heart really is. I saw this in the Pensacola outpouring in the 1990s. Many did not understand this fire because it came with many unusual physical manifestations. Critics of that revival got bound up in their thinking, focusing on the manifestations instead of what was happening in the hearts of the people.

"That the genuineness of your faith, being much more precious than gold that perishes, though it is tested by fire, may be found to praise, honor, and glory at the revelation of Jesus Christ..." (1 Pet 1:7).

Pure gold is soft and bendable. That is what the **Refiner's Fire** does; it makes the heart like that. Pure gold shines the brightest and reflects the light of God and of His kingdom. These refined hearts and lives make the most powerful witnesses on the Earth.

It's the Word and the Spirit functioning together that will activate the workings of God in people. When the Spirit of God is not allowed to move or manifest, there is no **Refiner's Fire** that turns hearts to pure gold. The Word and the Spirit is what cause this great preparation in every heart. For it is the Word that brings the instruction, correction, and reproof, but it is the Spirit that makes everything new, fresh, and alive again while burning out the chaff or the dross. Baptisms of fire burn away the chaff, until only the wheat remains. The sin, the mental strongholds, the traditions of men, the lusts of the flesh, and impurities of the heart, like pride, covetousness, jealousy, and every form of iniquity, are burned away in the **Refiner's Fire**.

The **Refiner's Fire** brings out the pure gold. It removes your blind spots and causes you to see. And it always results in a purity. And it is the pure in heart who see God (Matt. 5:8) and are not deceived.

Here's a personal word from the Spirit of God that moved in our hearts:

*"Look at the age of men you've admired. Look at their natural age and when they began to have a great impact. According to their degree of yielded-ness and holiness is how I used them. Flaws were overlooked because of their greatness in the anointing. That is why you must go to the **Refiner's Fire** and be purified more. For some things in your flesh will still cause some to stumble. Greater shall be the impact from things that fall off in the **Refiner's Fire**. Fleshly strongholds caused many to die an early death — lack of **Refiner's Fire**..."*

What precious, living words born in prayer and from conversations with God!

It is dangerous for ministers to have a strong anointing on their lives and not be in the **Refiner's Fire** and possess the character that matches their calling. Remember that God's gifts and callings are irrevocable. He will not take away the calling and the anointing that He has ordained for your life (Rom. 11:29). If someone with a strong calling and anointing on their life is not yielding to the Holy Spirit in the **Refiner's Fire** or praying to be more like Christ, his fleshly flaws could send him to an early grave.

The Lordship of the soul is taken away in the **Refiner's Fire**. There is a surrender and a submission to God. As I said, in the Old Covenant, this was done through discipline, hardship, and frustration experienced in the flesh. Moses and the children of Israel wandered in the wilderness for 40 years as a means of being refined through leanness of flesh so their souls could be brought low (Ps. 106:15). The blood of Jesus Christ had not yet been shed, and the Spirit had not yet come and quickened them, so God had to deal with them according to the deadness of their spirits.

In the New Covenant, this work is done through the exaltation of the spirit of man, where the seed of the nature of God matures until it takes over the soul and the flesh of a man. God will not work this in a man without his consent. If men will not yield to the Spirit of God and the **Refiner's Fire**, the work will not be done in them. Furthermore, if they will not yield but continue to pray to be conformed into the image of Christ, then God will have no choice but to send hardship and frustration in the flesh to accomplish the goal of submission, as He did in the Old Covenant.

Think about it. Even the original apostles of the Lamb were trained according to the deadness of their spirits. During the Earthly ministry of Jesus, none of them were born again yet, so Jesus had to deal with them differently. He taught them directly and trained their soul first. It wasn't until the Spirit had been imparted to them that they were trained in spirit by the Holy Spirit.

Frustration and leanness of the flesh as well as powerlessness in ministry will often bring men to a low place, where they are willing to surrender and go to the backside of the desert. Paul was an example of that in the New Covenant. Even with the Holy Spirit helping him, Paul came to a place where he was willing to surrender the reins of his soul and intellect and be trained on the backside of the desert. There he received great revelation of the New Covenant post-resurrection realities and the mysteries of God. He went to the **Refiner's Fire** and qualified himself for greater use to the Master who had called him.

This is a life-saving, ministry-saving word so that the body of Christ, led by the Ephesians 4:11 ministers, can mature to fullness of stature and bring the life and power of God to a lost and dying world.

CHAPTER TWELVE

THE SMOKESCREEN OF MINISTRY

HIDING REAL ISSUES

I want to continue addressing ministers in this chapter. The words you read do not come from one who has a personal axe to grind or a bone to pick, but they come from a heart that has been broken and transformed, and needs God's grace every day to remain in Him. I love the body of Christ, and I love fellow ministers. Knowing the obstacles and resistance one must continually overcome in ministry, in this season of my life, it is a great joy for me to see ministers fulfilling their callings in a maximum way to benefit and bless the body of Christ. In order to do that, a minister has to be stripped of every veil that has blinded him to his true identity in the Lord and to what godly success really is.

Are you paying close attention to your spirit and personal life, or are you caught up in the natural things of life, the world, and the smokescreen that ministry tends to produce? Look within, and examine yourself to see if you are really in the faith (2 Cor. 13:5). Are you being honest with yourself and living in the sight of God? Do you have sufficient communion with the Holy Spirit to even do that? Is your heart open to the dealings of God that comes through the Refiner's Fire? What do I mean?

TOO MANY MINISTERS ARE HIDING UNDER A FALSE PRETENSE

Many ministers are like spiritual orphans, standing in their pulpits and instructing others in spiritual things, while they themselves are lacking in spirituality. They are hiding behind a cloak of anonymity, where their real character is kept hidden and unknown to the public.

Many are like actors, with dual personalities, using the stage of ministry for a cover-up. Even sadder is that their spouses are compelled to cover up their failures at home and their real character issues while feeling trapped in a world that forces them to put up a front for the ones they minister to. What a prison that must be.

Not everything is as it appears. We have learned that in ministering to many people in many places over the years. Nearly everyone has a front. Nearly everyone wears a mask. Nearly everyone puts their best face on and their best foot forward in public. Nearly everyone will place themselves in the best possible light in their conversations with others. Everyone wants to look good and be esteemed in man's sight — so often at the expense of defiling themselves in the sight of God. My wife and I have personally been there, and have left there, and don't ever wish to return.

God is extending His hand to help many leave this place. It is an awful burden and yoke to carry. I believe it could be the biggest part of being burdened and heavy laden, and never having any inward rest, as Jesus said in His invitation to come to Him.

"Come to Me, all you who labor and are heavy laden, and I will give you rest. Take My yoke upon you and learn from Me, for I am gentle and lowly in heart, and you will find rest for your souls. For My yoke is easy and My burden is light" (Matt. 11:28-30).

BEING FREE FROM ONE OF THE BIGGEST HUMAN BURDENS

I believe the greatest burden all humans carry, outside of sin and trying to obtain salvation through their own self-efforts, could very well be self-image and self-esteem and the pretension and projection of a public persona. This is still an aspect of being under the law and being more conscious of yourself than you are of the Lord and others, and it rules the lives of so many. Jesus extends His invitation to be free from these yokes of man and the law, and to take on His yoke. A part of His yoke is to quit tinkering with your own soul by getting your eyes off yourself and learning to behold Him. This creates grace in you.

"But we all, with unveiled face, beholding as in a mirror the glory of the Lord, are being transformed into the same image from glory to glory, just as by the Spirit of the Lord" (2 Cor. 3:16).

If you humble yourself under the mighty hand of God by making the Lord Jesus Christ your all-sufficiency, and with an unveiled face behold Him, the Spirit of God will begin the process of transforming you into His image. The enemy will no longer have a handle or grip on your soul and access into your life through these false perceptions, pretensions, and projections. Beholding the glory of the Lord means to look on Jesus and His divine attributes, especially as you read of Him in the gospels, and allow His image to be shaped and formed within you by the Spirit of God. Gradually you will be free from the fear and approval of man. You will learn of the meekness and lowliness of the Son of God, and you will no longer fear abuse and rejection. After all, Jesus was the most abused and rejected of all men, and yet sinless and blameless in all His ways. He is very familiar with this state of suffer-ing and temptation in man.

"Therefore, in all things He had to be made like His brethren, that He might be a merciful and faithful High Priest in things pertaining to God, to make propitiation for the sins of the people. For in that He Himself has suffered, being tempted, He is able to aid those who are tempted" (Heb. 2:17-18).

This transformation begins with learning to commune with God from your spirit and receive the love of the Father. In order to do this, you've got to surrender more and more of yourself to Him, especially the public perception of your life and ministry. Serve Him from a position of already being loved and not from a position of trying to earn His love and approval.

The Holy Spirit, who is our Helper, will help you put on the image of Christ and die to your own perceived public image. It takes an initial surrender and coming under the dealings of God to strip you of all self-sufficiency, that will lead to years of burdens being removed from your shoulders and walking in a freedom you've never known before.

"When God brought me into a deeper experience with Him, He spoke by the Spirit, making me to know I had to reach the place of absolute yielded-ness and cleansing so that there would be nothing left." — Smith Wigglesworth

We are living in a time of an increased inordinate desire for an esteemed reputation among men and self-promotion — and where there's been an absence of the judgments of God, some people live in the lie and hypocrisy of Ananias and Sapphira and Simon the sorcerer all their lives. They are never really fully aware of it (refer to the introductory chapter of this book again). Masks of religion and veils of hypocrisy are all too common in today's superficial church culture and are counterproductive to the honesty, transparency, and unveiled face it takes for transformation.

Notice the expression in 2 Corinthians 3:16: *"with unveiled face, beholding Him."* "Transparency" is another word for "unveiled." No hiding. What happened to Adam and Eve must *not* happen to us. Adam and Eve hid from the presence of the Lord. In hiding, the veils hid God from them.

Transparency is the essence of true fellowship and freedom in the Lord. It is only in allowing your own heart to be exposed that you can walk in the light as Jesus is in the light. True fellowship with the Lord requires complete transparency. The same principle is true in our fellowship with others. It can hurt to be open and honest with God, yourself, and with others, but it is the sure pathway to lasting peace, freedom, stability, and wholeness. Many are deceived and unaware of the layers of pretension and hypocrisy that have kept them from being transformed into the image of Christ.

Furthermore, you will never really learn to commune with God from your spirit until you cultivate a sensitivity to Him and pay attention to those things He has put His finger on that keep coming up when you pray or talk to Him. This is part of your sanctification. It takes time to learn to commune with the Lord effectively, where there is little mixture from your soul and emotions. The beginning of this life change came about in my wife in 1995 and in me in 2002, when we came under the dealings of God concerning pride, selfish ambition, and the desire for the honor and approval of men. Of course, this is an ongoing work, but the power of it was first broken off of our lives during that time. This led to a great transformation, in which we began to operate and walk in the Spirit much more than we had before.

CAN LEADERSHIP BE OVEREMPHASIZED?

I know the question sounds preposterous since it's the popular teaching of the day that says everything rises and falls with leadership, but please hear my angle on this and what Scripture actually emphasizes. We have all met ministers in our lifetime who are stuck in the pride of who they are, or in their justification of error or wrongdoing. Influential leaders want to maintain their influence, and non-influential leaders are striving to become more influential. Influencing people toward God is commendable, but often pride and dark motives, as seen with Ananias and Sapphira and Simon the sorcerer, are lurking in our hearts. It's such a circus merry-go-round — everyone wanting to be influential and a success like the world counts success. And most of our conferences and seminars feed that awful ego of man.

Think about the time and money spent on such leadership conferences and seminars. It's a billion-dollar industry even in Christendom. Do we really need another book on leadership development? Can someone please point out clear Scripture references where we are to emphasize leadership, leadership, leadership? What about following Jesus? What about being His disciple? What about servanthood and obedience alone, and not as a stepping stone to leadership? Aha! But it is leadership that sells. Submission, servanthood, and obedience don't. We are to raise up faithful *followers* of Jesus, not faithful *leaders*. There's been much error in the way we train and lead others through overemphasis on leadership. Frankly, as I said, it feeds the ego and pride of man.

Must you always have your title attached to your name? Is your first name "Apostle," or "Prophet," or "Doctor," or "Bishop"? With all due respect for those who have earned or truly function in what these titles entail, must you flaunt it? Are you not happy just to be known or called by your first name or "Brother or Sister so and so"? It's nauseating to see the excess in what has become the pomp and pageantry of modern-day ministry.

The truth may be that you are an orphan in your own pulpit, making feeble attempts to lead others when you are in such a broken state of confusion yourself and mired in your own image and inordinate desire for success. But I love you and want to help you as God has helped me.

ORPHANS IN OUR PULPITS

We have a serious ministry problem, worse today than it's ever been. Fake ministers. Fake love. Fake faith. Superficiality and a lack of transparency and accountability. Years ago, I would've spoken out strongly against this, but now my heart breaks and weeps when I see how some got to be this way.

Through abuse, or a poor upbringing, hurts, rejection, failure and disappointment, unfulfilled desires, misunderstandings, and lack of validation, many project an image they want others to see — an image of a strong and confident leader who knows the Word of God and has it all together. Often their resume and life/ministry experience contain a list of accomplishments and achievements that belie the real truth of who they are.

Some ministers and leaders need constant validation and affirmation to prod them forward. Their peers must know how successful they are. Their peers must honor and respect their gifts and ministry. If not, they will subtly exalt themselves in self-aggrandizement to hide the real issues, insecurities, and fears of their own hearts. It's sad. Perhaps these are the minority; I'm not so sure anymore. You can be the judge of that. But I would call them "spiritual orphans in our pulpits."

These orphans can rarely be wrong. They are hesitant to admit their own mistakes. It is difficult for them to receive correction. Their leadership or personal life can never be challenged, even by friends. They defend their right to be who they are and justify their actions. There is very little accountability in their lives, because they make sure to surround themselves only with "Yes" men who constantly affirm them. To me, more often than not, these are symptoms of orphan hearts. In some way, many of us have experienced these things or have had to fight through them, but the Spirit of God wants to set us permanently free from this unnecessary burden.

Here's the mindset of orphan hearts. Often, many of us feel that, in order to be accepted, we must wear masks of perfection — especially in the context of public settings. Our modern society and media-driven world has taught us to curate and edit our lives, on and offline, in order to present an image to the world that we "have it all together." But in the process of curating this unrealistically perfect life — we find ourselves exhausted, isolated, and craving genuine connection that allows us to be known and accepted just as we are. In a world that applauds productivity, multitasking, and accomplishment, our culture is constantly pushing us to "do more" and "buy more" so we can "be more," causing us to "stress more."

The Word of God and the wisdom of Christ push back against this sort of culture by challenging us to create space in our lives by taking up His yoke. Grace is essential to overcome this soulish drive, but the first step is to refuse to hide away as Adam did when he sinned, and remain in fear, guilt, and shame. God loves us, accepts us, and works with us where we are to deliver us from such. With an unveiled face, let us behold His glory and be changed.

WARNING: BE CAREFUL WITH CON ARTISTS AND OPPORTUNISTS

Sometimes I don't know what to do with all the social-media requests for friendship and favors of one kind or another I receive, especially from ministers and pastors overseas. On one hand, as a minister myself and elder in the body of Christ you want to help those God calls you to help, but on the other hand, you don't know them, and from having lived on the mission field for years, I know there are many con artists and opportunists looking to latch on to anyone whom they consider to be in a position to help them, especially financially.

My heart has grown softer over the years toward these types of individuals in that the Lord has shown me that many of them are just spiritual orphans. Yet I know they are making the same mistake as many "ministers" here and the world over, in trying to fill their orphan hearts with position, titles, accomplishments, influence, power, significance, and on and on...you can fill in the blank.

Finding your identity in anything but the love of the Father is a disease, not necessarily and initially due to any fault of their own, but as I said, due to conditions of neglect, abuse, unfulfilled desires, or lack of validation and affirmation from others, especially a father. And many times, it is just a result of having grown up in abject poverty. That is when my heart really softens and Scriptures like Matthew 7:12 roll and rumble within me.

But I cannot coddle those opportunists (again, I'm not saying all are this way; there are a few genuine) or stroke their misidentified need for attention and affirmation and favors to build their personal kingdoms. That's not what they need. In fact, that may be the cruelest thing you could do to them. It will do more harm than good in the long run. Their greatest need is to be stripped of the layers of substitutes they've directed their inordinate desires toward that are replacements for the love of the heavenly Father and finding their identity in Christ alone.

In reality, most have never followed the leading of the Spirit into the wilderness and the school of testing and suffering. Jesus set that example, and John the Baptist right before Him. Think of it. We talk about having spiritual fathers, and, of course, I'm all in favor and have always seen the great need for them. But who fathered John the Baptist? I know he may be an anomaly, but the example is there, nonetheless. He was groomed in the wilderness for what virtually amounted to a six-month ministry. This training was critical for him to fulfill his call as the forerunner to Christ and true friend of the Bridegroom.

What of Jesus? A lifetime of submission to His Heavenly Father, but the 40 days in the wilderness was the clincher. Nothing to eat to feed the flesh, no one was following Him, no one to minister to in order to validate His place in the kingdom, no likes and shares on social media to affirm His approval (smile), no admiration from any beautiful women, no children to play with, etc. Just wild beasts — types of demons to harass Him.

That's the wilderness, my friends, and for us it can mean different things. But it's a type of testing so that no substitutes for our relationship with the Father remain. In my humble opinion, this is one of the greatest needs for all ministers today and one of the things we must pay closer attention to in equipping the next generation.

We are sending the wrong message and offering the wrong training to young preachers. Our paths are crooked. The focus has been on what we can do and who we can become — in other words, on the glory and deification of man, instead of the honor and glory of God. We talk about impartations, activations, anointings, and authority without the strong foundation of prayer and fasting and of the worth and excellence of the intimate knowledge of God. The constant modern focus of what God will do for you to make you great and fulfill all your dreams has trumped the deep desire to win and gain Christ, as Paul did (Phil. 3). This wrong focus will make orphans out of all of us.

Orphans will produce other orphans. False identities will produce more false identities. False apostles and prophets will produce other false apostles and prophets. We've got to get this right, or many more ministers will spend their lives on the performance treadmill, attempting to receive the validation of men at the expense of the validation of God. It will cost many their eternal reward.

MY PERSONAL TESTIMONY

I was an orphan, so I know of what I speak. In 2002, the Lord opened my spiritual eyes and delivered me after an extended time of prayer and fasting. In an inward vision, I was looking up through a glass ceiling at all the things I wanted in ministry — power, anointing, favor, significance, influence, etc., but the Lord directed me to the floor and my foundation. He spoke to me at length about my character, saying such things as:

"The reason I have not opened the doors you've wanted me to open for you in ministry is because if I did, you would have ceased to be a man after My own heart."

I broke down and wept when I realized He was keeping me from greater ministry opportunities, power, and influence because of His love and protection for me. He also said this:

"Take away 'ministry' over the last 17 years, and what do you have? Your character has not been sufficiently dealt the death blows that it will take to properly develop it to where I can impart to you the mind of Christ. You need more mortification to receive the mind of Christ."

When I heard this, I realized He was requiring crucifixion and death to what I perceived I wanted and for me to return to Him as my first love.

"Nevertheless I have this against you, that you have left your first love" (Rev. 2:4).

(My testimony and personal transformation are detailed in my book *The Journal of My Journey to His Holiness*).

IS JESUS ENOUGH FOR YOU?

Let me ask you a question: Is Jesus enough for you? If you didn't have a ministry, a vision from God, an esteemed reputation or occupation, a list of achievements you're proud of, riches, and possessions, how would it be with you? And if you don't have those things now, why are you so desperately reaching for them? Have you found your fulfillment in Him alone? And how would you know if you have?

More heart-searching questions, especially for younger ministers:

Why are you always talking about yourself? Why are you always defending who you are and what you do? Is it difficult for you to recognize the achievements of others and the honor they receive? Is it painful to celebrate a friend's success and accomplishments because you perceive you don't have as much? If so, you may be a spiritual orphan. You are insecure and need so badly to find your security in Christ and in the love of the Father. When you're secure in His love and who you are in Him, you want to lift up everyone else except yourself. You honor and respect others even when you're not honored and respected. You can take the lowest seat without feeling slighted and wash others' feet as Jesus did when your security is in Him alone. This is a miraculous transformation of major proportions.

You don't need further validation or the affirmation of friends. All that has done is cover up the real issues of your own heart and life, and cause the deception to become thicker. You need the outstretched hand of the love of the Father God to deliver you from the bondage of your mind and soul, and fill your heart with His glory. You need a fresh revelation of His deep love for you. You need to hear the words, *"This is my son or daughter in whom I am well pleased."* Yes, men will honor you and validate you, but then it doesn't move you in the wrong direction of pride or feed your sense of self-importance.

Full healing and restoration in a man or woman happens when they become established in the image of Christ and in the Father's love — and then have no need to be honored or affirmed by anyone. The honor of God will be enough. Jesus will be your all-sufficiency. This work can be done only through the meditation and revelation of His Word and in the closet of true prayer and tender intimacy with the Lord. It is a process that takes time, faith, and patience, and usually happens in the wilderness and through tests and trials. And it will work such a humility in you.

When they asked the people of the Yoido Full Gospel Church, in Seoul, South Korea, perhaps the largest numerical church in the world, what they loved the most about their pastor, Dr. David Yonggi Cho, they said it was his humility. When he makes a mistake, sins, or misses it with God, he stands in front of the congregation and asks for forgiveness, they said. How rare that is today, especially among leaders of large churches and works.

Why am I saying all these things? Because as I grow older, I not only want souls to be saved, but my heart grows increasingly burdened for ministers who are called to save souls. They should be the primary agents of change and reformation in the Church and society, exemplary models of Christ-likeness, but ironically, often they are the main hindrances. If change doesn't happen in them, it won't happen in many others because leaders transmit and impart what they are to others. In other words, if you save a ministry gift, you also save souls. If leaders don't change, God will allow the systems they have built with their own hands to come tumbling down and new works will be built through those who have truly humbled themselves and who've been content to labor in obscurity. God is going to shake everything that can be shaken, including the old political, backslid, ecclesiastical systems, and the formal mega-church structures. And He will judge all those who are engaged in self-serving and self-promoting ministries. It is those who've submitted themselves to the Refiner's Fire, who, after having preached to others, will not be disqualified (1 Cor. 9:27).

Real deep and lasting change is birthed in all of us when we begin seeing things as God sees them. Full restoration in a man begins with this revelation that leads to true repentance and surrender. When your character is refined and strongholds broken, there will be nothing for the enemy to hang on to. You will cut off his access into your mind, life, and heart. You will be free from the accuser and your past. Once you repent and die to your own reputation, the devil will have nothing to hold over you. You will be completely and permanently free as you abide in Him.

As I've said, the Lord saved the gifts in my wife and me from a certain defilement a number of years ago. We humbled ourselves and came under the deep dealings of God. It was painful. Sometimes there is a season of pain we must endure to lay everything down at the altar. As ministers, we have to be willing to lay down even our ministries and churches for a season if need be and be willing to reveal to the people where we went wrong.

Orphan hearts are everywhere. They fear the disapproval of men because they have not embraced the approval of God that comes when they humble themselves in His sight. Come to the Father, and allow His Spirit to anchor you in His love. I can testify that many old, life-long burdens will be removed from your soul and you will enjoy a newfound freedom and rest you've perhaps never had before. On that day, your greatest rejoicing and honor will simply be that you are no longer an orphan in bondage to fear but a child of God who has re-ceived the spirit of adoption and the love of His Father.

"For you did not receive the spirit of bondage again to fear, but you received the Spirit of adoption by whom we cry out, 'Abba, Father.' The Spirit Himself bears witness with our spirit that we are children of God" (Rom. 8:15-16).

IS THIS THE ROOT OF ALL OUR PROBLEMS?

When is the last time you walked into a roomful of people and all you thought about was them? *How can I be a blessing to them? How can I make their day? How can I help lift their burdens and bring joy and encouragement to their heart?* How deep can a man go into self-lessness, where he is no longer concerned about himself, thinking of himself — thinking of ways to get ahead, to put himself in the best possible light in all conversations and appearances, to look good, to impress others and to project an image of himself that perhaps belies who he really is? Did Jesus ever live a day with that sort of mindset?

Why do men do this? Could this selfishness and self-focus be the larger part of what Jesus came to free us from?

Is not this self-consciousness the larger part of the bitter fruit of what the law produces? Is this not what the devil bombards us with in moments of insufficiency, so that our sufficiency would be placed in ourselves instead of Christ? And is not cultivating a God-conscious-ness and beholding the glory of the Lord, as in a mirror, with your heart, the solution toward the sort of radical transformation Jesus came to bring (2 Cor. 3:18)? Is this not the bigger part of what it means to grow up into Him and mature?

"Let nothing be done through selfish ambition or conceit, but in lowliness of mind let each esteem others better than himself. Let each of you look out not only for his own interests, but also for the interests of others" (Phil. 2:3-4).

Is not coming to Him and learning to abide in Him what produces selflessness in our lives and a blessed rest, where we quit striving to be someone, to achieve something, to be great as the world counts greatness?

Here's where much of the body of Christ is at today:

"For ye are yet carnal: for whereas there is among you envying, and strife, and divisions, are ye not carnal, and walk as men?" (1 Cor. 3:3).

We argue, we fuss, we find fault, and we have a tendency to excessively engage in strife, disputes, and disagreements. Much of this is due to envies and jealousies, and comparison and competition with others. The root of this is plain self-centeredness and glorying in ourselves.

"He who speaks from himself seeks his own glory; *but He who seeks the glory of the One who sent Him is true, and no unrighteousness is in Him"* (Jn. 7:18).

God wants to purge us from seeking our own glory so we can seek His glory and grow up into Christ.

Our strife and division may be our most frequent and consistent witness to the world. But listen to what Jesus said:

"A new commandment I give to you, that you love one another, even as I have loved you, that you also love one another. By this all men will know that you are My disciples, if you have love for one another" (John 13:34-35).

How did Jesus love us? He denied Himself totally and completely to reconcile us to God. He brought to us the highest life by a firm committal to His death on the cross. His deepest motivation was to go as low as He could go to lift us up as high as we could go — the lowest death producing the highest life. He endured this death because we were His joy.

"Let us look to Jesus, the author and finisher of our faith, who for the joy that was set before Him endured the cross, despising the shame, and is seated at the right hand of the throne of God" (Heb. 12:2).

Should not this be our aim — to be like Him? To be conformed to His image? To love as He loved? How else will the world know that we are indeed Jesus' disciples (John 13:35)? It is time for this message to come to full maturity in the body of Christ and among His servant leaders.

Many churches are known for many different things. Some are known for prophecy or their charismatic gifts, some for their benevolence and outreach, some for their good singing or great preaching, etc. But how many are known for their love, not in word but in deed? For it is the revelation that we are loved by Him that will ultimately produce the beginning of this transformation in our lives. We must constantly be receiving His love in order to release His love. The greatest glory we can experience on the Earth is to know how loved we are by God. When we live loved, we will manifest His love to others.

When you truly commune with God and His Word, you lose what you don't need and gain what you need in His presence. You lose those burdensome, weary, burned-out physical and emotional feelings that come from constant striving and the unripe fruit of what each day can bring, and you gain real rest in your soul that comes from His grace and knowing His love. The following verses, quoted earlier but appearing here from a different Bible translation, blesses me immensely and gives me a glimpse into real freedom:

"Are you tired? Worn out? Burned out on religion? Come to me. Get away with me, and you'll recover your life. I'll show you how to take a real rest. Walk with me, and work with me — watch how I do it. Learn the unforced rhythms of grace. I won't lay anything heavy or ill-fitting on you. Keep company with me, and you'll learn to live freely and lightly" (Matt. 11:28-30, MSG).

If you do not get established in the image of Christ and grounded in the love of God, you will be like many other Christians. They pray and worship regularly, read the Bible faithfully, attend church consistently, and constantly show God how much they love Him, but still have no peace and mental freedom. What's the problem?

The revelatory truth of how much they are loved by God has not yet gripped them. They see themselves through their own weaknesses and shortcomings, or what they perceive as a lack of accomplishments and achievements, instead of through the eyes of the love of Christ. As I stated earlier, their pursuit of God is from a position of somehow try-ing to *earn* His love instead of from a position of *already being* loved.

Here is one of the greatest prayers that we can pray for ourselves and for one another that will change that:

*"That He would give you, according to the riches of His glory, power to be strengthened by His Spirit in the inner man, and that Christ may dwell in your hearts through faith; that you, **being rooted and grounded in love**, may be able to comprehend with all saints what is the breadth and length and depth and height, and to know the love of Christ which surpasses knowledge; **that you may be filled with all the fullness of God**"* (Eph. 3:16-19).

Notice the connection between knowing the love of Christ and being filled with all the fullness of God. Knowing the width, length, depth, and height of His love that passes your intellectual knowledge is how you will come to be filled with all the fullness of God. This is the greatest transformation anyone can receive in this life.

To be filled with the revelation of God's love is to be filled with all His fullness. There is nothing greater. As disciples of Jesus, we've got to move past identifying ourselves with anyone or anything outside of Christ — whether it be our failures, our greatest achievements/accomplishments, man's acceptance and approval, what we do or don't do, our jobs/careers and status in life, our churches, ministries, finances and so on — and move into a full-fledged identity with His love.

The heart that knows he is loved by God the Father and the Lord Jesus Christ ceases to look elsewhere for love, peace, and satisfaction. His delight is in the Lord. He has found his dwelling place and his rest in Him. When you receive a revelation of His deep love for you, it will put a pure delight and contentment in your soul. It is then that you will truly live free and full.

NOT ALL MINISTERS AND PASTORS ARE ORPHANS: SOME ARE JUST ABUSED

In closing this chapter, I'd like to share the other side of what I've witnessed in years of missionary service and in itinerant ministry, traveling to many churches. I'm going to share what many local pastors would like to share with their people but often don't or can't. There are some hirelings out there who leave God's sheep vulnerable and unprotected from the wolves, but there are also plenty of good shepherds.

"And I will give you shepherds according to My heart, who will feed you with knowledge and understanding" (Jer. 3:15).

I believe the Lord is saddened by how quick people are to criticize and degrade His local shepherds. It is certainly true that shepherds or pastors are real people with their own shortcomings and flaws, but I believe most people have no idea of the sacrifices most pastors have made to do what they are doing. They have no idea of the pressure they are under to meet a varied myriad of unspoken superhuman expectations by the people they serve. Most people just don't realize the heartbreak many pastors often endure at the hands of those they have poured so much time and effort into. They don't realize the constant criticism they endure from those who feel they know better and could do better. Moreover, most are clueless of the toll that ministry has taken on their own marriage and families.

Furthermore, many people are totally unaware of the countless hours pastors have prayed, the hours spent with marriages in crisis, families that are broken, rebellious teenagers, hospital visits, funerals, visitations, personal counseling, phone calls, or encouraging broken-hearted people who've been affected by some sort of tragedy or the death of loved ones. And yet they are constantly expected to be present at every prayer meeting, committee meeting, and church-wide event, as well as to be available in late hours, seven days a week — regardless of personal life or family schedule. Most do not know of the stress they carry to make sure all the church bills and staff are paid and that the offerings are enough to meet the budget.

Too often the common perception is that the pastor does next to nothing but teach the Bible a couple of times a week. The impression that most people have is that the average pastor works a few hours a week at most. He gets paid for very little effort, and he must make up for that by not living in a nice home or driving too new or nice of a car.

By far, most of the pastors I have known over the years have been above-average people who have given up much more than the normal person to do the will of God. Though far from perfect, most have been humble, God-fearing, and self-sacrificing. They have bypassed better opportunities, better income, and easier vocations with much less stress. They are expected to do what no one else wants to do, make up whatever is lacking in the church that everybody thinks needs done but no one else is willing to do. They mow lawns, move chairs, answer phones, visit people in distress, clean toilets, fix problems, and always have to be in a good mood for everyone else who isn't.

The next time you want to criticize one of God's shepherds or pastors, remember these things.

So not all are orphans; some are just abused.

CHAPTER THIRTEEN

THE WISDOM OF MAN VERSUS THE WISDOM OF GOD

The first order of life for every minister and saint is to put all your trust in the Lord — to keep your eyes on Jesus. That's so easy to say, easy to agree with, but many fail to see the importance of such a simple statement and the transformation it can bring to our lives.

"Blessed is the man who trusts in the Lord" (Jer. 17:7).

"Cursed is the man who trusts in man" (Jer. 17:5).

Modern Christians do not understand the distance of contrast between those two statements. "God helps those who help themselves" is about the only verse many can quote concerning this theme. Oh, wait a minute — that's not a Bible verse, is it?

Western Christianity is infamous for what it has been able to do without God. We know how to raise money and produce results; we're slick with our sales and know how to promote our product or service; we know how to market our churches and ministries, and the list goes on and on. We are experts on almost everything, or at least we think and act like we are. We boast in our accomplishments. We love to talk about things we know, experiences we've had, our own status, important places we've been, and important people we know.

Many are not happy unless they are talking about themselves, seeking for others to recognize them, acknowledge them, and be impressed with them. As stated in the last chapter, we are always trying to project and maintain a positive image of ourselves and hide that which we don't want people to see about us. When that positive image is threatened or challenged, we are so quick to defend ourselves — always careful to put ourselves in the best possible light.

Why is looking good and impressing others so important to us? If we can identify and extract that root of pride,we will have won a major victory and increase our chances a hundredfold of staying on the path of life.

The world and so much of our Western culture breed self-centeredness into us. We glory in ourselves. We worship man. Image is far too important to us. That is why God has chosen to reveal Himself through foolish things, the weak things, the base things, and the things that are despised. If He didn't, we would glory in our flesh (1 Cor. 1:26-29). There's a reason Jesus was born in a stable, where animals are, and not in an inn or a palace. There's a reason he was raised in the despised town of Nazareth. There's a reason he chose unlearned and uneducated men to train and commission.

In a scripture I quoted in the last chapter, Jesus said, *"He who speaks from himself seeks His own glory..."* (Jn. 7:18a).

Another way to say that would be, "He who speaks from himself glories in man and trusts in man."

The wisdom of man dominates our thinking. We think being clever and smart is the wisdom of God. The Western way and the "Western Gospel" have taught us that. But "smart" is often in conflict with the true wisdom of God. "Smart"may even be ugly, sensual, and devilish because it can be so man-centered. The wisdom that is from above is not self-seeking (Jam. 3:14, 16).

Let me simplify this even more for you. The beginning of the wisdom of God is when you fear the Lord and are not wise in your own conceits(Pr. 1:7, 3:7). Paul was a very learned man but put no confidence in his own flesh or "smarts." The fear of the Lord produces that in a person and is manifested when your eyes are fixed on Him and you put all your total trust in Him. That is how you get saved, and that is how you are to live. That is so easy to forget and lose sight of.

What troubles and heavy burdens would be released from us if we would simply learn to keep our eyes on Jesus. Much of this has to do with our projections and pretenses — projecting a positive image, pretending to be someone we're not, and always seeking to impress — as we've already discussed.

The wisdom of God affects how we relate to man. Most people, even Christians, govern their fellowship with man based on what they can get from them, not on what they can give. Here's a great truth: Eyes on man binds things up; eyes on the Lord looses things up in people's hearts and lives, and in our times of assembling with other believers.

Yes, as the body of Christ, we do receive from one another, but our faith and trust is to be in the Head of the body, Jesus. You don't put pressure on people or manipulate them to meet your needs or to serve your own agenda. You don't position yourself to receive some favor from them. You don't do any of these things even with the person you're closest to — your spouse. This happens in ministry and in life all too frequently.

When I was young missionary, I'd go to church or ministry conferences and catch myself trying to get close to someone influential or of financial means, or a pastor of a large church — in hopes they would help me, support me as a missionary, or promote my ministry in some way. I'd see others exchange their business/ministry cards and play the old game of "You scratch my back, and I'll scratch yours." When the Lord would let me see what I was doing, it was all so ugly to me. These things are all a manifestation of putting our trust in man.

Through the years, I've swung more in the other direction of making it more difficult for man to help me or promote me, not mentioning or even subtly hinting of my own personal needs to anyone unless asked, and just being content with a hidden life in God. Oh, what peace comes when your motive is no longer to be seen or heard — when you just don't care about whether men recognize you, promote you, or favor you. What peace comes when all you care about is being known by God and walking in obedience to Him. Oh, how I wish I had learned that lesson earlier and better! But God is gracious, patient, and long-suffering with each of us, isn't He? That's why I love Him so much.

Something as simple as not placing your total trust in the Lord is the reason for so much of the strife, division, and competition in the body of Christ and among ministry peers. That's why, in some cities, there are churches on every street corner. It is also the reason your mind has no peace or rest. It is all because men seek their own and not the things which are Jesus Christ's (Phil. 2:21). They've got their eyes on man and on themselves.

Have you ever asked yourself this question: Why do most people desire to minister in their gifts above their personal relationship with God? Why do people esteem talent above character? Isn't it because they desire an honored reputation above relationship? Isn't the root of this a desire to be seen by men and honored by men rather than live a private life with God, as Jesus first taught (Matt. 6)? These things are all a by-product of the "gospel of me" heard in the West and our self-centered culture. It is rooted in trusting in man. It is a departure from the Lord and making the arm of flesh our strength.

As you meditate on this and the rest of this chapter, allow the peace of God that comes from His wisdom to fill your heart and mind.

THE WISDOM OF MAN HAS NO MARKS OF THE CROSS

The wisdom of man has no marks of the cross. What do I mean by "marks of the cross"? The apostle Paul said that he bore the marks of the Lord Jesus or the cross on his body.

"But God forbid that I should boast except in the cross of our Lord Jesus Christ, by whom the world has been crucified to me, and I to the world....From now on, let no one trouble me, for I bear in my body the marks of the Lord Jesus" (Gal. 6:14, 17).

Whether one has actual physical marks on his body or not doesn't matter. Rather, the evidence of a "cross walk" is that you are dead to the world, its systems, and its supposed wisdom. This is what marks the core of a true disciple's life.

There is precious little in much of mainstream Western Christianity today that is cruciform or cross-centered in our theology and practice. Where is the cruciform life among us, where self-denial, servanthood, suffering, and sacrifice are shaping our lives? The cross, representing the crucifixion of Jesus Christ, is the soul-shaping substance of the genuine Jesus disciple. How does this tie in with the wisdom of God?

Sometimes there are spiritual deficiencies in the body of Christ that are not so easy to see or detect or articulate. For example, there are many things that sound good in Christendom today, even among so-called "Spirit-filled" people that have nothing to do with God. Some of our biggest "Christian" celebrity preachers and popular mainstream voices fool many people with their words. Just because someone has a reputation among men doesn't mean they are favored by God or even sent by God.

For instance, as I stated in the last chapter, "leadership" is always a hot topic, and everyone seems to want to excel in this area. Many will read some of the most popular leadership books by prominent authors and take whatever they write or say as gospel. Here's a recent quote on Twitter I read from a mega-church pastor:

YOU KNOW YOU'RE A HIGH-CAPACITY LEADER WHEN:

1. You Create

2. You Take Risks

3. You Live Your Passion

4. You Never Give Up!

This quote was retweeted hundreds of times by mainly Christians, many of them leaders and ministers. Honestly, that is a worldly and carnal quote. There is none of God's wisdom in it. It is not the mind of Christ. It is not cruciform. It is the way of the world. Heck, many entrepreneurs and highly successful business people do that. Anyone who has made a lot of money and obtained status and prestige in the world possesses those characteristics.

C'mon, saints! We've got to have more discernment. So many Christian people and so-called "ministers" don't even know the heart of the Lord. Whatever happened to cross-centered theology and practice? Whatever happened to self-denial, obedience, and even suffering so that others can be helped and served? Whatever happened to the real wisdom of God and the soul-shaping substance of the cruciform life of the genuine disciple? But as I said, it's "leadership" that sells. Once the Church becomes familiar with the true wisdom of God, the wisdom of man will be very distasteful to us. Most of the wisdom of man is filled with man's agenda to get ahead.

Some of the greatest Christians I know do not even have a platform in ministry. You'll never see them on TV or read books about them. You'll never hear of them in this life. They suffer and lay down their lives every day so that others might live. Some are just faithful husbands, fathers, wives, mothers, and sons and daughters who go to work every day to provide for their families. Some are praying grandmothers whom no one knows. Many of them just live normal, regular lives, but they are esteemed in God's eyes.

Let's quit being fooled by man's worldly wisdom and get real close to Jesus and learn His heart and ways.

In this day of great human ingenuity, it takes the wisdom of God and knowing His heart and ways to discern the difference between what is of man and what is truly of God. We are easily fooled by principles and techniques and the modern machinery of man that can be used effectively in man's own strength and prowess to accomplish great things — all without the Holy Spirit's involvement. We label so many things as originating in God when, in fact, God has nothing to do with it. We take pride in our own knowledge and abilities, or we are naive and lack godly discernment. For example, just because something is new, big, and grows fast does not necessarily mean it has its origin in God. It may even be emotionally thrilling, intellectually stimulating, and very financially and numerically successful — all without God's involvement. Savor this wisdom so that you will cultivate more discernment in your life.

Let's understand that there are principles, which, when implemented by anyone, will get results. The problem is not the principles, per se, but the motivating power and ethics behind the principles. Whom do they honor? Whom do they serve?

Human nature is easily fooled by a charismatic personality, the energy he exudes, the projection of a strong ministry gift, and crowd-stimulating and mind-controlling techniques. For example, often when people feel an excitement in a corporate assembly, they make the assumption that God is there, but that is not necessarily so. This happens many times, especially when the music or what we label "praise and worship" is emotionally stimulating. We believe and appreciate excitement that is born of the Spirit of God, but it can be difficult for a casual observer to discern the difference between what is of the flesh or the soul of man and what is truly of the Spirit.

Recently I came across a list of principles that shed much light on the very subtle differences between the world's version of wisdom versus the kingdom of God's version. In the words, I recognized these principles as the difference between man's wisdom and God's wisdom. Following is a contrast of those differences.

- The wisdom of man provides an identity in yourself. The wisdom of God establishes our identity in Christ.

- The wisdom of man provides a sense of uniqueness, specialness, and personal destiny. The wisdom of God admonishes us to lay down our lives and to shun personal advancement and self-aggrandizement.

- The wisdom of man provides strong leadership and a charismatic leader figure to follow. The wisdom of God delivers us from false identities and an inordinate dependency on man.

- The wisdom of man uses stimulating music and songs as a tool to rally people to a great cause or project. The wisdom of God uses music and songs to worship and glorify God, not human interest or selfish ambition.

- The wisdom of man calls us to great, world-changing endeavors. The wisdom of God calls us to die daily; it's irrelevant whether that involves greatness to change the world.

- The wisdom of man motivates us to overcome obstacles, challenges, and adversity (even the world does this). The wisdom of God leads us to the One who is our all-sufficiency, admonishes us to rejoice in Him in our trials, and overcomes evil with good by loving our enemies.

- The wisdom of man is capable of challenging us to personal discipline, hard work, and sacrifice. The wisdom of God instructs us to yield to our new spiritual nature and tells us that we can do nothing without Him.

- The wisdom of man calls us to greatness. The wisdom of God defines greatness as being the servant of all. Jesus is worthy whether we are called to be great or small as the world defines it.

- The wisdom of man conducts large-scale meetings to impart vision. The wisdom of God leads us to New Testament life and Scripture, which emphasizes being like Christ and being conformed to His image as the vision. (Do you realize there's not one New Testament Scripture on vision? Knowing Jesus intimately and making Him known is the vision. I know this is a shocker to some people, but Jesus modeled leadership by laying down His life for others, not by presenting a vision. (Calvary is the vision). The vision is doing what God tells you to do.

- The wisdom of man provides enticing speech and heightened oratory to inspire and stir people to a mission. The wisdom of God teaches lowliness and humility and a mutual laying down of our lives for each other as the ultimate virtue.

Do you know what releases maximum potential in the body of Christ, so that we are built up and equipped for service? It is lowering yourself and serving others as being more important than you. This is what brings complete restoration in the body of Christ.

The contrast that I show here between the wisdom of man and the wisdom of God is not intended to quench godly motivation and inspiration to a God-directed cause or a mission, but to show you the subtle differences between a man-centered and a God-centered methodology. The world uses some of these principles and techniques with great success and often for good causes, but we must understand that there is a subtle but large gap between what is good and what is God.

There is nothing cruciform or cross-centered in the world's methodology, and yet much of the Church has been guilty of very subtly imitating the world. For example, I've been to leadership conferences that are very similar to conferences the world conducts. The principles they teach, though often worded differently with Christian terminology, are the same as the world's. I've also been to "Christian" concerts that are similar to the world's concerts in that the spirit and motivating factor which gives it impetus with those in attendance is the same. The only difference is that we attach God to our concerts and emphasize the cause behind it. Much of it, however, is self-serving, driven by some ulterior agenda.

• The wisdom of man is popular and appeals to the flesh. The wisdom of God is hidden and must be searched out.

• The wisdom of man glories in the might, power, and riches of man, but the wisdom of God glories in the Lord.

• The wisdom of man often has the appearance of good and smart, while the wisdom of God esteems the foolish and weak things of the world that most cannot see or discern.

- The wisdom of man is aligned with the will of man and looks pretty and sophisticated, but in truth, it is actually more aligned with the glory of this world. The wisdom of God is aligned with the will of God and has the marks of the cross on it — humility, brokenness, sacrifice, and total dependency on God.

Here is a description of the wisdom of God:

"For you see your calling, brethren, that not many wise according to the flesh, not many mighty, not many noble, are called. But God has chosen the foolish things of the world to put to shame the wise, and God has chosen the weak things of the world to put to shame the things which are mighty; and the base things of the world and the things which are despised God has chosen, and the things which are not, to bring to nothing the things that are, that no flesh should glory in His presence" (1 Cor. 1:26-29).

The Bible shows a clear pattern in which God does not use the best, the most talented, the smartest, or the most expected and likely to succeed in the flesh. Even Moses was so insecure that he didn't want the calling God was offering him. Rather than using the most qualified, the pattern is that God uses the least qualified and least likely to succeed in the flesh, the insecure, the flawed, the depressed, the doubter, and the underdog, so that no man will glory in the flesh or in himself. Every single person can make a difference, especially those who think they can't. That is the wisdom of God.

AN EXAMPLE OF A MAN MOVING IN GOD'S WISDOM

Years ago, I read a testimony of a man who prayed in the Holy Ghost (tongues) hours upon hours every day. By edifying himself to such an extent, this man put himself in a position to hear from the Lord and to receive the interpretation and revelation of what he was praying. He was called to the ministry and was seeking the Lord for direction. He had a very small cassette-tape ministry at this time and not much money. Here are the instructions he heard from the Spirit of God:

"Take up no offerings from these people. Sell no tapes. Mail everything freely, and do not even put in a return envelope. Never let a human being know of any needs that you have. I am your Source! If you will precisely obey these instructions of Mine, I will speak to the hearts of the people I choose to support both you and the needs of the ministry." — Gary Carpenter

Now the Lord does not speak to everyone the same way, but this is a wonderful and compelling example of unconventional wisdom given by the Spirit of God to a man of prayer. The wisdom of God often comes wrapped in that which seems illogical and even foolish to man. Based on the contrast I've made in this chapter between God's wisdom and man's wisdom, can you see how the instructions this man received from the Lord are cruciform, bear the marks of the cross, and fit into the wisdom of God? This is so rare today.

Many times, the wisdom of man will even masquerade itself as a great opportunity for more influence, power, and money, but, again, it has no marks of the cross.

EXAMPLES OF OTHER MEN WHO UNDERSTOOD THE WISDOM OF GOD

Here are four other examples of men who understood the wisdom of God and refused such good and glamorous opportunities in order to obey God.

1. Many years ago, Dr. Billy Graham was offered 6 million dollars by someone to build a university. After praying about this offer, which was contingent upon building a university, he rejected it because it would have interfered with his evangelistic calling. Sadly, most minis-

ters today would probably not even pray about an offer of considerable means like that, and to refuse it wouldn't even be an option. Dr. Graham loved souls more than mammon, and obedience to God was most important.

2. Mr. J.R. and Carmen Goodwin, affectionately known as Dad and Mom Goodwin, pastors of an Assembly of God church in Pasadena, Texas, in the 1950s and 60s, were offered television time to widen the influence of their prolific and supernatural ministry. They prayed about it, and the Lord let them know that this was not His will for them.

Again, most ministers today wouldn't even pray about such an opportunity but would automatically assume that it was a promotion from the Lord. After all, how could such an opportunity to reach many more people not be from the Lord?

The Lord's ways are not man's ways. The Lord's wisdom is not man's wisdom.

3. Smith Wigglesworth, to whom I've already referred in this book, reached the world from his humble home in Bradford, England, in the first part of the last century. God never told him to have a big organization, build a large ministry headquarters, or squeeze money out of people to support his ministry. On the contrary, he gave away much of the offerings he derived from his ministry to missions works and the poor and needy.

4. Then there's the late Kenneth E. Hagin's reluctance to build a Bible college, even though the Lord directed him to do it. He begged God to let someone younger than him do it to no avail.

He never wanted to be a prophet. He never wanted a big ministry. For a man who was widely known for teaching faith, healing, and Biblical prosperity, few know of the spiritual stature and maturity of this General of Faith. Unlike multitudes of ministers today, he never wanted the limelight. Here again is the direct quote from him that I provided for you in the preface of this book. It has blessed my life immeasurably, and I still feed on it today:

"I could care less if God used me. I wish He'd take me off the platform. I'd be perfectly happy in a prayer room never being seen or heard. If you want to be seen or heard, you shouldn't be on any platform. The people don't need to see and hear you but Jesus, anyway."

Again, notice the cruciform nature of this man's heart and character. How refreshing are these statements in a day when so many are insatiably covetous for more power, more influence, and more money, and are always endeavoring to climb higher on the ministry ladder. We need more reluctant ministers, in a sense, who are still willing and obedient to the Lord but who have been stripped of selfish ambition.

Jesus was taken up to a high mountain by the devil, who offered Him all the kingdoms of this world and all its glory, if He would only worship him (Lk. 4:5-7). Jesus refused it, and so will all those who truly love the Lord and bear the marks of the cross in their lives.

Oh, people of God! Resist those men who have no marks of the cross in their lives and preaching. Resist those voices that are diabolically aligned with the spirit of this world. Beware of men who constantly strive for higher positions, bigger and better possessions, the finer things of this life, and more and more success and popularity. Flee from them!

As I've said before, if we all did this, we could shut down every huckster and charlatan ministry in the body of Christ overnight. The landscape of Christianity would be cleansed.

Instead, find that man whom the devil has taken to the top of the mountain and offered him all the things of this world — and he turned it all down. Find that man, and listen to him. Or better yet, *be* that man.

May God give us such men of wisdom and no compromise in this hour who are known not only in heaven but in hell as well (Acts 19:15).

The Church and the world are waiting for them.

SECTION IV

BECOMING A HOUSE OF PRAYER

CHAPTER FOURTEEN

WAITING ON THE LORD:

THE KEY TO HEARING HIS WISDOM AND COUNSEL

One of the great keys to true kingdom increase is to pray and wait on the Lord, hear, and then obey the Lord's wisdom and counsel.

For example, when the widow obeyed the word of Elisha to go around and collect empty vessels from her neighbors, the oil was multiplied and sold to pay off her creditors (2 Kings 4:1-7). The key to this miracle was the faith of the widow to obey the commandment of the Lord through Elisha and go and gather *empty* vessels. This pattern of hearing from the Lord and obeying what He says is the thread of fabric that operated first through the prophets in the Old Testament and then through the ministry of Jesus and the apostles. This pattern runs throughout all of Scripture. It is the key to God's power and kingdom increase. This account is a story of financial provision coming from obedience to a word of wisdom, but it can also be applied to spiritual increase as well.

The Spirit of God made the following statement to our hearts:

"There will be enough oil (Holy Spirit), grain (the living word of God, fresh manna), spiritual and numerical growth/increase, provision, and protection for the churches who will hear and obey the counsel of the Lord in this hour."

FRESH OIL

As with the account of this widow and Elisha, and in a spiritual sense, fresh oil will follow the obedience to the counsel of the Lord. Water will be turned to wine when we do what Jesus says (Jn. 2:5).

Spiritually speaking, the increase of the oil of the Holy Spirit revives people and causes them to become eternally minded, thus becoming an asset to the church and the work of God. Revived workers is one of the greatest needs of the Church in this hour.

In a great house there are vessels of gold and silver, and of wood and clay, some to honor and some to dishonor (1 Tim. 2:20). **In the same way the widow went around to collect empty vessels, so it is that the honorable vessels who qualify for more oil are those who are empty of themselves.** The dishonorable vessels are those who are carnal, full of pride and conceit, the wisdom of man, and self-sufficiency. There will be little to no oil for them.

Again, spiritually speaking, we know oil represents the Holy Spirit. We can see this more clearly in the parable of the 10 virgins (Matt. 25:1-13). Naturally speaking, oil is purchased with money, and money represents what everyone needs to live in this world — symbolic of your life. There must be a surrendering of your life (Lk. 14:26) and an emptying of yourself, so that you can be filled with fresh oil. Frankly, many in the body of Christ and even ministers are too full of themselves to receive fresh oil. Humility is required to receive the grace that produces the oil of the Holy Spirit in your life (Jam. 4:6). And the measure of the Holy Spirit you will receive is also in proportion to you hearing and obeying the Lord's counsel. It is important we understand this.

Having just enough oil is not enough for the midnight hour and the coming darkness. The foolish virgins found that out the hard way. They were unprepared in the midnight hour for the coming of the Bridegroom. In addition to oil in our lamps, we need an added vessel as the wise virgins possessed for the supply of extra oil.

PROTECTION AND MULTIPLICATION COMING TO THE TRUE CHURCH

I see the Lord providing great protection, spiritual and financial increase, and multiplication to the praying and uncompromising Church of today. The majority of that increase will come to numerically small churches because their foundation has not been set in stone and can be more easily reset. Conversely, numerically large churches and, in a greater measure, denominations, have traditions and systems built into them that are much more difficult to be broken up, reset, and changed in order to accommodate the true counsel of the Lord. New wineskins are needed to contain the new wine.

There will be a divine protection and a multiplication for churches who are following the pattern that Jesus and the apostles laid down in the beginning. The pattern is Acts 6:4: *"But we will give ourselves continually to prayer and to the ministry of the word."*

Churches who truly become houses of prayer will receive words of wisdom that will result in great protection and provision for the body of Christ and the people of God. Just as the Christ-child was protected through warnings, and direction given to Joseph and the wise men in dreams (there are at least five dreams given in Matt. 1 and 2), even so shall it be for the true churches in this hour who've stood in the counsel of God and refused to compromise. Not only will there be divine protection, but there will also be divine spiritual and numerical multiplication and the undeniable power of God in manifestation, as we see in the early Church.

"Then the word of God spread, and the number of the disciples multiplied greatly in Jerusalem, and a great many of the priests were obedient to the faith" (Acts 6:7).

"And with great power the apostles gave witness to the resurrection of the Lord Jesus. And great grace was upon them all" (Acts 4:33).

FALSE COUNSEL OF MAN VERSUS THE TRUE COUNSEL OF GOD

"Blessed is the man who walks not in the counsel of the ungodly, nor stands in the path of sinners, nor sits in the seat of the scornful; but his delight is in the law of the Lord, and in His law he meditates day and night. He shall be like a tree planted by the rivers of water, that brings forth its fruit in its season, whose leaf also shall not wither; and whatever he does shall prosper" (Ps. 1:1-3).

Listening to and obeying the counsel of man diminishes — or rather, *prevents,* a thorough planting and fruitfulness — and the glory and power of God from manifesting. Listening to and obeying the counsel of God causes a deep planting and lasting fruitfulness — and increases His glory and power. Here's an example of the subtle false counsel that is being prescribed to many pastors today:

Pastors talk to their congregations about connecting with visitors and engaging in community. They go to conferences, and they hear things like, "Unless your visitors make several friends in the first few months of coming to your church, they will leave." So, they make every effort to create community in their churches by building cafes and coffee houses and setting up lounges for people to connect socially. There's nothing wrong with any of those things, for they can be useful and helpful, but what is your motive, and why are you putting emphasis on the building that you use for services? Is that the only place people can connect? If it's just to have more people to grow your church, to pay for your building, and expand your programs, then you have been corrupted by worldly methods. That is not a gospel-motivated church.

True community is created with people who love God's ways and want to be true disciples. Christ followers with burning kindred spirits bond in true community, and they can do that anywhere, not just in the church building. Can you imagine Peter and John or any of the early apostles sitting down and strategizing about how to keep the 3,000 new converts that came into the church at Pentecost from leaving? Yet this is what many of these church conferences teach you. In Jerusalem, they had just experienced a mighty outpouring of the Holy Spirit, and Peter's message was so freighted with the Spirit of God that it produced genuine repentance and conversion as people began seeking God with all their hearts. That is how the Church is supposed to grow.

There is great temptation out there for pastors who see their churches dwindling in numbers to compromise their values and use worldly means to try to grow their churches or keep the people from leaving. There is no Scriptural standard for drawing more people into the local church, or for building a bigger audience, in order to keep the funds coming in to maintain salaries and buildings, and to expand programs. These motives are tainted with man's wisdom that runs the church like a for-profit business.

Here is the word of the Lord again: When pastors and ministers return to the pattern of Acts 6:4 in their churches and ministries today, they will see a restoration of God's glory and power, and the protection and multiplication of the work of God.

When we obey the counsel of the Lord, there is glory, power, protection, financial provision, and spiritual multiplication for the Church. There are many Scriptural instances of how the wisdom and counsel of the Lord brings increase, even financially. Hearing and obeying is all that is required. As I stated, this is one of the great secrets that runs through the fabric of the entire Bible, but today men don't pray much, and they don't listen to the counsel of the Lord.

PERSONAL EXAMPLE OF THE COUNSEL OF THE LORD THAT CHANGED THE COURSE OF OUR LIVES AND MINISTRY

A number of years ago, we were struggling financially in our itinerant ministry. Prior to the time of launching out into a full-fledged traveling ministry we were trans-local — meaning we were doing church work and traveling only limitedly. When we fully launched out, not many doors opened for us to minister at first, and invitations were few. I did not like to call pastors of local churches for meetings. Eventually we did start calling, more out of relationship than anything else. Still it was a struggle. Our expenses seemed to always outweigh our income.

Over a process of time, I became discouraged and began wrestling with the idea of leaving the ministry and getting a job to provide for my family. However, that was not a good proposition, either, as the ministry was all I had ever known and had been fruitful in doing for most of my adult life. It seemed that now, in a later season of my ministry life, when I should be prospering, I found myself between a rock and hard place.

Finally, after much consternation, I went away on a minister's retreat and spent some time praying and waiting on the Lord. I rolled up my sleeves and meant business with God. It seemed to me that He rolled up His sleeves as well. He knew I was in a desperate situation and in need of wisdom and direction.

I had a notebook that I carried to prayer, and I made two columns — a negative one, with my complaints, and a positive one, with what I was thankful for. I must say that the negative one was much longer, and, like Hannah of old, I poured out my complaints before the Lord (1 Sam. 1). After a day or two of flushing out my frustrations and emptying myself of myself, my mind got quieter, and I heard a word.

"What was the last thing I told you to do?"

I had learned a principle back in my Bible-school days that, often, the Lord won't say anything much to you if you're not obeying what He's already told you to do. In other words, until you're walking in the light you already have, no more light will be given. We must walk in the light as He is in the light (1 Jn. 1:7).

The first thing that came to my mind when I heard this question was the call to write. Years before, I had heard the Lord tell me that writing was my life's greatest work, but I didn't believe it. I reasoned it away by questioning how that could possibly be. No one knew me. I wasn't on television. I didn't have a large platform. Who would read what I wrote? How could writing possibly be my life's greatest work? So, I dismissed that. Now years later, the Lord brings it up in the form of a question. After pondering that question, I went back to my journal and realized the Lord had not only said that writing was to be my life's greatest work but that there were some other things He'd said about it that I had forgotten. After being convinced that it was, indeed, the Lord who had spoken to me and was now getting my attention, I made a pact with Him.

"I'll tell you what I'm going to do, Lord. I'm going to give You five years. I'm going to write diligently and give myself to it (I had already written some things in the way of articles and portions of manuscripts, and a couple of books that didn't go anywhere, etc.), but if I don't see reasonable progress within that time, I am going to leave the ministry and go get a job."

I know that sounds pretty bold and arrogant, but we have a working relationship with God. And if you're sincere about it, I don't believe He minds you speaking to Him that way. I was proving the Word

I believe I heard from the Lord. The Word says, *"Let us reason together, plead your case…"* (Is. 43:26).

After praying this way, with God as my witness, the following month, a young man asked me if I wanted him to publish my books through a small publications ministry he ran on the side. He told me I wouldn't even have to pay him but that he'd do the work on a donation basis. Praise the Lord!

Shortly after I published a couple of books, the Lord opened a door for me to be a featured blogger with *Charisma* magazine, the largest Christian magazine in the world at the time of this writing, with a subscription of four million people. Many people began to read my articles, and some invitations to minister opened up to us. One invitation came from a popular Christian television program, and my appearance on the program led to a spike in our book sales. Soon I was publishing about a book a year, which led to other invitations. I could see that my obedience to the Lord was now having a bit of a domino effect.

Then the Lord spoke to my wife and me about our traveling ministry; what He said gave us a fresh focus and refined our purpose for traveling in ministry. We didn't want to be just another one of many traveling ministries who fall into the trap of doing it for a living, but we desired to distinguish ourselves in an already-crowded market through specialized ministry according to a God-ordained purpose. The strategy and specialization the Lord gave us led to further success and fruit in the churches and nations He sent us to. Our financial situation also changed, as our meetings and offerings increased. The five-year period passed, and God more than met His end of the bargain. He is faithful to His Word. Our responsibility is to hear and obey.

Obedience to a true word from God can catapult you into years of fruitful ministry or business or whatever it is you do. Obedience to a word from God can revolutionize your life. God wants you to be successful and fruitful in whatever it is He has called and directed you to do. The key is to wait on the Lord and receive His wisdom, counsel, and direction.

One of the Lord's simple directives — and the main emphasis of this book — is to return to the original pattern so that we will see the original results they saw in the gospels and in the book of Acts. Fervent effectual prayer, staying filled with the Spirit, and obedience to God's wisdom and counsel will produce fruitfulness and the power of God, which, in turn, will bring provision, protection, and a multiplication to the Church.

Here's another Holy Spirit-inspired utterance we received in prayer:

"And as the three in the fiery furnace came out, so will those who stand in the counsel of God come out, in spite of the adversity, the opposition, and the bewitching (Gal. 3:1-3) that is going on in the Church today. There will be a great increase of spiritual activity to those who have made their churches houses of true prayer. There will be financial increase and greater provision for pastors who've refused to compromise and give place to man's wisdom and who have placed all their confidence in the power of God. The true churches will be known by these foundations: Prayer and obedience to God's Word and counsel, following the leading of the Holy Spirit, and a Christ-centered gospel (building their churches on the Rock of Jesus Christ). This is the foundation that will manifest the glory of God and not be shaken during the coming storm."

What a word.

We must return to the pattern of the Son and the early apostles, who knew they could do nothing in and of themselves. They sought God, and, as long as they sought God, they prospered.

"He (King Uzziah) *sought God in the days of Zechariah, who had understanding in the visions of God;* **and as long as he sought the Lord, God made him prosper"** (2 Chron. 26:5).

WAITING ON THE LORD

"You'd be appalled if I were to show you how few ministries worldwide are on the path of life." (Holy Spirit-inspired utterance)

This statement floored me. It shook me to the core. It put the fear of God in me because it left me to ask myself, "Am I among those few, or am I on the outside looking in? Am I truly on the path of life?"

The path of life does not refer to being born again or baptized in the Holy Spirit. It has more to do with this statement: *"Unless the LORD builds the house, they labor in vain who build it"* (Ps 127:1). Is what I'm doing in life and ministry at the direction of the Lord, or am I laboring in vain?

Any labor not in line with the Lord's direction for your life and ministry is vain or futile. Any plan, agenda, or will apart from the Father's will is wood, hay, and stubble. It won't survive the Judgment Seat of Christ (1 Cor. 3:12-15).

Jesus is the pattern Son. His life and ministry are the perfect example for all of us to follow. While it is good and profitable to have earthly mentors in our lives, let us not forget that Jesus is our primary mentor. He is the Head of the Church and is to be the Lord of our lives.

Here is how Jesus lived His life: *"Then Jesus answered and said to them, 'Most assuredly, I say to you, the Son can do nothing of Himself, but what He sees the Father do; for whatever He does, the Son also does in like manner'"* (Jn. 5:19).

Our problem has been that we don't really believe this. I mean, we believe that *Jesus* lived this way, but we don't believe *we* can live this way. Without Him, we can't, but let me submit to you once again: That is exactly the main reason He sent the Comforter, the Holy Spirit.

Jesus knew we could not do it on our own. So why do we even try? Again, isn't it because we don't believe we can have the same relationship with the Father and the Holy Spirit as Jesus did? But think logically now: Would Jesus give us any less than He was given to get the job done?

*"And I will pray the Father, and He will give you **another** Helper, that He may abide with you forever — the Spirit of truth whom the world cannot receive, because it neither sees Him nor knows Him; but you know Him, for He dwells with you and will be in you."* (Jn. 14:16-17).

The Greek word for "another" is "*allos*," which means "One besides me and in addition to me, but (also) one just like me." And here is the part I love, written in the margin of my Bible: **"He will do in My absence what I would do if I were physically present with you."** In other words, the Holy Spirit's coming assures continuity with what Jesus did and taught.

Do we really believe that? And if so, why do we see so little of the Spirit's operation in life and ministry today?

Honest answer: Because we don't know the Comforter.

And why don't we know Him?

Honest answer: Because we don't spend time cultivating communion with Him. In a word, we don't wait on God.

Waiting on God is a lost art to this restless generation. Yet it is our greatest need.

Let us be foundational and realistic for a moment. Without knowing the written Word of God and walking in the light of it, we can never progress in our life with God. The more we get to know the voice of the Word, the more we will know the voice of the Holy Spirit, who inspired that Word. We can never get away from this foundational truth. People have gotten weird and gone astray attempting to do so.

I encourage young ministers to build their life and ministry on the Word of God, not on the anointing or the gifts of the Holy Spirit. Nonetheless, the Word without the Spirit is dead, so they do run hand in hand. Without a Holy Spirit-inspired ministry and His gifts, young ministers will become like every other preacher — lots of talk but no demonstration of the Spirit and power of God (1 Cor. 2:4-5; 4:20).

For example, a Christian who has never been baptized in the Holy Spirit, with the evidence of speaking in other tongues, is at a great disadvantage in life, and their spiritual progress will be seriously hampered. Without the baptism in the Holy Spirit, much of the evangelical world will stay dry. Similarly, without the strong foundation of the Word of God, much of the Charismatic/Pentecostal world will be too sensational and even flaky. I am sometimes appalled at what passes today for the Holy Spirit in Charismatic/Pentecostal circles.

The number-one problem we have in Christianity today and the reason for every failure among those who claim His Name is that we don't know Him. You know Him through His Word and His Spirit.

We are not talking about a *general* knowledge of Him. Of course, when we are born again, we come into new life in Jesus, and we know Him as our Savior. Thank God that we receive eternal life and an assurance of our salvation. But to intimately know Him will move us into another realm of the Spirit's operation in our lives.

ARE YOU SACRIFICING THE LIFE OF CHRIST ON THE ALTAR OF YOUR OWN WILL?

What have you done with the eternal life of Christ that is in you? The majority of the Christian world has sacrificed that life on the altar of their carnal mind and their own will. Many have never yielded the life within them to the Lordship of Jesus Christ and the Spirit's direction.

Do you understand that it was unthinkable for Jesus to attempt ministry without the direction of the Father through the agency of the Holy Spirit? Just as it is unthinkable for a man to produce a baby without a woman, so it was unthinkable for Jesus to minister and to produce life without the co-laboring of the Holy Spirit.

Jesus understood that He was not on the Earth to do His own will but the will of the Father. He also understood that He was not here to do His own will in the Name of the Father, which is the more common error today.

The first step toward knowing God intimately is to *surrender* the life of Christ within you on the altar of the *Father's* will. The reverse is what most Christians do. They *sacrifice* the life of Christ within them on the altar of their *own* will. They have life in their spirits, but the direction of their lives comes mainly from their own will and carnal mind, resulting in the works of the flesh.

The same pattern is also true in ministry today. Thus, the works of man and of the flesh are plentiful, while the true works of God and of the Spirit are rare.

The sure word of the hour for the body of Christ is that this counsel I'm sharing now would come to maturity — that all ministers and saints would learn to commune with the Holy Spirit and minister to the Lord until they hear and know the mind of Christ for their own lives, situations, and ministry.

WHAT IT MEANS TO WAIT ON THE LORD

"Trust in the Lord with all your heart, and lean not to your own understanding; in all your ways acknowledge Him and He shall direct your paths" (Pr. 3:5-6).

Everything in our lives — absolutely all the will of God — is locked up in these two verses. Everyone wants the last part of that verse — *"He shall direct your paths,"* but they don't know how to fulfill their part. The Bible reveals the *general* will and plan of God, but the specifics of our lives must be personally received from the Lord by taking the time to wait on Him.

"Those who wait on the Lord shall renew their strength; they shall mount up with wings like eagles, they shall run and not be weary, they shall walk and not faint" (Isa. 40:31).

Waiting on the Lord helps us to receive His wisdom and counsel for our lives, but it also renews our strength. But what does it mean to "wait on the Lord"? Somebody once said that it means to just remain stationary, doing nothing until God visits you like He did the 120 disciples in the upper room. I can't really agree with that. First of all, the 120 were not just sitting quietly doing nothing. They were in prayer and supplication (Acts 1:14).

How did they pray? Luke's account gives us insight into how they prayed after witnessing the resurrection and ascension of the Lord Jesus Christ and receiving His instructions to wait for the promise of the Holy Spirit:

"And they worshipped Him, and returned to Jerusalem with great joy, **and were continually in the temple praising and blessing God"** (Lk. 24:52-53).

Most of their prayer time was taken up in praising and blessing the Lord, and this was all before they had even been baptized in the Holy Spirit. Ministering to the Lord is a big part of what we do when we wait on the Lord. That is when His plans begin to come into your heart, and you will usually receive direction.

"As they ministered to the Lord and fasted, the Holy Spirit said..." (Acts 13:2).

The larger part of ministering to the Lord means to focus your powers of concentration on just loving and praising and worshipping Jesus. Saul (Paul) and these other ministers added fasting to their time of ministering to the Lord for the purpose of seeking God in a more concentrated way.

The first thing we must remember is that, when we minister to the Lord or come to Him in prayer, we must believe that He is there — present in the now. In other words, we must come to Him in faith.

"But without faith it is impossible to please Him, **for he who comes to God must believe that He is, and that He is a rewarder of those who diligently seek Him"** (Heb. 11:6).

There must be a faith and an expectation in your heart to meet with the Lord and for Him to manifest Himself. Believing that He is indeed present, is what takes you into the Spirit and makes you more

God conscious than you are man conscious. Our greatest reward is when we experience God's presence in manifestation, and when we hear from Him as we pray and wait on Him.

The word "ministered" (Acts 13:2) in the Greek is a very interesting word. It is "*leitourgeo*" — from which we get our English word "liturgy." The first-century meaning of this word is the key to understanding the greater fullness of this verse. The deeper meaning of this word is not even close to the traditional prayers and vain repetition we see in some denominational services today. In Paul's time, this word meant: "To employ public office or perform public service at one's own expense."

In ancient Greece, the city officers and public officials were not paid a salary, so they paid their own salary for the privilege of serving the people. Therefore, this phrase *"as they ministered to the Lord"* implies that these five men were focusing 100% on the Lord, giving of themselves in complete devotion, which was also noted by their fasting. That is the reason the presence of the Holy Spirit came upon them and gave them direction.

They were worshipping the Lord at their own expense. There was nothing of self-centeredness or "me" oriented at all — 100% of their focus was on the Lord alone. It is the same principle we see when Araunah offered King David his land (the threshing floor and his oxen) for free, but David renounced it by saying: *"I will not offer the Lord that which costs me nothing"* (2 Sam. 24:24).

This same principle should govern our lives. The greatest generosity in giving, for example, is when it costs you something. That is why Jesus commended the poor widow for her gift of two pence, for it was all her substance and greater than the offerings of the rich, who gave from their abundance (Mk. 12:41-44). It is also the reason for inviting the poor, the maimed, the lame, and the blind to a great supper instead of your relatives, friends, and rich neighbors, who can pay you back (Lk. 14:12-14). That is also why Jesus told His disciples to not merely love those who love them, for even the wicked tax collectors do that, but to love our enemies who hate us, so that we would be perfect, as the Father is perfect (Matt. 5:43-48).

Our lives are supposed to cost us. That is what being a disciple and adhering to the Lord's ways is all about — laying down our lives, counting ourselves dead to sin and the world, and denying ourselves, in order to be like Jesus. Is it any wonder in this self-centered genera-tion that many of the songs we refer to as "worship" are mostly "me" focused? The Acts 13:1-2 men were not focused on themselves but they ministered to the Lord in whole-hearted devotion. That is why they heard from the Holy Spirit — because the Spirit comes to glorify Jesus and testify of Him. To turn and minister wholeheartedly to the Lord with an unveiled face is to be open to the Spirit of the Lord (2 Cor. 3:16-17).

DON'T BE MOVED BY THE DRY PROCESS

The challenge with most believers and ministers is that they don't wait on the Lord very long because they don't feel His presence. They give up when they don't get a quick breakthrough. Here is a word of encouragement for you: Don't listen to teachings that tell you that, just because you don't feel His presence, He's not there, or He's not pleased with you, or that you're doing something wrong. The dry process you may feel is nothing more than change you're going through.

What makes you think that, just because you don't feel Him, He's not receiving your worship? This has nothing to do with whether you've broken through or not. In fact, some of the times you feel His presence less are the times you've actually broken through more, because you're dealing with your fleshly nature that kept you from His presence before. You are changing realms of operation.

For example, as you begin to wait on the Lord, you may sense very little of His presence at first, but as you continue on in faith and in the light and knowledge you possess, you will start to pass from the natural realm into the spiritual realm. You will be lifted up into the realm of the Spirit, where you are more conscious of the Lord than you are of yourself.

As you continue waiting on the Lord your spiritual senses will be sharpened, and you will begin to understand the love and desire the Lord has toward you and toward all humanity. But it is essential that you first go through a "processing" time where the desires of the flesh and distractions of the soul decrease so that your spiritual desires will increase. When this starts to happen, you will experience the release of spiritual life from the Lord. He will become your delight, and ministering to Him will actually become addictive.

Let me say this another way. As you wait on the Lord to receive this impartation of spiritual life and strength that is so necessary to your overall spiritual development and well-being, there must also be a parallel crucifixion of your natural, fleshly life. This is accomplished through a direct, firm committal to the cross and a renunciation of anything you have knowledge of that is contrary to God's will in your life — including anything that would hinder your times of waiting on the Lord.

DIFFICULT TO WAIT ON THE LORD WITHOUT YOUR PRAYER LANGUAGE

Let me admonish you, though, that it will be more difficult to wait on the Lord when you have not been initially baptized in the Holy Spirit with the evidence of speaking in other tongues. That is the gateway into the realm of the Spirit and the doorway to being able to commune with the Lord in supernatural utterances.

Personally when I wait on the Lord, most of my time is spent speaking forth mysteries in tongues and then ministering to the Lord in psalms, hymns, and spiritual songs as I sense the unction of the Spirit. As you fine-tune your spirit by praying in tongues at length, there will be a bubbling up from inside of you that needs to be released through speaking or singing forth supernaturally inspired utterances or prayer with your understanding.

Paul said that he prayed and sang with his spirit and with his understanding also (1 Cor. 14:15). This means that Paul actually interpreted what he spoke or sang in tongues. These utterances and songs are not from a songbook or rehearsed, but they flow from your own heart to the Lord by the inspiration of the Holy Spirit (Eph. 5:18-19) (Col. 3:16).

True worship is to flow from the existing intimacy and vibrancy of each person's closeness to the Lord. A true worshipper can break forth spontaneously in their own words of love and adoration for Jesus without any accompaniment of a band or music. Finding your own words and singing with melody from your heart to the Lord will increase the likelihood of the manifest presence of the Holy Spirit in your life. In most churches today and in assembly with other believers, very little time is given to these expressions. Thus, by mere example, people are taught that all worship is dependent on someone else's music and lyrics. Most believers don't know how to use their own words to worship Jesus and the Father.

Here's how it happens and how you can cultivate this expression: As you pray with your spirit in tongues at length, you will eventually get to a place where you hear a word or phrase in English or whatever your native language is. As you speak that word or phrase out in faith, more words will come by the spirit of prophecy. The words will usually be a Scripture or a particular theme or thread from the word of God. Sometimes the words will just be words of love and adoration toward the Lord. You can speak or sing the words you receive by the unction of the Holy Spirit.

As you develop your spirit in these things, you will come to a place where you will get in the Spirit more quickly, and you will begin to see and know things supernaturally. Songs will come to you more quickly, especially as you continue to meditate on the Scriptures. You will even hear precise instructions from the Holy Spirit as to what He wants you to do. You will be quickened and renewed with the life and strength of the Lord, your peace will be great, and your joy shall be full.

(If you have not yet received the baptism in the Holy Spirit, go to YouTube and type in "Joel Crumpton" [at this writing, he is still on there]. He's a good friend of mine who specializes in ministering the baptism in the Holy Spirit to believers. Watch the video to receive his excellent instructions).

TWO ELEMENTS THAT INCREASE YOUR ABILITY TO WAIT ON THE LORD

"For John truly baptized with water but you shall be baptized with the Holy Spirit not many days from now...You shall receive power when the Holy Spirit is come upon you" (Acts 1:5, 8).

"And they were all filled with the Holy Spirit and began to speak with other tongues, as the Spirit gave them utterance" (Acts 2:4).

The Christian life is not difficult. It is difficult only for those who've not been transformed by the empowering grace of God. And as great as being born again is, it is still not enough. Jesus left us with more than the new birth and forgiveness from our sins. Your degree of effectiveness in prayer and as a witness of the Lord Jesus Christ is severely hampered without the baptism in the Holy Spirit with the evidence of speaking in other tongues.

Jesus told His disciples not to depart from Jerusalem until they had received this baptism of power (Lk. 24:49). Why would He tell them that, if they could be effective without this power? Our churches have gotten away from prioritizing this sacred baptism.

The baptism in the Holy Spirit was an essential in the early Church. It would have been surprising to the early apostles and believers to find someone in their assemblies without it. They didn't wait to pray and minister the baptism in the Holy Spirit to new converts.

For instance, in Acts 8, Philip the evangelist was conducting a great soul-winning campaign in Samaria with power and miracles. Many believed on Jesus and were born again and baptized in water, but then Peter and John came down shortly thereafter to Samaria to minister the baptism in the Holy Spirit to the new converts(Acts 8:14-17). Half of the Church today has been hoodwinked by the devil and man's traditions, thinking they can minister effectively and live a consistently victorious Christian life without the power of the Holy Spirit.

When one receives the power of the Holy Spirit, he also receives his prayer language of tongues. That is the pattern in the early Church (Acts 2, 8, 9, 10, 19).One of the signs given by Jesus that would follow all believers was that *"they shall speak with new tongues"* (Mk. 16:17b). Those tongues are the language of the kingdom of God. A brand-new kingdom needs a brand-new language.

Before Pentecost, in Acts 2, there were officially no citizens of heaven. Paradise was below the Earth until Jesus trans-located it to the third heaven after His resurrection and ascension. The disciples all received the power of the Holy Spirit after Jesus' ascension. The tongues came with this power and is a personal expression of the Holy Spirit for our own personal edification. Why am I saying all this?

Because it is very difficult to wait on the Lord without this supernatural prayer language called "tongues."

Praying and singing with tongues is one of the greatest vehicles for getting you in the Spirit. Believers who don't pray in tongues have no longevity in prayer, very few breakthroughs spiritually, and no empowerment. They usually live from crisis to crisis, and life's circumstances tend to rule them.

The more you pray in other tongues, the more you will walk in the Spirit and accelerate in your life and calling, especially as you get established in the Word. The more you utilize your prayer language, the more fluency and diversity you will obtain in it. I've met many Spirit-baptized believers who are stuck in their prayer language — stuck on the same few syllables they've been praying for years. There's been no advancement in their prayer life because they haven't yielded properly to the Holy Spirit and practiced or exercised praying at length in other tongues.

There is a higher walk and a higher path all saints are called to — a path that transitions you from the carnal mind to the mind of the Spirit. With every hour you give the Lord, especially in praying in other tongues and worship, He will begin moving you there.

Praying in tongues and learning to minister to the Lord will increase our ability to wait on the Lord.

CHAPTER FIFTEEN

THE POWER OF FASTING AND PRAYER

Fasting is hard on the flesh. This is the number-one reason Christians don't do it. Something happens to you when you take away food. Your body and emotions are immediately buffeted and shut down. There will always be a fight between the spirit and flesh, especially in the beginning. One of the great benefits of fasting is that there is a purging from things that bind and hinder your spiritual life.

The body has been declared dead because of sin (Rom. 8:10), but fasting is a tool that executes that position of death by the Spirit(Rom. 8:13).

The devil has a way of tracking a man and using his flaws and weaknesses to continually trip him up. Men have fallen short of fulfilling God's plan and purpose, and some have even died prematurely because the enemy found something in them that eventually took them out and cut their lives short.

There are what men of old termed "darling lusts" that can rule us — an uncontrollable appetite for food, sexual immorality, a bondage to pornography, or any addiction; anger or greed and a love for money, power, and fame; or something more subtle, like unbelief and indifference that limits our effectiveness for God and results in a lack of power. Impatience, unforgiveness, bitterness, being easily offended — all are habits of the flesh that keep us out of the Spirit. Other such strongholds can limit a man from growing and going further in God. We all have shortcomings and flaws. As I've heard it said, even the greatest of men have feet of clay. Fasting is a mystery that deals with such things.

As I said, the devil tracks people all their lives and is familiar with their vulnerabilities and wounds, entry and access points,that he badgers them with over and over again.

"For the ruler of this world is coming, and he has nothing in me"(John 14:30). Satan had no access points into Jesus' life. He learned obedience through the things He suffered (Heb. 5:8). He sympathizes with our weaknesses because He, too, was tempted in all points as we are, and yet without sin (Heb. 4:15).

One of the great benefits of fasting is that you come out of hiding from your own flesh (Is. 58:7), and you allow God to access your weaknesses and flaws and purge you from them.

When I was first saved, I fasted one or two days per week, and, occasionally, longer. I did it simply out of a desire for more of God in my life, but then I got away from the consistency of it, until a number of years ago, when the Lord began to steer me back to it. He said that the fullness of His calling would not come forth in my life without it. That got my attention. Like so many Christians and ministers, I dragged my feet on it, was slow to get back into it,and eventually even came to a place of unwillingness to do it. After all, what's going without a pizza or a hamburger got to do with the presence and power of God? The voice of the flesh justifies itself and is deceptive, and no good thing dwells within it. In addition to this insight and warning from the Lord, He also recently gave us counsel regarding fasting.

The Lord stirred our remembrance to times past and major victories that were obtained. We began to realize that they were all manifested in times of prayer and fasting. It was during those times when the greatest power and change were released personally and ministerially to impact people. It makes you wonder why we don't fast more. Even fasting a meal or two a week would help some people. The Spirit of the Lord called fasting "His principle of power" and highlighted Acts 13:1-12 and Matt. 17:20-21 as a mystery that only those who've walked in it understand.

This is the way of setting heaven's order in your life and ministry. That's why Paul could go and pronounce judgment on a sorcerer who was hindering the gospel (Acts 13:10-12). He had come under heaven's order for his life and ministry and was empowered and sent by the Holy Spirit after a time of prayer (ministering to the Lord) and fasting. And because he was under the influence of heaven's order, the effectual working of God's power was manifested through him.

This is God's way, and this is His plan. Let us walk in it.

THE THREE-DAY FAST: A PRINCIPLE OF SUSTAINING POWER

It was December 1987 when I began my missionary assignment in Liberia, West Africa. As a young zealot for God, I decided to shave my head and fast my first two-plus weeks in that nation. As a result, a ministry of fire was manifest that launched me into fruitful ministry for the next nine years of missionary work.

Let's move ahead to 1995 now, in Gambia, West Africa. During this time, my wife, Carolyn, went into a season of repentance and received a new touch of the Holy Spirit and personal revival in her life. We led our team and staff into three days a month of prayer and fasting for a breakthrough in that tiny Muslim nation. In one prayer session, Carolyn heard my prayer language of tongues in English as I spoke the name of the principality of that region, and by the direction of the Spirit, we addressed it and exercised our authority over it in the Name of Jesus. From that day forward, instead of being persecuted and stoned as in previous outreaches, our evangelistic street team began to experience new favor and miracles among the Muslims. Things opened up for us in that nation and remain open for others until this day.

One *imam* — the Muslim equivalent of a Christian pastor or a priest — was visited by an angel who told him to go ask for Jesus at one of our evangelistic street outreaches. The angel gave him the address of where our team was ministering. Glory to God! This *imam* received Christ and was baptized in the Holy Spirit. This is an account similar to what we read of in the book of Acts. This happened shortly after our time of prayer and fasting.

Isn't that much better and sweeter than using Madison Avenue tactics, seeker-friendly methodology, and the wisdom of man to try to influence people for Jesus? This brand of miracles and wonders doesn't just happen. They are a result of focused prayer and fasting and exercising our authority over the devil by the Spirit in the Name of Jesus.

Let's move ahead to 1999, in Pensacola, Florida, when we were part of the faculty at the Brownsville Revival School of Ministry. There was an evil spirit that came to test me on a book that I had written called *Soulish Leadership*. God was requiring me to become one with the message of that book. Satan was allowed to test me. It was a hard battle that lasted for about three years.

Finally, out of desperation, at the beginning of 2002, I went into an extended time of prayer and fasting. I did what some call "series fasting" — three days on, three days off, two days on, two days off, one day on, one day off, and then back to three. God gave me grace and a hunger to do this. Strongholds were broken off my life and ministry, and I became more unified with the message of my own book. I entered a new room in the Spirit and a transformation into a deeper love and walk of humility. I've never been the same since. The testimony and revelation I received during that time is written in another book I wrote called *The Journal Of My Journey To His Holiness.*

Every major breakthrough we've had in life and ministry has come from a time of prayer and fasting. It is a principle of power that God has established for the believer and for His Church and ministers.

There is divine activity and power and authority released during a fast. The dealings of God are also released, just as it was with Saul being blinded on the road to Damascus and not eating and drinking for the three days after his miraculous encounter and conversion (Acts 9:9). Do we have any idea what happens when our flesh shuts down like that? Paul could not see and did not eat or drink for three days. The vision and encounter he'd just had with the glory of God was ingrained into the deepest part of his being.

The same dealings happened with Peter on the rooftop during a time of prayer and waiting on God (Acts 10:9-16). There is no way the impulsive and impetuous Peter would be praying on the rooftop while lunch was being prepared. He had some kind of burden and stirring to go up there and pray. A vision was given to him as he was suspended in a trance, and God's dealings caused Peter — and then the rest of the early apostles — to preach the gospel to the Gentiles and receive them as God's people. It totally revolutionized their "Jewish-only" mindset.

Did it ever occur to you that perhaps God was moving on Peter because another man, named Cornelius, was fasting and praying?

"So Cornelius said, "Four days ago I was fasting until this hour; and at the ninth hour I prayed in my house, and behold, a man stood before me in bright clothing, and said, 'Cornelius, your prayer has been heard, and your alms are remembered in the sight of God. Send therefore to Joppa and call Simon here, whose surname is Peter. He is lodging in the house of Simon, a tanner, by the sea. When he comes,

he will speak to you.' So I sent to you immediately, and you have done well to come. Now therefore, we are all present before God, to hear all the things commanded you by God" (Acts 10:30-33).

Peter would probably not have received the men Cornelius sent to the house if the Lord had not dealt with him in such a spectacular way through a vision. He had to know that the Gentiles were no longer considered unclean but were now included in the universal plan of God for mankind. It was on the fourth day of Cornelius's time of fasting and prayer that the angel appeared to him with specific directions from God. I often wonder what would've happened if Cornelius had stopped fasting and praying on the third day. Perhaps God would've had to find someone else to speak to. Oh, what we miss when we fail to fast, and pray, and wait on God!

In Acts 13:1-3, ministry gifts of prophets and teachers in Antioch ministered to the Lord and fasted. I'm sure they did so because they had a burden and sensed a change that was coming. The Holy Spirit spoke, and Saul and Barnabas were separated, empowered, and sent as the Church's first missionaries. An incredible judgment miracle followed and confirmed Saul's calling and authority (v. 8). We've got to get back to this principle of power called fasting, with prayer.

Some have tried it and even seen some success. But like us at one time, they dropped it and forgot the results they initially had. Others attempted it but soon quit. Some do not know how to go there and do not understand the power of this spiritual principle of fasting with prayer. Truly this is where a blow to unbelief is dealt (Matt. 17:20-21), and great advances are made in the Spirit.

Great prayer giants of the past such as Rees Howells and Father Nash, co-laborer in prayer with Charles Finney, obtained degrees of faith, power, and effectiveness in prayer because of the added element of fasting that overcame unbelief.

Many go and work for God, but they go without the power. They're content to do without the help. They don't want to put a knife to their throats and sever their appetite for even a short time. The negligence of this principle of power has robbed many from walking in God's higher-kingdom plans and purposes.

The Church must return to this principle of power that deals with unbelief directly and puts us in a position for far greater effectiveness and fruitfulness.

TWO SECRETS TO PAUL'S MINISTRY: TONGUES AND FASTING

I believe there were two great secrets to the apostle Paul's ministry that we need to pay close attention to. The first is his continual use of praying in tongues. He said it this way:

"I thank my God I speak in tongues more than you all..." (1 Cor. 14:18)

The Amplified translation reads even more strongly:

"I thank God that I speak in [strange] tongues (languages) more than any of you or all of you put together..."

As the principal writer of the New Testament, the apostle Paul's private use of speaking in tongues was his key to revelation knowledge and to his understanding of the mysteries of God. How do you think he received revelation of the post-resurrection truths and the new-creation realities he lays out in the epistles? No other apostle received these revelations — not even the original apostles of the Lamb and those who walked with Jesus in his earthly ministry. How do you suppose Paul received the mysteries of Christ and the Church where he understood them enough to write them on paper? I propose to you that one of his great secrets was how much he utilized his private prayer language and use of tongues. It is a key to revelation knowledge.

The late Lester Sumrall was asked how often he spoke in tongues. His response was rather terse but poignant: "when I'm not preaching." Let us take a lesson from him.

When you speak in tongues, you speak mysteries. Many of those mysteries concern the plan of God for your own life that is processed by speaking much in other tongues.

"For he who speaks in a tongue does not speak to men but to God, for no one understands him; however, in the spirit he speaks mysteries" (1 Cor. 14:2).

FASTING

The second great secret to the apostle Paul's life and ministry was fasting. While rehearsing his many trials and tribulations that he suffered for the gospel, he says this:

"In weariness and toil, in sleeplessness often, in hunger and thirst, **in fastings often**, *in cold and nakedness"* (2 Cor. 11:27).

"But in all things we commend ourselves as ministers of God: in much patience, in tribulations, in needs, in distresses, in stripes, in imprisonments, in tumults, in labors, in sleeplessness, **in fastings...***"* (2 Cor. 6:4-5).

Paul encouraged the saints to imitate him as he imitated Christ (1 Cor. 11:1) and to follow his example (Phil. 3:17) and pattern and purpose of life. Fasting and prayer were a constant in his life.

He is not giving these instructions only to ministers but also to the churches and to all believers. He even admonished husbands and wives to fast and pray:

"Do not deprive one another except with consent for a time, that you may give yourselves to fasting and prayer; and come together again so that Satan does not tempt you because of your lack of self-control" (1 Cor. 7:5).

We have been too busy with religious activities and have fallen short of following Paul's example, which will lead us to the highest kind of power for the highest kind of service.

We have many Bible conferences, evangelistic campaigns, fellowship meetings, potluck suppers, dinner banquets, and musical concerts, etc., but why not have fasting and prayer times and consecration fasting meetings and conferences? It will give birth to astounding fruit and results as it has throughout the ages when men have ventured into such consecrated times of fasting and prayer.

How will the whole creation ever stop groaning and travailing and the sons of God ever be manifest without fasting and prayer (Rom. 8:19-22)? For it is fasting and prayer that will cause us to identify deeply with the whole creation and enter into the same groaning and travailing to give birth to what God wants to do. You can be a believer and a child of God all your life and never manifest this way as a son. Even Jesus did not begin to manifest His Sonship until after He had fasted for 40 days and nights. Let us follow His example (not specifically in the sense of a 40-day fast — unless the Lord leads you that way — but rather the lifestyle of fasting). Let us also follow the zeal and fervency of Paul and enter into a life of fasting and prayer.

Remember this is how Paul began his new life and ministry (Acts 9:9). Would to God that all new converts would follow this example of a three-day fast and pray and meditate on the Scriptures! There would be far less backsliding and more chosen vessels thrust into the Lord's service.

MORE UNDERSTANDING AND BENEFITS OF FASTING

"Then Jesus, looking at him, loved him, and said to him…" (Mark 10:21).

Deeper and more consistent fasting leads to a transformation of love. Perhaps this is the most forgotten benefit of fasting.

The outward man cracks like a shell. The inward man's life oozes out. The heart softens and melts as you submit to Jesus. Intimacy with Him becomes your obsession and beholding His magnificent beauty your quest.

Fasting is hard on the flesh but removes impurities and hindrances that hide Jesus from you. It allows you to see Jesus in a magnified way and to sense His Spirit more acutely.

When you fast and pray the right way, you see beyond the façade of religion and the veil of hypocrisy more distinctly. You are not as easily fooled by the hype, glitter, and the showmanship of the flesh any more.

Fasting is not a cure-all, but it's certainly one of the most misunderstood and neglected practices of the carnal church. And I believe that, when it is done for the right reasons and with pure motives, it is the master key to the impossible. At first it is hard for the novice or the carnally ruled Christian to do, but by reason of use, practice, and experience, it will become a much-lighter burden, especially when you see the fruit and results it brings.

When you receive the revelation of how much of a hindrance your flesh is to the life of Christ within you, you will fast, especially when your spiritual hunger is sufficient. One of the great purposes of fasting is to bring forth that life and manifest Christ's character on the Earth.

When you allow His life to exceedingly grow in you through fasting, many burdens you've been carrying for years and decades will be removed from you. All that is not the will of the Father will begin to be stripped from your flesh and soul, and your spirit will gain ascendancy.

The life of Christ was sown as a seed in your heart when you were born again, but the Father's great desire is to bring forth that seed into full harvest until you are transformed into His image. Fasting is a great purging tool to accelerate this process.

One caution: Never base your worth or value in the kingdom of God on whether you fast or not, but also understand that the perfect will of God in your life will not be accomplished without it. The Father's love for you remains steadfast whether you choose to implement fasting into your life or not, but without it, you will fall short of walking on the highest path of the upward calling of God in Christ Jesus for your life (Phil. 3:14). You see, until certain areas of your flesh are purged, you cannot even begin to take up your cross and follow Jesus in order to fulfill His perfect will for your life.

Some believers understand the positional truths of the physical body being declared dead because of sin and your spirit being made a righteous new creation because of the life of Christ within you (Rom. 8:10). But many do not understand that fasting enforces these positional truths in your life, so that you can walk above the realm of the works of man and begin to operate in the works of God.

Fasting greatly enhances the power of the Spirit in your life to manifest the perfect will of God. Your own will and aspirations begin to die when you truly fast, and His perfect will becomes your consuming desire.

Fasting is one of the great secrets of transformation in the believer's character. Yes, it is difficult on the flesh, but the power of the blood of Jesus has gone before you and will strengthen you in your weakness, cleanse you, purge you, and transform you. Call on the power of His blood in times of fasting.

Consistent fasting in your life will progressively and eventually bring you into the mind of Christ as you spend time in prayer and also in the Word. A new man will emerge within you, and what appeared at first to be a heavy yoke will, indeed, be easy and light.

You will be transformed into a deeper love walk and be led more perfectly in the way of the Lord. Light will break forth on your path, and even your health shall spring forth speedily (Is. 58). That which right now seems like a heavy and grievous affliction to you will be as nothing compared to the exceedingly eternal weight of glory that fasting will work in you (2 Cor. 4:17).

CHAPTER SIXTEEN

SENSITIVITY AND COMPASSION: THE OUTFLOW OF

TRUE PRAYER AND COMMUNION WITH GOD

"Then the blind and the lame came to Him in the temple, and He healed them" (Matt. 21:14).

When the Church truly becomes a house of prayer, it will drift farther and farther away from being a place of business or a house of merchandise where the purpose seems to be more about attendance, buildings, and cash — in other words, presentation and production rule. True prayer is walking with God and communing with Him from your heart. When you truly commune with God, you receive His heart, you are taught of Him, and you understand His ways. You see beyond the veil. You see beyond outward appearances. You see things clearer from God's perspective. You have discernment.

Becoming a house of prayer is much more than conducting local, regional, or even national corporate prayer events. It's more than a mid-week prayer meeting that has more form than substance. Corporate prayer meetings and events are vitally important, for real power is released through united praying, but change must also happen at the grassroots level with each individual heart and life. The outflow of real prayer and communion with God is not only power but holiness and compassion toward humanity.

Even when we add fasting to prayer, we have to be careful we are doing it with the right attitude and motive. When Israel fasted wrongfully, God brought correction.

"No, the kind of fast I want is that you stop oppressing those who work for you and treat them fairly and give them what they earn. I want you to share your food with the hungry and bring right into your own homes those who are helpless, poor, and destitute. Clothe those who are cold, and don't hide from relatives who need your help" (Is. 58:6-7).

In my book *The Real Spirit of Revival*, I wrote the following:

"For most of my life, I have felt like a square peg in a round hole. I'm sure that, when I was younger, this was due in part to my own idealism. Some of it, however, was due to the integrity of my own heart for the things of God. The 'out of place' feelings I've had in different settings and situations over the years were simply a spiritual 'disconnect' my spirit would feel to what was going on. At times I just couldn't get excited over the things that others would get excited about. I witnessed too much Hollywood and the spirit of the world in the Church, and it always grieved me.

At first, I thought there was something wrong with me, but as time went on, I realized that the grieving I often felt was coming from the Lord. Hype, showmanship, appearance, and all the slick professionalism that is so often a part of the production of the traditional Church culture has never impressed Jesus. What truly impresses Him is meeting the deepest needs of the heart and *real-life* issues in people's daily struggles. Helping a friend out with monthly rent, paying for a widow's groceries, transporting an invalid person to a church meeting, assisting single parents with their small children, visiting the sick in hospitals, clothing the naked, feeding the hungry, and visiting those in prison are some of the things Jesus gets excited about. We are part of a kingdom that places great value on these things. The reason many Christians don't get excited about these things is that they require a certain amount of personal sacrifice and, therefore, are not closely attached to their emotions. Rejoicing in the Spirit does often involve your emotions, but there is an emotional rejoicing that has nothing to do with the Spirit of God.

The Word of God uses the aforementioned acts as the criteria to identify the righteous (Matt. 25:31-46) when Jesus comes to set up His Earthly Kingdom. What these verses do *not* say is this: Enter into the kingdom the Father has prepared for you because you performed many miracles, cast out many devils, prophesied in the Lord's name, had a television ministry, preached to thousands and even millions of people. You may have never missed a church service, sang faithfully in the choir for 30 years, went on several mission trips, were prophesied over by a popular TV evangelist, or received a debt-cancellation prayer cloth with a promise of prosperity. By the way, there is nothing wrong with most of these acts except, obviously, the last one. However, the kingdom we are a part of does not place high value on the sort of acts that are greatly esteemed in much of ministry today. You can do all these things and still have a corrupt heart.

There is a part of our Christianity that is very low profile, routine, even a bit mundane, with very little fanfare, and always including in our daily affairs opportunities to help and serve others. Feelings are not always involved, but a quiet confidence and a rejoicing in the Lord will accompany your love and service for others. When you choose to serve the least of all people, you are, in fact, serving Jesus.

A PROPHET'S VISION

I have a prophet friend of mine who received a visitation from Jesus several years ago. He was in a church service located in a red-light district, where most of its members were former drug addicts, prostitutes, homeless people, and prisoners. *My friend was on his knees worshiping when Jesus said: "I love these kinds of people."*

There's something about Jesus that is so different than natural man. He loves the poor, the broken, and the lowly because they have no pretense and no airs about them. They are real. Jesus found His joy and pleasure in meeting and serving such people. This is where much of His rejoicing was anchored.

Amongst all the hype so prevalent in ministry today, whatever happened to just loving and serving Jesus because He saved you from sin and hell or just loving Him for who He is? Whatever happened to just simply loving your neighbor as yourself and doing unto others as you would have them do unto you because that's what Jesus said to do?

There is a great need in the Church today to simplify our lives and our faith, to return to the simplicity of the cross and of loving Jesus and serving others. Unplug your emotions from being impressed by big names, big productions, all the professionalism and showmanship of the modern Church enterprise system, and start plugging yourself into meeting the real needs of hurting people around you.

Isn't this what Jesus exemplified when He cleansed the temple, and then the blind and the lame came to Him and He ministered to them? Although the blind and lame represent real physical needs that require the manifestation of the power of God to heal, symbolically, the blind and lame also represent those who cannot spiritually see and spiritually walk. That describes the real need of lost humanity. Jesus ministered to crowds, but He also ministered to many individuals.

JIM AND LYDIA: IT'S ABOUT MEETING REAL NEEDS

Jim and Lydia are a godly couple who live near me and have had church in their home for years. Recently their grassroots efforts in effectively making disciples caught my attention.

One day while I was getting a haircut, I found out my hairdresser had been converted and was being discipled under the tutelage of this husband-and-wife team. She told me her story of how she'd been a homeless drug addict trying to care for her little son she had out of wedlock. As a sinner, when she first met Jim and Lydia, she hated them. When they took her into their home and provided for some of her daily needs, she still hated them. She told me that she hated their God and their Jesus.

What did Jim and Lydia do? They exercised great patience and long-suffering and continued to love this young woman. She started attending the church in their home and eventually gave her heart to Jesus. Soon thereafter she met a young man in this home church and got married. Her life has been radically transformed and her feet set aright on God's path and destiny for her life. She is now a true disciple of Jesus.

This is what Jim and Lydia do. They spend their lives for others. Besides raising their four young children in the fear and admonition of the Lord, at one time they had 17 homeless and troubled people staying in their small home. Their constant sacrifice and being inconvenienced for the sake of others is a real testament to what it means to be a true disciple of Jesus. Their life is a testimony to what true love and compassion is.

THE GOOD SAMARITAN

Isn't it interesting and revealing how, in the account of the good Samaritan told by Jesus, it wasn't the professional religionists, exemplified by the priest and the Levite, who helped care for the man who'd fallen among thieves, was wounded, and nearly died. But it was the despised Samaritan who came to the wounded man's rescue and demonstrated practical love and compassion for the man (Lk. 10:25-37).

The lawyer in question, who initiated the conversation by asking Jesus what he must do to inherit eternal life, seemed more interested in theorizing than in acting. Seeking to justify himself and perhaps relieve himself from his responsibility to love his neighbor, he asks, *"Who is my neighbor* (v. 29)?" Jesus then flips the question on him and changes the emphasis through a parable, from "Who is the neighbor to be cared for?" to "Who proved to be the neighbor who cared?"

It's not theory Jesus is looking for but action and practical demonstration of our love and compassion. Words and theoretical discussions are empty and cheap. Much of the Church needs to learn this lesson today.

Unplug yourself from the hype and professionalism of man-made religion, and plug yourself into the practical demonstration of loving your neighbor as yourself. This is the great lesson of this parable told by Jesus. We have too much theorizing and not enough action in the body of Christ.

For instance, there are many differing views and theories on eschatology and the return of the Lord today, and I myself have passionately debated and discussed these views with friends. It is very unlikely, however, that I will be on this Earth when the Lord returns and at the end of the age. Therefore, all I have is today and this moment. I can't control when or how the end comes, but I can control how well I am loving others right now.

If I should know my eschatology and how it is all going to play out in the end — but I don't even know my neighbors' names or their pain and struggles — what good is knowing and theorizing about it? Absolutely nothing whatsoever. What good is "being certain" about the end when all it leads to is a lack of tolerance and strife between professing believers of differing opinions, and we ignore the clear mandates of the Lord and choose instead to focus on speculation? When we fail to obey the Lord's simple mandate to love others, we actually ruin the testimony of the Lord's name before an unbelieving world as it watches our foolish religious and internal wars and our constant theorization of such things. What good is being sure about what the Bible teaches on eschatology or any other doctrine if the process does not lead to love? We become sounding brass and clanging cymbals (1 Cor. 13:1-3).

I am content to leave all views of eschatology and the future in the hands of God. I don't need to understand it except to know that He is coming and that we must keep ourselves ready, which the Scriptures do emphasize. I don't need to give my energy to things I can't affect one way or the other, especially when there are so many other things in the present moment where I *can* have an effect. I am actually foolish enough to believe that a present moment of demonstrating love, compassion, and kindness to others actually builds the future and heaps up for me eternal rewards far more than theorizing about pre-tribulation vs. post-tribulation raptures. Redeeming the time by loving others today or at any given moment creates the future for both them and me.

A PASTOR DEMONSTRATES TRUE LOVE AND COMPASSION

Here's another example of this love in action. Some time ago, a pastor named Bob shared this incredible story of how he loved one lady back to health. It made such an impression on me that I never forgot it. I asked him to write out his testimony in his own words. It is a great example of the practical demonstration of loving your neighbor and leaving the ninety-nine to minister to the one.

"When I came to pastor this church 16 years ago, I met a lady who was in her early 40s named Sandi. Sandi had been adopted at the

age of 26 by a couple she now lives with. Sandi had suffered with numerous physical and mental issues most of her life.

"Her parents asked me to visit with her and pray for her because of the debilitating state of her mental condition. She had tried to kill herself many times and was being treated with electroshock treatments twice a week. I began meeting with her weekly for months, and we witnessed a notable improvement. The only issue was that, every time she went for her treatments, we had to start our conversations all over again because she'd forgotten what we'd talked about before. Needless to say, this was beginning to frustrate me, so I told the family that, as long as she is on the treatments, I would have to change the weekly visits to monthly.

"The family talked with the doctor, and they decided to stop the treatments; to our surprise, her mental and physical health improved within a few months. After a couple of years, she no longer required monthly visits to her psychiatrist, and her medications had been reduced to one quarter of what they had been for most of her life.

"Now here is the kicker. I met with Sandi for 15 years, and all we ever talked about was everyday life. No deep Bible studies, and no hour-long prayer sessions. We would talk about family, weather, or current events and then say a little prayer. All she needed was a friend — someone who would love her for who she was and connect with her on a human (but spiritual) level.

"Sandi graduated to heaven in 2017, and I will miss my friend. I learned a lot from her, such as that people don't need the preacher to have all the answers; they just want to know he cares."

Pastor Bob visited this woman every week for about eight years and then every other week for several more years. What a heart of a true shepherd! What a practical demonstration of love and sacrifice!

You cannot develop this kind of sensitivity, patience, and compassion without true heart communion with the Lord. Bob's temple was a house of prayer, and he possessed the heart of the Lord by leaving the ninety-nine for the one who was hurting. When the Church corporately and individually becomes a house of prayer, we will be known even more for these kinds of practical demonstrations of love and compassion.

THE UNDERGROUND MOVEMENT

I believe there is an underground "grassroots" movement in the Church today to return to authentic Christianity that is void of the greed, hype, and Hollywood that has infiltrated it. Compare this to the many ministerial practices outlined in this book that steal from the sheep. This is a word, especially for the Charismatic/Pentecostal Church, where these kinds of excesses, extremes, and abuses seem to be more common.

Someone recently asked me what I see for America and the Church's future. Right now, I am seeing the beginning and mushrooming of an underground move of God and an evolution of sorts concerning both the Church and the nation. Not everything is as it appears or as many have spoken.

Here's a powerful word from the Spirit of God I've shared before that illustrates this point:

"Do not look at the TV and larger media ministries to try to understand what I am doing in my body today. They have a part to play, but they are the visible to the eye veneer of the body that people see. Those who are carnal and immature see the outward appearance and are impressed, thinking that these are the height of ministry and where the Spirit is concentrating today. But they are mistaken.

"See what I see — many small churches and ministries investing in relationships, walking in love, pouring their lives into each other; this is where the Spirit is moving today. There is a revolution taking place in my body, a revolution of relationships, discipleship, and love. This will affect whole communities and economies." — John Fenn, Church Without Walls International

The Church will remain under divine discipline until then, as God awaits an earnest and heartfelt response. He is separating the wheat from the chaff. There must be a greater distinction between the world, the false and worldly church, and the true disciples of Jesus through the work of the cross. The glorious Bride of Christ must come forth without spot and blemish. Both His severity and kindness are manifesting simultaneously (Rom. 11:22) as people choose whom they will serve. A large segment of the Church is being upbraided for her worldly ways, worldly thinking, and her departure from the real faith.

God is preparing an underground church and a loving, consecrated people against an increased time of trouble, and a great harvest and glory that is yet to come. This is a necessary work and, more importantly, a manifestation of God's mercy to the masses, because when the Church is judged and cleansed, that is when we will have the greatest impact on the world.

"For the time has come for judgment to begin at the house of God, and if it begins first with us, what shall the end be for those who do not obey the gospel of God? And if the righteous one is scarcely saved, where shall the ungodly and the sinner appear?" (1 Pet. 4:17-18).

The absence of true judgment is glaring in many places, and sheep are starving for the true word of life. Holiness has been replaced by hype. Appearance has been exalted above the true anointing of the

Spirit and the real love of God. And there's been an obvious absence of the fear of the Lord.

On the positive end of things, it's been very encouraging to witness struggling pastors of smaller churches who are laboring in obscurity, pressing into God in the Spirit, and taking an uncompromising stand for the Lord — while others are growing increasingly discouraged or compromising for numerical growth or just giving up and quitting. Conversely, some pastors of larger churches who have a platform and means to make an impact on their community and nation have grown comfortable and self-congratulatory in their false success.

We need fire and holiness in the pulpits of America right now and a restoration of the fear of the Lord, but much of what we seem to be getting is smoke and noise, as men are caught up in their own self-importance and image. We have some of the largest churches and ministries we've ever had in the history of our nation and yet the greatest departure from the true faith. What a paradox! One of the reasons for this departure is simply that many professing Christians hardly read their Bibles any more, have no private life of prayer, no oil of the Holy Ghost, and provide virtually no gospel witness. Many just depend on what their favorite popular celebrity preacher or pastor says. Moreover, many preachers in their quest to keep their churches and ministries going have left off intimacy with the only One through whom this is possible, and instead have substituted the machinery of men and organizational abilities for their conquest. They need to heed the call to prayer from R.A Torrey:

"The devil is perfectly willing that the Church should multiply its organizations and its deftly contrived machinery for the conquest of the world for Christ, if it will only give up praying. The devil is not afraid of machinery; he is afraid only of God. And machinery without prayer is machinery without God."

THE CALL TO A DIFFERENT KIND OF PRAYING

We need to unplug from the noise, hype, and machinery of men and plug into the love and compassion of Jesus and what true holiness births. But we also need to plug into the kind of prayer that produces the power of God to convert souls to Christ. We need love and holiness, but we need praying that produces the power of God, too. For this motivation and incentive, we need only listen to the words of one of the greatest soul winners in American history.

"In regard to my own experience, I will say that, unless I had the Spirit of prayer, I could do nothing. If even for a day or an hour I lost the Spirit of grace and supplication, I found myself unable to preach with power and efficiency or to win souls by personal conversation. In this respect, my experience at that time was what it has always been since — I found myself having more or less power in preaching and in personal labor for souls just in proportion as I had the Spirit of prevailing prayer. I have found that unless I kept myself — or have been kept in such relations to God as to have daily and hourly access to Him in prayer — my efforts to win souls were abortive. When I could prevail with God in prayer, I could prevail with man in preaching, exhortation, and conversation." — Charles Finney

Finney's life and words outline the house of prayer the Church must become in this hour. It is not a form. It is not a show. It is not an event. It is true worship and holy intimacy with God. It is a spirit of prayer. It is being pregnant with birthing power to save souls. And it outflows into the practical love and demonstration of the gospel, as noted in this chapter. A people of true prayer are content and satisfied to minister in obscurity, never being seen or heard from. This heart is what will change the Church and the world. Contrariwise, prayerless people are usually shallow people, who like the mighty rapids of a free-flowing river, make much noise and theorize, but cannot discern between hype and holiness. But prayerful people are deep, and like the still waters of wells, silence and quietness rules their hearts, and acts of compassion mark their lives.

My point is this: It's going to take a consistent and deeper kind of praying to give birth to the purposes of God on the Earth.

THE CRY OF THE LORD

Here is my narrative of what is happening now and the time of awakening we are in:

The Bridegroom is running desperately through the streets looking for His Bride, but most do not recognize Him or know Him. The Bridegroom weeps as He did over Jerusalem long ago because they missed the time of their visitation (Lk. 19:41-44). Interestingly, it was shortly thereafter that Jesus went into the temple and cleansed it (v.45-46).

This is what the Lord is doing now in preparation for His glory and His coming. That is the cry I am hearing that is greater than any other cry because much of His Church is not ready for Him and do not recognize Him. And why don't those who profess His Name recognize Him? Why aren't they ready for Him?

It is because many prophets and priests (ministers) have lulled His Bride to sleep by teaching them these modern, false concepts of love and grace that allow them to do what they want and live how they want. There is no mention of the judgments of God and His wrath or severity. It is because of the unleashing of these kind of seducing spirits and doctrines of demons that many can no longer endure sound doctrine, but having itching ears after their own lusts, they heap up to themselves teachers (2 Tim. 4:3).

A deep cleansing followed by a loving devotion and consecration to God are what will prepare the way for the manifestation of the true glory of God in these days before Jesus returns.

THE OLD CLEANING WOMAN PROPHECY

"Lo, I will come to your door as a cleaning woman, yes, an old cleaning woman, to clean out the house you inhabit, says the Lord. In a time which is inopportune to you, I will arrive at your door with bucket and mop, with duster and scouring cloth, with soap and rags, with broom and polish; yes, I will stand at your door, and you will not recognize Me. You will see an old woman, not desirable and young to match your style. And she will begin the cleaning up of the dirt and the dust, of the rubbish and the filth, and bring order into each room and compartment of your dwelling place. From behind every hidden doorway, she will sweep away every venomous snake and scorpion and poisonous spider, and shake out with her strong hands the very carpets of crimson and gold. With a ladder, she will climb to the very top and sweep clean that which for many years has accumulated and wash with soap and water the windows until they sparkle. So she will do and continue to do until I am satisfied. For her labour will be for My reward.

"See, I come swiftly at a time you do not expect it, and I will demand from each an account of the time and labour of your service for which you have received reward.

"Hold fast unto your faith, and do not waver, oh faithful ones of the Lord, for see I come, yes I come quickly, and I will take charge of My Church. Every habitation which has been broken down and neglected I will cleanse and restore. I will turn out the false prophets and the false priests so that every heart will mourn and be silent and fearful at the mention of my Name!" — A. Smit

CHAPTER SEVENTEEN

RECOVERING THE SPIRIT OF PRAYER

Many things have been introduced into Christianity today that have greatly diluted the glory of God and the power of His Spirit — the greatest of them being the dearth there is on the Earth of the true spirit of prayer. All spiritual activity not born of prayer and communion with God rarely contains the heart of God. Similarly, all that's done in life and ministry without love and pure motives cannot please God. Only obedience to God's Word and the leading of the Spirit is authorized and approved by heaven.

INCREASE OF KNOWLEDGE AND TECHNOLOGY HAVE DIMINISHED THE SPIRIT OF PRAYER

With the great increase of knowledge on the Earth, there has also been a great increase of pride, for it is knowledge that puffs up or makes one proud (1 Cor. 8:1). God resists the proud but gives grace to the humble (Jam. 4:6). We cannot pray in the secret place and serve God acceptably without grace and humility.

In this superficial age of social media, pride is the state of many Christians as they freely voice their opinions from their comfy environs behind their laptop or iPhone keys. They will often do so, even to an elder or a person whom they don't know, without any thought, honor, and respect to their age or wisdom. And doctrinal disputes, vain babblings, empty chatter, and useless striving and argumentative rhetoric is prevalent — all symptoms of this ugly pride. Pride puffs us up and engenders conceit, and we start operating in the same strife and hatred the world does, forgetting that it is love that edifies. But even more importantly, this sort of strife and contention diminishes and desensitizes us to the spirit of prayer.

Not only does the pride of knowledge desensitize us to true prayer, but the immense increase of media and technology has also greatly diluted the spirit of prayer in comparison to days of old. In spite of all the attention given today to public prayer events, the spirit of prayer has vastly diminished since, say, a century ago, when the distractions that media and technology have produced were non-existent. These things tend to cause indifference and carnality, and they have a numbing effect on our spirits.

Again, there must be a deep purging and cleansing and an uprooting of pride and covetousness, followed by a fresh consecration, before a new planting can occur.

EXCERPT OF A MOST REMARKABLE REVIVAL WITH LASTING FRUIT OBTAINED THROUGH THE SPIRIT OF PRAYER

Some of the greatest revivals in American history manifested through the ministry of Charles G. Finney. We've made mention of him earlier in this book and quoted him in the last chapter. But as we near the end of this book, I wanted to share a remarkable example of the real spirit of prayer that was at work, not only in his life but in the lives of two other prominent men of deep prayer who were the backbone and fuel of most of his revivals. Their names were Daniel Nash and Abel Clary.

Here is an excerpt from a book about the life of Daniel Nash and the mention of a few others like him who obtained the spirit of prayer (obtained with permission from Dr. Michael Yeager through prayfor-revival.org.uk).

The most remarkable revival of this period in American history was that which occurred in Rochester, New York, in 1830-1831. *"Rochester was a young city,"* wrote Finney, *"full of thrift and enterprise, and full of sin."* Nash and Clary were well aware of this, as they teamed up for the praying with the assistance of others, as we have noted. These two men were so similar in their praying that one is often described to explain the other. Such fervent praying in agony of soul brought sights that may seem strange to our eyes today.

Our gentle prayers accomplish so little, but then they cost us so little. Finney wrote: *"I have never known a person sweat blood; but I have known a person pray till the blood started from his nose. And I have known persons pray till they were all wet with perspiration, in the coldest weather in winter. I have known persons pray for hours, till their strength was all exhausted with the agony of their minds. Such prayers prevailed with God. This agony in prayer was prevalent in Jonathan Edwards' day, in the revivals which then took place."*

During the Rochester meetings, there are several accounts of these two men in deep agony of soul while praying day and night. Some accounts name Nash, some Clary, others both. It seems they were together in fasting and prayer much of the time, weeping and crying out to God. Sometimes they lay prostrate without strength to stand up. Their concern over sinners being lost brought great stress to their minds and souls.

They groaned under the load, they risked health, and they gave up comforts that the battle of the heavenliest might be won. Sometimes they *"would writhe and groan in agony"* over souls. God honored their burden-bearing and poured out His Spirit. The Spirit of prayer was poured out so powerfully that some people stayed away from the services to pray, being unable to restrain their feelings under the preaching. Privately they prayed, and publicly God answered.

The results of this awakening were incredible. One of the first results was the coming together of the different churches, which constituted a huge breakthrough in those days. As the awakening swept through the town, the great mass of the most influential people, both male and female, were convicted and converted. It seems almost impossible to believe, but *"it began with the judges, the lawyers, the physicians, the bankers and the merchants, and worked its way down to the bottom of society, till nearly everybody had joined one or other of the churches."* Consequently, the public affairs of the city were put, to a large extent, into the hands of Christian men.

Because the awakening was so powerful and gathered in such great numbers of people, especially the most influential people, it created great excitement. Like the Welsh Awakening in 1904-1906, many people came in from near and far to witness the great work of God and were converted. The *New York Evangelist* reported that *"Almost every town within 40 or 50 miles of Rochester is favored with the special presence of the Lord."*

Finney preached in as many places as he had time and strength to do, asserting that *"the work spread like waves in every direction."* Wherever he preached, he was astounded that, *"in every instance, the Lord has come down and commenced a work upon the spot."* Finney was only too well aware of the opposition of the evil one and how that had to be dealt with first. Therefore, he knew that a huge breakthrough had been made in the heavenlies, so that the Lord was free to come down and do His work.

Years later, Dr. Beecher, the renowned preacher of Boston, remarked that the 1830-1831 Rochester Revival was the greatest work of God and the greatest revival of religion that the world has ever seen in so short a time. 100,000 people were reported as having joined themselves to churches as a result of the awakening. *"This,"* he said, *"is unparalleled in the history of the Church. Moreover, these were not shallow conversions, but genuine works of God, for the most ungodly sinners had been convicted of sin."*

"So manifestly were the great mass of the conversions sound, the sinners really regenerated and made new creatures; so profoundly were individuals and whole communities reformed; and so permanent and unquestionable were the results, that almost universally it was acknowledged that this was the work of God. There were so many instances of conversion that were so striking; such characters converted, and all classes, both high and low, rich and poor, so thoroughly subdued by the Spirit, as to silence all opposition."

The proof of all this was seen in the effects on society. The only theatre in the city was converted into a livery stable, the circus into a soap-and-candle factory, and the bars and taverns were closed. But it is in the realm of crime that the most astounding results were seen. The most full and careful census of crime in the city, both before and after the awakening, was taken by the most competent men, including the prosecuting attorney for the city.

This census showed that, during the period 1830-1842, the number of prosecutions for crime decreased to less than a third of the number prior to the revival. That is amazing enough, but what is astounding is that this took place during a period when the population of the city increased threefold. The population of the city in 1830 was 10,863, so that means the population by 1842 was about 32,000. If the prosecutions in 1829 were about 300, i.e., 3%, this means the prosecutions in 1842 were less than 100, which would be a prosecution rate of only 0.3%!

This means that the awareness of the presence of a holy God was so strong and so powerful that it continued for years afterwards, so that all the new people who were coming into the town, who would have included many different kinds of characters, including violent criminals, were so subdued by the manifest presence of God, that almost no crimes were committed. Nothing like this has been seen in the history of the world.

All this was due to a few people, including Daniel Nash, really praying, and one man preaching. Within a few months, Daniel was dead. He, like John Hyde, had literally prayed himself to death. But he had left his legacy. The world would never again see an awakening like that at Rochester. If we refuse to strive in prayer, we should not be surprised at the lack of God's mighty stirrings.

Is it not amazing that we have no problem with people wearing themselves out in sports for pleasure, work for money, politics for power, and programs for charity, but think it fanatical to so pray for souls? Is it any wonder we see so little of God's great working? Daniel Nash would pray until he had to "*go to bed absolutely sick, for weakness and faintness, under the pressure.*"

Finney told of this relationship of intense prayer and successful preaching. Speaking of Nash, he wrote: "*I have seen Christians who would be in an agony when the minister was going into the pulpit, for fear his mind should be in a cloud, or his heart cold, or he should have no unction, and so a blessing should not come. I have labored with a man of this sort.*"

"*He would pray until he got an assurance in his mind that God would be with me in preaching, and sometimes he would pray himself ill. I have known the time when he has been in darkness for a season, while the people were gathering, and his mind was full of anxiety, and he would go again and again to pray, till finally he would come into the room with a placid face, and say: 'The Lord has come, and He will be with us.' And I do not know that I ever found him mistaken.*"

Nash had great confidence in a God who heard and answered prayer. He was not satisfied to stop praying until God answered in mighty power. Praying day and night, great struggling and weakened health were but prices to be paid that God might move in power. The results were opened heavens, glorious power, souls saved, and God glorified. This may well explain why more than 90% of Finney's converts stood without ever backsliding and may also explain why less than 10% of today's converts only last a couple of years.

We must ask God to help us recover the real spirit of prayer such as Father Nash and these men possessed.

HOW TO OBTAIN THE SPIRIT OF PRAYER

Charles Finney, in his excellent book *How to Experience Revival*, compares the spirit of prayer to the great conviction sinners often feel. Sinners are especially convicted when they think about their sins. Finney equates this to a spirit of prayer that a Christian may obtain as he also thinks on the condition of lost souls. In other words, if the believer will cultivate a deep awareness by thinking on their state and cherishing the slightest impressions, he will come into a spirit of prayer for the conversion of sinners. He encourages Christians to go through their Bible and find verses of Scripture that describe the conditions of a world without God. *"Look at the world, your children, and your neighbors, and see their condition while they remain in sin. Then, persevere in prayer and effort until you obtain the blessing of the Spirit of God."*

Finney explains that, with most Christians, this is a progressive and prolonged process. Gradually they cultivate a burden about something until it consumes them in sighing out their desires to God during their daily activities. He likens it to a mother who sighs as if her heart is broken because her child is sick. If she is a praying mother, her sighs are breathed out to God all day long. If she leaves the room where her child is, her mind remains on the child. If she sleeps, her thoughts are still on the child. She will even jerk in her dreams, thinking that perhaps her child may be dying. Her mind is absorbed with that sick child. Finney says that this is the state of mind in which Christians can enter into the real spirit of prevailing prayer for the lost.

This burden is the natural result of great benevolence and a clear view of the danger sinners are in. This is a reasonable sentiment, Finney says. He compares it to the average Christian witnessing a family shrieking with agony in a burning fire. He would become extremely burdened and moved to action to save them. No one would consider these actions strange but, rather, cold-hearted if there was no powerful response or reaction.

This depth of concern and burden for souls is thoroughly Scriptural. The apostle Paul was familiar with it.

"I tell the truth in Christ. I am not lying, my conscience also bearing me witness in the Holy Spirit, that I have great sorrow and continual grief in my heart. For I could wish that I myself were accursed from Christ for my brethren, my countrymen according to the flesh..." (Rom. 9:1-3 - KJV).

The psalmist of old was familiar with it.

"Horror hath taken hold upon me because of the wicked that forsake thy law" (Ps. 119:53). *"Rivers of waters run down mine eyes, because they keep not thy law"* (Ps. 119:136 — KJV).

The Old Testament prophets such as Jeremiah also experienced great sorrow because of Israel's sins.

"My bowels, my bowels! I am pained at my very heart; my heart maketh a noise in me; I cannot hold my peace, because thou hast heard, O my soul, the sound of the trumpet, the alarm of war" (Jer. 4:19 — KJV).

In light of these Scriptures, why should it be considered fanatical or abnormal when Christians become burdened this way and pray fervently unto groanings and travailings when they contemplate the wrath of God on sinners and the misery of those nearing eternal damnation?

Occasionally the Spirit of God may initiate a burden to pray, but more often than not, you must cultivate it and move into it by faith and learn to yield to the Spirit of God. It's usually not all God, and certainly not all man, but a cooperative work between God and man. The Holy Spirit does not pray, but He helps us mightily in prayer.

"Likewise the Spirit also helps in our weaknesses. For we do not know what we should pray for as we ought, but the Spirit Himself makes intercession for us with groanings which cannot be uttered" (Rom. 8:26).

"My little children, of whom I travail in birth again until Christ be formed in you" (Gal. 4:19).

"As soon as Zion travailed, she brought forth her children" (Is. 66:8)

Groanings and travail of soul are elements of prevailing prayer. Persistence and perseverance are usually required. These elements of intercession are often extensions of praying in tongues. Finney believed and taught that this travail of soul in prayer was the only real revival prayer, and if anyone does not know what that is, he does not understand the spirit of prayer, and he is not in a revival state. That is, until he understands this agonizing prayer, he does not know the real secret of revival power.

We don't learn to pray that way by just hearing about it or reading about it. As with most skills, we learn by doing it.

For example, you don't learn to drive an automobile by reading the handbook on it. No — you must get behind the wheel and start driving.

You don't learn to cook a delicious meal by just reading a cook book of recipes. You must actually prepare the food and various ingredients and cook the meal.

It's the same way with prayer. Unless this spirit of prayer and certain elements of intercession are passed on by those who understand and operate in these dimensions, it will be lost to the next generation. This is probably the primary reason why we are no longer witnessing the great depths of revival and outpourings of the Spirit that was seen in Finney's day. Let us consecrate ourselves to the Lord and cultivate the spirit of prayer. Perhaps God is calling some to make prayer your business and to labor fervently this way for the conversion of souls and true revival.

CONCLUSION: MOVING FROM PROCRASTINATION

TO CONSECRATION AND PRAYER

I conclude this book with an incredible prophecy on procrastination, consecration, and prayer. The Holy Spirit spoke the following words through the late Kenneth E. Hagin years ago to the church world. They still apply today. Whosoever will, let him hear what the Spirit of God is saying to the Church.

"Don't draw back. The time is near, the time is at hand. No longer can you wait; no longer can you procrastinate. No longer can you say, yeah, in another day I'll consecrate. In a later day, I'll wait on the Lord more. In another day, I will spend more time with Him. In another day, I'll put my flesh under. No longer. Don't draw back and don't pull back.

"The Spirit of the Lord pleads with you. Come forward, more forward. Answer the call you hear in your heart. Respond unto the Spirit of God. It is not bad. It is good. The price that would be paid in the flesh is nothing compared to the glory which shall be revealed. It is not bad. Do not dread it. Do not draw back from it. It is a lie. It's a deception that has held you back. It's a lie. It's a deception that has caused you to draw back. Go on in. Taste and see that the Lord is good.

"Oh, the treasures of the things He has laid up for you. The things that your heart is hungry for. Nothing else will satisfy your soul. Nothing else will give you the answer in your heart. Nothing else will satisfy what you seek. Nothing.

"Oh, push in. Respond unto the Spirit of God. Just lay those other things aside. Humble the pride and fall before Him and wait upon Him. And as you do, your soul will blossom. Your spirit will spring

forth. Yea, you will be a greater blessing unto your spouse. You'll be a greater blessing unto your family because you will bloom forth. And you won't be restricted like before. And you won't be vexed like before. And you won't be hindered like before.

"Yea, you've done some things for them (your family). You've drawn back and you said it was for them. But you have not been a blessing to them in that the full blessing of the Lord was not upon thee. But if you shall press in, though it might seem to cost that price in the beginning, it might seem like it costs you. It might seem like it costs them. Yea, but that's the only way to get to the things that they desire and the things that you desire and the things that are needed.

"Yea, the things that must be in this hour, it cannot be delayed. It cannot be delayed. It must be now. Now, now is the time. So heed the call of the Spirit's cry in your heart. Don't say, 'I'll do it by and by.' But the time is now. Do not dread or fear. It is good. Taste and see that the Lord is good. Taste and see that the Lord is good!

"Don't think it's too high a price. It's nothing in comparison to the light and the glory that shall be revealed. Draw nigh unto Him. He shall draw nigh unto thee. Seek His face. He shall reveal Himself unto thee even in a greater way. And you shall rise up and you shall be enabled to be a far greater blessing.

"And your latter end shall exceed and it shall overflow and it shall be abundant in blessing and glory and grace. And the evil one that thought to deter you and thought to lie to you and keep you from it, you shall look at him and you shall say, 'Ha, ha, ha, ha... Your plan did not work. Ha, ha, ha, ha... It did not succeed. Ha, ha, ha, ha... I did not believe it. Ha, ha, ha, ha... I obeyed... Ha, ha, ha, ha... I ran my course. Ha, ha, ha, ha... I finished my job. Ha, ha, ha, ha. I have ac-

complished His will and with His glory I am filled. His grace, mercy and glory is with me day by day.'

"And those things that once held you, those things that for years, years, and years deceived you and held you out; you shall look at them from that higher place. And they shall seem nothing to thee. They shall seem small and despised in your eyes. You shall look upon them in dismay and you shall say, 'Ha, ha, ha, ha, ha, ha." You shall see far, ha, ha, ha, ha... And you shall know well, and you shall move sure, and shaken shall be hell. And their power shall be confused for His authority you've used.'

"And that which they greatly feared (hell's demons) shall have happened. For they feared, they feared that the revelation of truth would come into the Earth. They feared that it would come through the heavenly host that would withstand it. They feared that someone would stand. They feared that someone would seek. They feared that some would penetrate into that realm.

"When the revelation comes, the truth doth set the captives free. And that which they have greatly feared, it shall even come to pass. It'll come to pass. God shall reveal His truth unto His people. Yea, we've rejoiced in the light. And we've seen a little bit. And we moved, but, oh, there's so much more. There's so much more. And the enemy would have us just revel in what we see and what we know and not push and penetrate to hold fast to receive more. But it shall not be for a glimpse we do see. And we shall not be satisfied until the truth in our hearts abides. We shall not draw back, and we shall not fear until we have all that God would give year by year...increasing glory to glory, light to light. Not doing it in the flesh, but by the good faith fight.

"And His plan shall be accomplished and His ways shall be straight. And then it shall be ready. He shall come. He'll not be late.

And His people shall have done His bidding, and His people shall have heard His voice. And His Spirit shall have reaped the harvest through the church and His people shall rejoice. He calleth thee higher. Continue to look down on lowly things on the ground, but look up and see what He has reserved for thee. And by faith, let your heart reach out.

"His Spirit lifts you up. Your heart has craved to know him. You shall know what your mind has hungered to know. You shall do what you were created to do."

After reading this prophecy and this book, perhaps now the cry of your heart is so intense you find yourself exclaiming, "Lord, purge us from mammon worship, every form of pride and iniquity, the wisdom of man, and false success. Purify us once again, and make us a house of prayer!"

In this modern day of increased media and technology, where platform, popularity, and public ministry are valued and promoted far above prayer and private ministry, we need to return to our roots.

May your own personal temple and the corporate temple of God be consecrated to Him and become a house of prayer in this hour.

REFERENCES

Chapter 9, © 2019 by Dr. Anthony G. Payne. All rights reserved. This article is a truncated version of a longer one copyrighted in 2018 by Dr. Anthony G. Payne.

The original article can be found at:

https://biotheorist.files.wordpress.com/2018/06/unholy-hype-by-dr-anthony-g-payne-june-20181.pdf

Chapter 17, Daniel Nash, *A Man Mighty in Prayer*, compiled and written by Dr. Michael Yeager, independently published

Thoughts on how to obtain the spirit of prayer in Chapter 17 taken from the following two books:

How To Experience Revival, by Charles G. Finney, compiled by E. E. Shelhamer, published by Whitaker House

Power From On High, Charles Finney, published by Whitaker House

Other quotes and excerpts from articles or books are noted with the name of the person or author who stated it.

ABOUT THE AUTHOR

Bert M. Farias, together with his wife, Carolyn, graduates of Rhema Bible Training Center, founded Holy Fire Ministries in 1997 after serving for nine years as missionaries in West Africa, establishing nation-changing interdenominational Bible training centers with an organization called Living Word Missions.

From 1999 to 2003, Bert served as the internship coordinator on the senior leadership team of the Brownsville Revival School of Ministry and Fire School of Ministry in Pensacola, Florida, a school birthed from a massive heaven-sent revival that brought approximately four million visitors from around the world with an estimated 150,000 first-time conversions. There, Rev. Farias and his wife taught and mentored young men and women in the call of God and trained them for the work of the ministry.

Bert is a messenger of the Lord carrying a spirit of revival to the Church and the nations. Before being separated to the full-time preaching and teaching ministry, Bert experienced a unique and powerful baptism of fire. His consuming passion is for human beings to come into a real and vibrant relationship with the Lord Jesus Christ through the power of the Holy Spirit and to become passionate workers in His kingdom, thus preparing them for the second coming of Christ, being among the wise virgins and a part of the first-fruits harvest who will gain an abundant entrance into glory and receive a sure reward.

Bert currently resides in Windham, New Hampshire, with his beautiful wife, Carolyn. They are proud parents of one precious son of promise.

MINISTRY INFORMATION

To become a monthly partner with Holy Fire Ministries, schedule a speaking engagement with Bert and/or Carolyn, receive a free monthly newsletter, or follow Bert's blog, please visit our website:

holy-fire.org

HOLY FIRE MINISTRIES
PO Box 4527
Windham, NH 03087
Email: holyfiremin@comcast.net

OTHER BOOKS BY BERT M. FARIAS

SOULISH LEADERSHIP
PURITY OF HEART
THE JOURNAL OF A JOURNEY TO HIS HOLINESS
THE REAL SPIRIT OF REVIVAL
THE REAL SALVATION
THE REAL GOSPEL
THE REAL JESUS
MY SON, MY SON: FATHERING AND TRAINING A HOLY
GENERATION
PRAYER: THE LANGUAGE OF THE SPIRIT
PASSING ON THE MOVE OF GOD TO THE NEXT GENERATION

To order any of these books or to view a synopsis of them, visit our website or Amazon books. If this book or any of Bert's other books have been a blessing to you, kindly post a review on Amazon.

CPSIA information can be obtained
at www.ICGtesting.com
Printed in the USA
BVHW031305030820
585354BV00001B/14